THE GOLDEN AGE OF
RADIO
IN THE HOME

THE GOLDEN AGE OF
RADIO
IN THE HOME

JOHN W. STOKES

Printed and produced in New Zealand

CRAIGS—PRINTERS AND PUBLISHERS
1986

Also by John W. Stokes
70 Years of Radio Tubes and Valves

ISBN 0 473 00389 9

Printed and distributed by Craig Printing Co. Ltd
67 Tay Street, Invercargill, New Zealand

1986—34012

Acknowledgements

In the preparation of this book I have received much help from many people; some lent photographs or other data, while others kindly allowed me to photograph radios in their collections. To all of the following in New Zealand I express my thanks: Alan and Stan Brehaut, Ian Browne, Harold Boyd, Noel Curtis, Lindsay Erasmuson, Leigh Hodgson, Eric Kirby, Ray Knowles, Peter Lankshear, Des Leonard, Mark Maloney, Ray Marett, Miss Joyce Martin, Reg Motion, Fred Pond, Eric Reynolds, R. S. Richards, Mark Thomson, Arthur Williams. In the U.S.A. I thank Alan Douglas and Floyd Paul.

A special thanks to Peter Lankshear who provided invaluable help by correcting factual errors in the typescript, and to George Weston who assisted by correcting typographical and spelling errors.

Thanks are also due to the Editor of *Wireless World* for permission to use material from that journal. Other material was obtained from long defunct periodicals and manufacturers' sales literature of both local and overseas origin.

As in the case of my previous book, my final thanks are reserved for my wife who continues to assist as before.

J.W.S.

A word of explanation

Because this work is concerned with only the so-called 'entertainment' or in-home aspect of radio communications, no more than passing reference has been made to the period preceding the advent of broadcasting.

In general, the period encompassed in this book lies between 1923 and 1958, a span of only 35 years, but a very important one which saw the rise and fall of the radio valve, the vacuum tube, as the key device upon which broadcasting itself was founded. Particularly during the first ten or twelve years of this period the pace of technical progress was extremely rapid and nearly all the significant developments had occurred by about 1935.

And now a word about what is *not* to be found in this book. Ham radio, although it was, and still is, usually an in-home activity is an entirely different development having little in common with home radio as such. Reference to radiograms and record players is minimal because, before the advent of the long-playing record, the playing of records was a relatively unimportant part of the entertainment scene in this country. Although reference to transistor radios occurs occasionally, no attempt has been made to cover the subject in detail as developments in this area are too recent to come within the time span of this book.

Finally, due to limitations of space, it has been impossible to illustrate more than a fraction of the many different models of sets made by each manufacturer. For this reason there are bound to be some seekers after information who will be disappointed not to find what they are looking for.

Contents

Introduction

The magic of radio! As one of the twentieth century's modern miracles, radio's ability to bring information and entertainment to everyone everywhere has for many years been a part of everyday life, long since taken for granted. Yet, when the first wireless signals crackled through the 'ether', nearly 100 years ago, who could have foreseen such a development? For more than 20 years after Marconi had transmitted the first wireless signals across the Atlantic in 1901, radio's only application had been purely one of 'communications'—the sending and receiving of messages—simply an extension of the telegraph which had already linked the Old and New Worlds by submarine cable many years earlier.

It was not long after the introduction of radio telephony, first used during World War I, that the idea of transmitting entertainment by radio became a reality. Initially the idea met with considerable disfavour in certain quarters where it was considered that such frivolous use of the new medium of communication was quite unwarranted. In Great Britain the main opposition came from the Post Office and the Royal Navy whose concern was that listeners-in might overhear confidential messages. In New Zealand, too, a similar concern was evinced by the Post and Telegraph Department, and for as long as receiving licences remained in use they carried a warning to listeners to observe the secrecy of public correspondence.

Previous books written on the history of broadcasting in New Zealand have dealt almost exclusively with the transmitting side and in particular with the three Ps—personalities, programmes and people—yet reception is the essential other half of broadcasting. Even though the receiving side, perhaps because of its passive nature, may be less interesting to read about, it nevertheless has its own appeal and its own story, much of it concerned with the necessary 'hardware' used for reception.

In the days before television and transistor sets the household radio, or 'wireless' of even earlier days, was a domestic god of no mean order and for many years 'listening-in' held its own unique appeal to those families fortunate enough to own a receiver.

To people interested solely in what comes over the air—the programmes—the end must always be more important than the means, but even so, once receivers evolved from the experimental stage manufacturers were soon dressing up their products in elegant cabinets so that radio became more than just a receiving instrument and could hold its place in any well-appointed living room. In fact, as time went on, cabinets tended to become more and more elaborate, with the larger and more expensive models sometimes becoming status symbols. At the other end of the scale was the humble crystal set—the poor man's radio—which could be purchased for a few shillings and which for many people was the only type of set they could afford.

But, right from the the beginning, there was more to radio than just listening in, even in the days when there was little if anything to listen in to. Quite early on three separate classes of 'listener' started to develop, probably all of whom were initially attracted by 'the wonder of it all'. Those who found the lure of logging distant stations irresistible became known as DX-ers; those who delighted in the building and rebuilding of receivers and experimenting were known as home constructors; those who became licensed amateur radio transmitters have long been known as 'hams'.

Originally a ham was largely indistinguishable from a hobbyist constructor or DX-er, for he was something of both himself and could also on occasions be a broadcaster as well, sometimes providing 'gramophone concerts' for the benefit of both fellow hams and casual listeners alike.

Home constructors came into existence even before broadcasting began and nowadays one may wonder at the enthusiasm of those who made their own 'apparatus' when there was then no thought of using the airways as a means of providing entertainment.

Getting 'bitten by the radio bug' it used to be called, and that same bug was still around nearly a quarter of a century later, though by then much of the virulence had gone out of its bite. During its heyday this interest amounted to almost a passion in some cases, a thing later generations can perhaps only dimly imagine.

To cater for the needs of home constructors a plethora of radio parts manufacturers and publishers of radio literature soon sprang up, particularly in the United States and Great Britain, during the 1920s. As an illustration of the growth taking place the American monthly magazine *Radio News,* which had been founded in 1920, had by June 1925 increased in size to 239 pages and carried advertisements for no less than 364 different firms, mostly components and accessories manufacturers.

Today the hobbies of ham radio and DX-ing are alive and well but the days of the home constructor are long gone, at least as far as radio proper is concerned, the nearest modern counterpart being the electronics hobbyist.

And now radio has become old enough to have histories written about it, and for early artefacts to become museum pieces. Inevitably, it would seem, old radio receivers have become, like any other old man-made articles, 'collectibles'.

They have joined the vast field which encompasses anything from stamps to steam engines, from bottles to barbed wire, and become collectors' items in their own right.

Strange, when one comes to think of it, how a 1930s 'cathedral' model cabinet once despised as being old and ugly is now again seen as being attractive, even beautiful. It was a Dutch poet, J. Cats, who said—"All beauty lies in the beholder's eye", so perhaps we can join another poet, Keats, in his belief that—"A thing of beauty is a joy forever. . . . "

Although many of today's radio collectors may be hams, hobbyists or DX-ers, many have no other interest in radio, but almost without exception all are interested in finding out more about the sets in their collections, about the manufacturers who made them and about what went on in the early, and not so early, days. It is for them that this book has been written.

John Whitley Stokes, Auckland, N.Z. 1986

How broadcasting began

For nearly 20 years after the advent of practical wireless telegraphy in 1903 there was nothing to be heard on the air but the dots and dashes of messages being transmitted by Morse code. The earliest form of these transmissions was by means of a spark generated by an induction coil, the spark being stopped and started by the manipulation of a Morse key. The spark generated a wide band of frequencies known as 'damped' waves, the resultant radiation being effectively self-modulated which allowed reception on a simple 'detector' such as a carborundum crystal.

Later, from about 1910, when arc transmitters began to replace the earlier spark type the new transmissions were in the form of 'undamped' or 'continuous' waves which could only be rendered audible in the receiver by a process known as 'heterodyning'. To receive 'CW' it was necessary to use an oscillating valve coupled to the detector, or else a regenerative triode detector which combined the functions of heterodyning and detection in one valve.

This, then, was the state of the art which set the stage for the next development in wireless, the transmission of the human voice. While it is true that attempts at voice transmission had been made as early as 1906 using arc transmitters modulated by means of a specially constructed carbon microphone these efforts were purely experimental and held no promise of future development. Not until a small fragile glass bulb, containing a sort of specially adapted electric lamp, was found capable of generating electrical oscillations was any real progress made. It was the same device, the triode valve, which had earlier been used as a detector and 'local' oscillator that now became a transmitting oscillator, capable of being easily modulated for the transmission of speech.

Some of the earliest successful efforts in transmitting speech had been made during the closing stages of World War I between aircraft in flight and the ground and it was not many years after the end of the war that the first civilian work was being done. Initially it seems to have been the sheer novelty as much as anything else which led to many of the early workers making

voice transmissions, for no one could have foreseen that an entirely new medium of entertainment, and indeed an entirely new industry, was to evolve from their pioneering efforts.

Of recent years there have been various claims made as to which person or which country was the first to have 'broadcasted', but before such claims can be settled it is necessary to define the term 'broadcasting'. In the absence of anything better, a definition put forward by the Antique Wireless Association of New York in December 1969 forms a useful yardstick in assessing claims to priority. The criteria contained in this definition are:

1. The station must have been authorised by the government of the country concerned to broadcast news and entertainment.
2. The station must have been allocated an official call-sign.
3. The station must have published details of its programmes in advance.
4. The station must have maintained a regular schedule for a reasonable length of time.

Using these criteria the world's first broadcasting station was PCGG The Hague, Netherlands whose owner, Hanso Idzerda, commenced operations on 6 November 1919.

Probably the best-known of the early broadcasters was station KDKA Pittsburgh, U.S.A. which commenced broadcasting almost exactly a year later in November 1920. In England the Marconi Co. had been making experimental speech transmissions from their station in Chelmsford as early as 1920, and from another location at Writtle, call-sign 2MT, during 1922. However it was not until the establishment of the British Broadcasting Company in November 1922 that the first official broadcasting commenced in that country. Another early broadcaster was the Canadian station CFCF Montreal which was licensed and began broadcasting in 1919.

WHAT HAPPENED IN NEW ZEALAND

In New Zealand the first experimental transmissions of radio telephony were made by Professor Robert Jack from the Physics Dept of Otago University. Dr Jack had received official permission from the Post and Telegraph Dept to transmit vocal and musical items for research purposes but it is quite clear that he had in mind that his transmissions should have entertainment value. To this end he broadcast a series of two-hourly 'gramophone concerts' each Wednesday and Saturday evening which were continued for nearly a year.

Following this a group of enthusiasts known as the Otago Radio Association took over from Professor Jack and with his help set up a station and commenced broadcasting in October 1922. Today it is their proud claim to be "The Oldest Radio Organisation in the British Empire". The original call-sign used was 'DN' but after the introduction of licensing early in 1923 the call-sign 4AB was allocated which in 1926 was changed to 4ZB. Following the establishment of the National Commercial Broadcasting Service in 1937 the Otago Radio Association voluntarily relinquished the use of 4ZB to allow the NCBS to complete their network of 'ZB' stations. From 1937 to 1948 the call 4ZD was used and then 4XD, which remains in use to this day.

It was the pioneering work of Professor Jack which undoubtedly encouraged others to get in on the act and during 1922 there was quite a flurry of activity. In Wellington Chas E. Forrest of the International Radio Co. commenced transmitting in this year using a 15-watt De Forest radio-telephone set. His activities created sufficient interest to encourage a group of local businessmen to form a company known as Wellington Broadcasters Ltd which in 1923 established a station licensed as 2YB. The people concerned were importers of radio apparatus who were looking for ways and means to promote the sale of components, and in the case of Mr Forrest, De Forest receivers as well.

Another early Wellington station was established in 1922 by a group calling themselves the Federal Radio Co. with Arthur McClay at its head. In November 1923 they sold out to the Dominion Radio Co. who then operated under the call-sign 2YK.

In Dunedin, which may aptly be called the birthplace of New Zealand broadcasting, there were three stations on the air in 1923: 4YA of the British Electrical and Engineering Co., 4YB of the Radio Supply Co. and 4AB of the Otago Radio Association. Christchurch was represented by station 3AC, originally operated by the Radio Society of Christchurch and later by Mr M. I. Smaill under the call-sign 3YA.

The first station to be licensed under the 1923 Radio Regulations was 1YA Auckland, owned and operated by the Auckland Radio Service Co., a group whose aims were identical with those of Wellington Broadcasters Ltd. This station remained in operation until it was taken over by the Radio Broadcasting Company in 1926 and today it remains the only station still operating under its original call-sign.

In addition to 1YA there were two other Auckland stations in operation in the early days. The first of these, 1YB, was licensed in September 1923 and owned by Mr Charles Pearson of the La Gloria Gramophone Co. In 1925 the call-sign was changed to 1ZB and in 1933 the firm's licence was sold to the Friendly Road Broadcasters. The other Auckland station was owned by Mr Roy Keith who had previously operated in Hawera before moving to Auckland in 1926. Between 1922 and 1929 Roy Keith had used no less than seven different call-signs, including two self-allotted ones, before being assigned 2BZ in 1925. His first Auckland call was 1AL, then followed 1YD, the latter being changed at his own request to prevent confusion with 1YB. Later still, when all B class calls were required to have 'Z' prefixes it became 1ZQ and so remained until closure of the station in 1933.

Apart from the stations which had been established in the four main centres there were also some in other parts of the country, mainly in the North Island. For example in Gisborne there was 2YM owned and operated by Percy Stevens under the name Gisborne Radio Supply Co., later changed to the Atwater Kent Radio Service. This station later became 2ZM and finally 2XM. It was one of the few stations which was not put off the air by government decree when the private stations were taken over and closed down during the 1930s.

During the first two or three years following the introduction of the 1923 Radio Regulations much enthusiasm for the new medium of entertainment had been apparent and by March 1926 there were no less than ten radio societies in existence throughout the country. But more than just enthusiasm was needed, for there was mounting dissatisfaction with the skimpy service being provided by the existing stations, some of which were on the air for only two or three hours a week. Lack of money was the universal reason for the inability to provide a better service to listeners, for no stations had any income apart from that provided by their owners. In some cases groups of radio dealers formed companies which were financed by levies on members, as in the cases of the Auckland Radio Service and Wellington Broadcasters Ltd. In those days no

A radio shop window in 1932. Harringtons N.Z. Ltd were agents for Pilot and Raycophone radios. On this occasion the film *Sunshine Susie* was being advertised.

advertising of any sort was permitted apart from mention of the station owner's name at the beginning and end of each programme.

Initially the licence fee for 'receiving stations' was five shillings and all of this was required by the P. & T. Dept to cover administration expenses as licensing authority. However, following the gazetting of new radio regulations in February 1925 the licence fee was increased to thirty shillings and provision was made to pay up to two-thirds of this amount to the broadcasting stations. In return the stations were required to be on air for a period of not less than 12 hours a week, excluding Sundays.

By this time the government of the day was beginning to realise that a demand existed for an improved broadcasting service and in August 1925 this led to the establishment of a body known as the Radio Broadcasting Company of New Zealand. The company received a five-year contract to establish a national broadcasting service with stations located in each of the four main centres. Revenue was to be obtained from listeners' licence fees on the basis of 25/- from every 30/- licence. In addition 90% of the amount paid by radio dealers for an annual licence went to the company. In passing, it may be remarked that the amount charged for a listener's licence represented nearly half a week's wages to some people in those days and also, in the case of crystal set owners, amounted to as much as twice what the set itself cost. No wonder there were many unlicensed listeners!

By all accounts the Broadcasting Company achieved excellent results during the period of 6½ years that it remained in existence. In this time the number of licensed listeners increased from about 3,000 in 1925 to over 60,000 in 1931. However, the government decided not to renew the company's contract and instead set up a Broadcasting Board to take over and run the existing stations.

Privately-owned 'B' class stations continued to operate as before, though except for a few located in areas where reception of the board's stations was poor and who received subsidies as a result, without a crumb of income from licence fees. Rather naturally the board regarded private stations located in the main centres as competitors and opposed the idea that they should receive any part of the licence fee. And, as if this were not enough, the gramophone companies in 1933 decided to enforce a copyright ban on the playing of gramophone records over the air in the belief that broadcasting was hurting the retail sales of records, not realising that it was mainly the depressed economic conditions that was responsible for the drop in business. A far cry indeed from more recent times when record manufacturers fall over themselves in their eagerness to get 'air time' for their latest releases.

In the event, copyright restrictions were enough to force some B stations off the air permanently, but in 1936, following the election of New Zealand's first Labour government, hopes for a better deal arose. The owners of B stations had come to believe that Labour, if elected, would be sympathetic to their cause, but the reality proved otherwise. The country's new Prime Minister, Michael Joseph Savage, was also the Minister of Broadcasting and as such was well placed to carry out his pre-election promises to allow the B stations to continue and shortly after taking office publicly voiced his approval of the idea that they should be allowed to earn revenue by means of advertising.

In taking to himself the portfolio of broadcasting M. J. Savage was obviously well aware of the medium's growing importance, and in line with Labour's policy was opposed to the idea of private ownership of radio stations. Before long it was apparent that the new government itself was going to put broadcasting completely under state control. Apart from taking over the established 'YA' network to carry a 'National' programme service, a second 'Commercial' service was established, the stations originally being known as 'C' class. These stations were to earn revenue by the sale of advertising on a fully commercial basis.

To implement the new policy the Broadcasting Board was replaced by two new organisations—the National Broadcasting Service (NBS) headed by Professor Shelley, and the National Commercial Broadcasting Service (NCBS) headed by the Rev. C. G. Scrimgeour. Thereafter the two services remained separate entities until the abolition of the NCBS during World War II when they were combined.

Colin Scrimgeour was a man whose name was by then already well known to many thousands of Aucklanders, largely through his extremely popular Sunday night 'Man In The Street' sessions broadcast from the 'Friendly Road' station 1ZB which he had almost single-handedly established. As a Methodist minister 'Scrim', as he was popularly known, had first become acquainted with the microphone early in 1931 when he began conducting a devotional service from Lewis Eady's station 1ZR.

When, in 1932, the government of the day purchased and closed down 1ZR, Scrim was forced to establish his own station which he did by purchasing the moribund 1ZB from the La Gloria Gramophone Co. In later years it was revealed that the price paid was £50, the money being raised by Scrim selling his wife's piano!

After the election of the Labour Government at the end of 1935 the continued existence of the B stations was still in doubt because 1ZB, along with the others, was under pressure to sell out. Although Scrim publicly stated that he was not, and had never been, a member of the Labour Party, he was certainly sympathetic to Labour's policies and was on extremely friendly terms with the party's leader, M. J. Savage. So, although 1ZB was purchased by the government, Scrim made a deal with Savage that the sale was conditional on the Friendly Road organisation being given special status and was himself guaranteed air time for his 'Man In The Street' sessions.

Thus it was that in October 1936 1ZB became the 'flag' station of the new commercial service, followed by 2ZB, 3ZB and 4ZB in 1937, and 2ZA in 1938. Scrim's Sunday evening 'Man In The Street' session was then carried by all five stations.

Initially there had been some resistance to the introduction of advertising over the air but when it was realised that the continuance of the new style of 'popular' programmes depended on it the objections soon vanished. As Controller of the NCBS it was Scrim who was largely responsible for the introduction of the new programme format of the commercial stations, but in spite of the workload which the job entailed he not only retained a continuing interest in the Friendly Road organisation but even went to Australia to set up a counterpart in that country.

For a few years things went well for Scrim but following Savage's death in 1940 it was not long before he fell foul of the new Prime Minister, Peter Fraser. In March 1943 Scrim was suspended as controller for the NCBS but proved a hard man to get rid of. After being shanghaied into, first the army, and then the air force during the final stages of the war he went into voluntary exile in Australia from which he did not return until 1968.

In spite of the continuing difficulties facing their owners, a number of privately-owned stations managed to remain in existence during the final years of the 1930s, though as ever their hours of transmission were usually quite limited. Although by the end of 1938 there were 16 government controlled stations on the air there still remained nine in private hands; the continuing existence of the latter being due in part to revenue derived from the then permitted 'sponsored' programmes which they were allowed to broadcast. However, the number of B class stations continued to decline and by the end of 1940 only four remained—2ZJ and 2ZM in Gisborne, 2YB in New Plymouth and 4ZD in Dunedin. With the exception of 2ZM all these stations are still in existence.

The history of the re-establishment of privately and commercially owned broadcasting stations in New Zealand is too recent to warrant a detailed coverage in these pages. It has proved to be a continuing story with applications for new licences being lodged ever since it became legalised. By 1984 there were 25 B class stations in operation, including five non-commercial ones and three newly licensed FM transmitters broadcasting in stereo. The latest development, introduced in the same year, has been broadcasting in AM stereo, an Auckland station, 1XI, claiming to be the first outside the U.S. with the new sound.

14

As the story of the 'National' government-controlled service has received adequate published coverage over the years readers seeking information on this aspect of New Zealand broadcasting are referred to the listing of relevant publications contained in the bibliography at the end of the book.

CHAPTER TWO

The hardware

CRYSTAL SETS

As mentioned previously, it was the humble crystal set which provided many people with their radio entertainment in the early days of broadcasting, but the use of a crystalline mineral as a detector of radio signals goes back quite a long way further than this. Carborundum, a commercial form of silicon carbide, was used as early as 1906, while at much the same time another early detector, the Perikon, used two different crystals in contact with each other.

By far the most commonly used type for broadcast listening was the galena detector which used a crystal of lead sulphide in conjunction with a wire 'catswhisker' contact. Crystal detectors of this type were made in vast quantities during the 1920s and formed the basis for both home-made and factory-built crystal sets. The only drawback was that the operator had to search for a sensitive spot on the crystal surface on which to place the catswhisker and once the spot had been found it could easily be lost by the slightest jarring of the receiver.

Because its simplicity made the crystal set ideal for the home constructor there were probably more home-made than commercial products in use throughout the 1920s. Either way its low initial cost and zero running expenses made it especially popular with schoolboys, many of whom acquired a lifelong interest in radio as a result of their early experiences. Although in some cases the crystal set did duty as a family radio as it was possible to use more than one pair of headphones, headphone listening was inherently somewhat unsociable as well as being rather tiring on the ears, bearing in mind the heavy-weight 'phones of the day. Apart from this, volume was strictly limited and selectivity sometimes insufficient to prevent two stations coming in together.

And now, over 60 years later, crystal sets are still being built by schoolboys, albeit with germanium diodes in place of galena detectors.

Although the crystal set formed many people's introduction to 'listening in' there were others who could not be bothered with fiddling with catswhiskers and who were not content to

This amateur receiving station, owned by Morton Coutts of Taihape, shows what 'wireless' looked like in 1922. On this occasion the apparatus has been moved into the garden to have its picture taken.

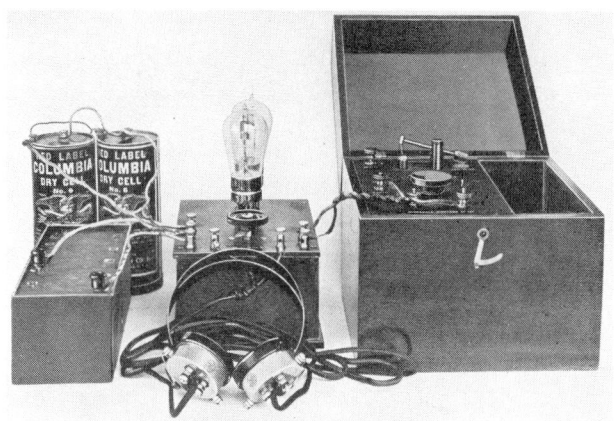

A crystal set coupled to a 2-valve amplifier. This was 'wireless' in the early 1920s.

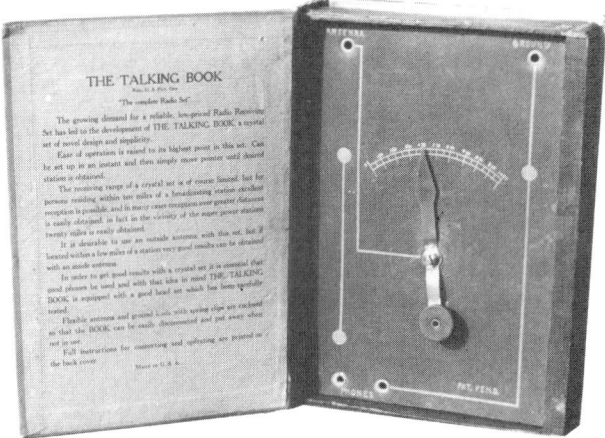

"Talking Book" crystal set c. 1923.

listen to only the local station, which in any case may have been on the air for only an hour or two daily. The owners of valve sets fell into two classes, those who had the enthusiasm and ability to make their own receivers, and those who bought factory-made sets. The very early experimenters and 'hams' were forced to 'roll their own' as before about 1924 there were very few commercially made receivers available in any case.

For many years the hobby of building and rebuilding receivers became almost an end in itself which continued in popularity up until the 1940s. Throughout this period home constructors were catered for by a variety of publications and by the availability of suitable components and accessories, many of which were produced specially to suit their needs. By 1950, however, the days of the home constructor were almost over.

EARLY BATTERY SETS

Initially, all receivers using valves were battery operated, and many years were to elapse

before batteries could be dispensed with and operation from household electric mains supply could be achieved. Because the early valves were expensive to buy, and were of low efficiency which made them expensive to run, the first receivers usually had no more than two or three valves.

Owners of battery sets were faced with the need for frequent renewal of the dry-cell high

Earliest known advertisement for a New Zealand-made crystal set 1923.

RadioCraft
Regenerative Radiophone* Receiver
TYPE D-6

RECEIVER D-6 utilizes the "honeycomb coil" system of tuning and employs the "three circuit" hook-up of tuning units. At the right hand end of the grained bakelite panel, one finds two bakelite knobs with pointers which control the coupling or proximity of the coils, two celluloid dials with knobs which vary the capacity of two De Forest vernier variable condensers, and an eight-point double arm switch that connects the larger condenser in series or across the "primary" honeycomb coil.

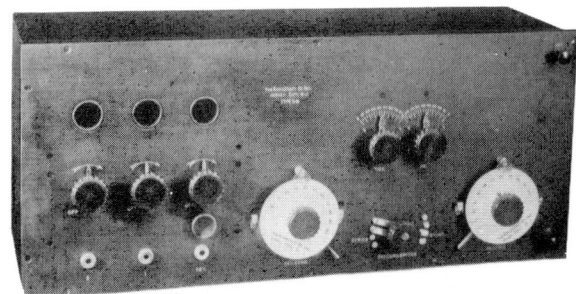

Radio Craft D-6 radiophone, 3-valve regen. 1922.
Made by the De Forest Radio Tel. & Tel. Co.

17

From *N.Z. Wireless & Broadcasting News* March 1923.

tension 'B' batteries, three 45-volt blocks of which could cost over a week's wages in those days and require replacement twice a year. In addition there was the problem of the low-tension 'A' battery, usually a heavy 6-volt car battery, which required transporting to the local garage for recharging at all too frequent intervals. As in the United States, the smaller, lighter 2-volt 'accumulators' never became popular in this country, though they were extensively used in the U.K.

Although in later years battery set owners could avail themselves of more economical valves, the replacement of the 'B' batteries and the recharging of the 'A' battery remained a constant expense. Even though HT battery eliminators, operated from the AC mains, became available from about 1927 their cost was often quite high and they were sometimes not entirely satisfactory

in operation. Similarly, 'A' battery eliminators were even more expensive and never became popular.

For those listeners living in remote areas where no battery charging facilities existed, 'all-dry' operation was often essential. In such cases 1½-volt general-purpose dry cells, as used in manual telephones and Ford model T ignition systems, were pressed into use as 'A' batteries to supply the filaments of special 'low-drain' valves.

Up until about 1925 reproduction was generally obtained through the use of headphones, and this method continued in popularity for some years after loudspeakers had come into general use.

Although smaller two or three-valve sets could sometimes drive a loudspeaker satisfactorily, it generally required a larger set to do the job properly. Most of the first loudspeakers were no more than a headphone unit fitted with

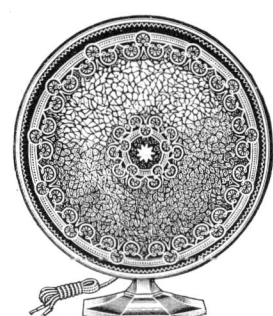

Above: Typical cone speaker of the late 1920s.

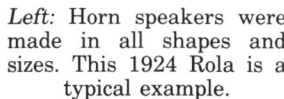

Left: Horn speakers were made in all shapes and sizes. This 1924 Rola is a typical example.

The latest thing in 1925. A Stewart Warner model 300 5-v TRF with matching horn speaker.

a horn, and it was the use of such an appurtenance which in later years gave rise to the term, horn speaker. As time went by improved types of horn speakers were developed, including the so-called 'balanced armature' types. One manufacturer, Magnavox, actually marketed a moving-coil horn speaker as early as 1921, though it was rather too expensive to become popular and, furthermore, required a fairly heavy current from a 6-volt battery to energise the field coil.

Following horn speakers came the so-called 'magnetic' or 'cone' speakers which used a cone-shaped paper or parchment diaphragm, usually about 12 to 14 inches in diameter, though sizes up to 24 inch were produced. Speakers of this type gave considerably improved reproduction of the lower musical frequencies, though it was not until the introduction of moving-coil 'dynamic' speakers, which came into use from 1928 onwards, that really good bass response could be obtained.

It was the combination of high running costs, coupled with comparatively difficult operation, not to mention frequent unreliability, of the early battery sets which set the stage for the introduction of the 'all-electric' receiver.* New Zealand was well placed to take advantage of the convenience and low running costs of mains-operated radios as by 1930 most of the country had been covered with a national electricity 'grid', leaving only the 'backblocks' unreticulated.

In this country, as in the U.S., people could not get rid of their old-fashioned battery sets quickly enough, even though most of the early electric receivers were quite expensive. In most cases the superior performance, particularly in the matters of tone and volume, left battery sets well behind and it was not long before the latter became obsolete.

* For the purposes of this book the term 'all-electric' is defined as a receiver using AC type tubes, as distinct from a mains-operated one using battery tubes.

Radio in the Home. A Philco model 20 All Electric 1930.

THE ALL-ELECTRIC RADIO

Initially the first all-electric radios bore some resemblance to their battery-operated counterparts as they were housed in small boxes, though of metal not wood, and were equipped with separate speakers. By 1929, however, American AC radios were housed in large and often ornate consoles, the so-called 'furniture' cabinets which also contained a moving-coil speaker. Yet within a year or so a complete revolution occurred. The advent of the Great Depression at the end of 1929 brought with it the need for a cheap, and that meant small, radio priced to suit the prevailing hard times. Thus the 'midget' was born. It was small, it was simple, but above all it was cheap and its production put all-electric radio within the reach of all but the poorest American families.

The first midget radios appeared in 1930 and by 1931 had captured a large share of the market. It is not quite certain which company actually produced the first midget, though Los Angeles is generally considered to have been their birthplace. The Automatic Radio Company's 'Tom Thumb', released in November 1930, is generally considered to be the first midget produced in the east.

When compared in size with those produced only two or three years later the first midgets do not seem to justify their description, but by comparison with the bulky 1929 console models they were indeed small. Most had cabinets measuring no more than 18 inches high by 14 inches wide which were often of the so-called 'cathedral' style.

By 1933, however, the introduction of transformerless (AC/DC) circuitry using tubes with series-connected heaters enabled even smaller and cheaper models to be produced. Sets measuring no more than 9 or 10 inches wide by 7 or 8 inches high became commonplace, and for the first time some manufacturers started using bakelite cabinets.

As economic conditions improved radios started to get bigger again and by 1936 console models were capturing an increasingly larger share of the market. Midgets remained popular though they grew even smaller and were relegated to the status of a second set.

Throughout the 1930s radio listening continued to increase in popularity, ranking second only to the movies as a provider of family entertainment. On the technical side improvements in circuitry, coupled with the production of more efficient and reliable valves and components had brought the domestic radio to a performance peak which was never really excelled in later years. The superheterodyne circuit had been tamed, moving-coil speakers had been reduced to manageable proportions and circuit refinements, chiefly the introduction of automatic gain control (AVC) had all helped to

bring about a high standard of performance coupled with ease of operation, making radio ownership almost universal in the United States. These were the years of radio's 'Golden Age'.

MULTI-BAND RECEIVERS

Because there were no long-wave broadcasting stations in the U.S., or anywhere in the entire Western Hemisphere for that matter, American radios, unlike their European counterparts, originally covered only the broadcast (MW) band. Any American sets which did have long-wave coverage were export models which became available from about 1934 onwards.

Although receivers incorporating short-wave bands had been available as early as 1928 (the Pilot 'Super Wasp' was an example) mains-operated models did not become common until after 1934. Depending on how the term 'short-wave' is defined, receivers capable of tuning to higher frequencies were seen a year before this when someone hit on the idea of producing a modified version of a standard broadcast receiver to enable reception of police calls which were transmitted just below the HF end of the broadcast band. In those days the police departments of many American cities had introduced one-way radio telephone services ("Calling all cars") and these transmissions could be received on a suitably modified receiver; all that was necessary was to tap the secondaries of two coils and fit a wave-change switch. Thus came 'police-band' reception. The idea was quickly taken up by most manufacturers and became an extensively advertised sales feature during 1933.

The following year, 1934, saw the general introduction of the first 'all-wave' models by most manufacturers, and by 1937 all but the smallest and cheapest sets included at least one short-wave band. It was the threat of war in Europe and its eventual outbreak at the end of 1939 which really boosted interest in short-wave reception, when for the first time many people found they could experience the thrill of listening directly to foreign countries.

CAR RADIOS

Although one or two American manufacturers had produced radios specifically for use in motor cars as early as 1930 these were really no more than a specialised form of battery set, one make at least being intended for use only while the vehicle was stationary. These first car radios made use of a mixture of standard 2.5-volt AC tubes and 5-volt battery tubes, while the HT supply was provided by three 45-volt dry-cell batteries, and in addition a bias battery was

*The "AUTO PILOT" goes on your running board and does not
lessen the car's trade-in value when taken off to go on your next car*

"Auto Pilot" Full Screen Grid Radio
LICENSED UNDER R.C.A. PATENTS
Increases Your Automobile Pleasure

Nobody will have a more up-to-date automobile than yours when you have assembled this powerful "AUTO PILOT" Screen Grid broadcast receiver kit, placed it on your running board in its attractive black japanned case and connected its remote control dial and speaker.

Even the specially designed PILOT "undercar" aerial attaches between the axles without necessity for harming your car's exterior or interior.

This new and advanced "AUTO PILOT" not only has every up-to-date feature of radio to assure you distance, selectivity, tone quality and volume—but the welfare and future trade-in value of your car has also been a chief consideration of design. The New "AUTO PILOT" requires no mutilation of floor, instrument board or upholstery to make a solid installation—convenient to operate, taking up no foot or seat room.

You Can Install the "Auto Pilot" in Your Car in An Evening.

Four-224 A.C. Screen Grid Pilotrons comprising three stages of radio frequency and detector give the "Auto Pilot" tremendous pick-up and distance range. A. C. Pilotrons are operated from the car's battery instead of battery type tubes because they are rugged and non-microphonic.

Auto Pilot Kit 47⁵⁰
Complete with aerial less
Pilotrons and Speaker

Thick sponge rubber mountings take up road shocks. The audio amplifier system gives enough volume for outdoor dancing, with tone quality of the highest order. Filament current drain from car's storage battery is only 4 amperes. Plate current is 20 milliamperes from three 45-volt "B" batteries.

Inquire of your local Pilot Radio Dealer or write direct to

PILOT RADIO & TUBE CORP.
323 BERRY ST., BROOKLYN, NEW YORK
Chicago Office: 234 South Wells St.   *San Francisco Office:* 1278 Mission St.
FACTORIES AT LAWRENCE, MASS.

PILOTRON RADIO TUBES
Endorsed by Professionals

July 1930

21

needed.

Within three years further development of this new class of radio was greatly accelerated by the introduction of a new range of special tubes having 6.3-volt heaters and the development of 'vibrator' HT power supplies. By 1933 self-contained receivers operating directly from the 6-volt car battery were available. Car radio had arrived.

As a nation of car lovers the United States was naturally the first country to produce and develop receivers specially designed for permanent installation in motor cars, with the result that by 1936 all major car makers were making provision for the installation of so-called 'custom-built' models by including a space for the control head on the dashboard. Furthermore, in the days before all-steel bodies many car makers included built-in aerials concealed in the fabric roofs.

General Motors acquired a radio factory in the early 1930s and established its United Motors Division especially to manufacture car radios, and later entered the domestic receiver market as well. Philco supplied Ford and other car manufacturers with custom-built models, and many other radio manufacturers entered the car radio market by producing 'universal' models designed to be fitted to any make of car.

It is of interest to note that even in the U.S., the home of the car radio, there was some initial resistance to the idea of having a set capable of operation while the vehicle was in motion. If, as was usually the case, the radio was under the control of the driver it was feared that his attention might be distracted from the road ahead as a result. In 1930 for example, one manufacturer, the Pilot Radio and Tube Corp., issued the following warning in their publication *Radio Design:*

VIBRATOR OPERATED HOME RADIOS

An offshoot of the car radio was the vibrator-operated home radio which came into use from 1936 and largely replaced the old type of battery set which used separate LT and HT batteries. Most of the New Zealand-made vibrator sets used ordinary 2-volt battery valves, though some used special low-drain 6.3-volt valves. In both cases the total current consumption was under two amps from a 6-volt battery, which meant that recharging was needed no more frequently than with the older sets, and of course no expensive dry-cell HT batteries were required.

This type of radio became popular in unreticulated rural areas, provided battery charging facilities were available. Vibrator sets were manufactured up until the early 1950s, but after this time a lessening demand made continuing production uneconomical even before the advent of transistor radios.

PORTABLES

Portable radios have a surprisingly long history, extending back almost as far as any sort of battery-operated set, though it was not until nearly 20 years later that they achieved any real degree of popularity.

In 1924 RCA introduced their model 24, a portable version of the 'Radiola Super', and also another superhet portable, the model 26. One of the best known early American portables was the 'Trav-Ler', a 4-tube TRF, the first model of which appeared in 1925.

For one reason or another portables did not become popular in the U.S. in the early days, probably because of their bulkiness and comparatively high price, and it was in England that they really flourished.

By 1928 there were over 25 different makes of portable receivers on the British market, not counting the so-called 'transportable' models, some of which could be pressed into use as portables. The average weight of a 1928 portable, as calculated by *Wireless World*, was 26 lbs.

The first British portable was made by the Rees-Mace Mfg Co., a firm which has the distinction of being the only British manufacturer to export any sort of radio to the U.S. in pre-war days. Two models of Rees-Mace portables were imported by the New York department store of John Wanamaker & Son in 1929, the circuit diagrams of which, incidentally, appeared in Vol. I of Rider's *Perpetual Troubleshooters Manual.* Ten years later, in March 1939, a Rees-Mace portable unexpectedly made the front cover of *Radio News,* but not surprisingly no one on the staff could recognise it.

A distinctive feature of British portables made before 1940 was the use of a 2-volt non-spillable jelly acid accumulator for the filament supply, but this type of cell was easily ruined by over charging or neglect.

It was the production of a line of special 1.4-volt dry-cell tubes in the U.S. late in 1938 that led

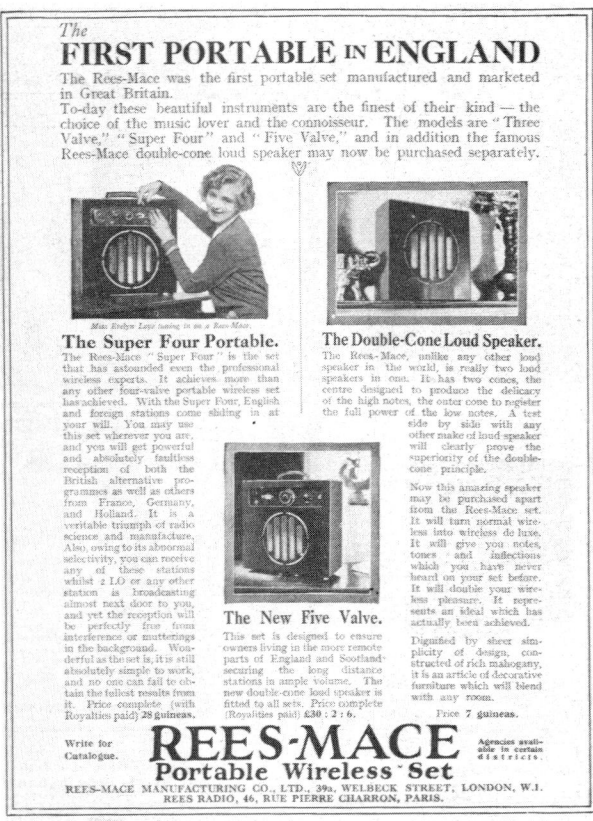
to portable radios becoming popular in that country. By 1939 many of the leading set makers such as Crosley, Emerson, Philco, RCA and Zenith had marketed sets using the new tubes. But it was the development of combined mains and battery-powered models from 1940 onwards which greatly increased the appeal of the portable radio and ensured a steady future market.

LISTENING TO RECORDS

Although the introduction of the all-electric radio was a serious threat to the gramophone/phonograph* industry it was not long before a marriage of convenience took place when the first combination radio-phonographs or 'radiograms'† appeared. Actually 'radio' had had an earlier connection with the phonograph industry when 'electrical' recordings, made using electromagnetic cutting heads fed by amplifiers using radio tubes, had been produced as early as 1925.

One of the earliest electrical reproducers was the Brunswick 'Panatrope', which first appeared in 1926. In the same year the Victor Company produced their 'Electrola Hyperion' which included a radio tuner, making it the world's first combination model. Another early electric phonograph was the 'Kolster' made by the

Brandes Products Corp. for Columbia Phonograph Co. It is interesting to note that all three were marketed by phonograph companies, but their high prices put them out of reach of the average owners of acoustical machines.

Apart from being expensive these early models were also bulky and inefficient by comparison with those produced a few years later. But, electric phonographs, as such, were used mainly for commercial purposes and only when combined with a radio tuner did they achieve any degree of popularity for home use.

Phonograph 'pickups' became available separately from 1927, but for all that was heard of them during the next few years they might not have existed. Some of the first types marketed were in the form of an attachment which could be used in place of the 'soundbox' fitted to ordinary gramophones, thereby enabling owners of acoustical machines to play records through a radio. By this means better reproduction could be obtained, but the bugbear of surface noise or hiss remained because the nature of the 78 rpm records themselves was unchanged. In addition, most of the early pickups were as heavy as, or even heavier than, the average soundbox and thus the problem of rapid record wear remained.

By the late 1930s some improvements in pickup design had taken place; pickup heads had been decreased in weight and needle compliance

---

* These terms are interchangeable, the latter being used in the U.S.

† The term 'radiogram' is used in English-speaking countries outside the U.S. and Canada.

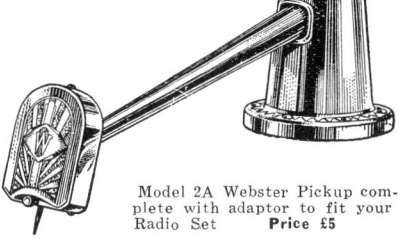
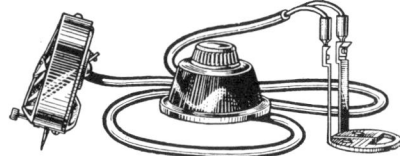
In 1929 records could be reproduced through a radio set by means of an electric pick-up.

Two early Radiograms. At the left is an Ultimate which sold for £69-10 in 1932. The other is a 1940 table model made by Collier & Beale Ltd which sold for £36.

had been increased. Crystal pickup cartridges, which gave improved bass response, came into use from 1935 and by the early 1950s had undergone many refinements. Lightweight magnetic pickups using miniature steel needles capable of playing up to 60 records also appeared in the early post-war years.

However, it was not until the advent of long-playing microgroove records in the late 1940s and early 1950s that the ownership of radiograms became commonplace. The introduction of the new records also resulted in an upsurge of interest in high-fidelity amplifiers, or Hi-Fi as

The Ultimate 'Concert Grand' radiogram was first issued in 1951 and continued in stereophonic form until 1961.

they came to be called, an interest which has seemingly been little affected by the later introduction of television and video recorders.

VALVES

No description of radio hardware would be complete without mention of the one essential device upon which all radio transmission and reception once depended—the thermionic valve or vacuum tube. Domestic receivers were invariably rated by the number of valves they used, from the earliest one-valve sets to giant 30-valve models. For over 40 years the valve reigned supreme and it seemed as if its position was impregnable, yet by the 1950s a challenger was in the offing.

For the first 20 years of their existence all valves were battery operated and it was not until the invention of a specialised type having what is known as an 'indirectly-heated' cathode that mains operation of receivers became feasible. From about 1927 battery sets gradually gave way to receivers capable of being operated directly from the household electric supply. This was a turning point in the development of radio receivers which led to their rapid acceptance as a household necessity throughout the world.

The majority of receiving valve development took place during the decade 1927 to 1937, and thereafter the main change was in the matter of size reduction, although certain new types of multiple and multi-electrode types continued to be developed.

By the late 1950s, however, although valve factories throughout the world were still going full blast, the first hint of a new device which was to challenge the supremacy of the valve became known. This new device was the 'transistor', a tiny object only a fraction of the size of a valve and sometimes known as an amplifying crystal. Later it was dignified by the name 'semiconductor' but its functioning depended on its essentially crystalline nature in exactly the same way as did the first crystal detectors which had been used in the earliest days.

Because, by comparison with valves, transistors required very low operating voltages their first application was in battery-operated portable radios. Within a few years, however, transistors had made great strides and by the early 1960s the production of valves and valve-operated radios was being seriously affected. Five years later valve radios had all but disappeared from the scene; solid state had arrived.

Although, at the time of writing, valves are still in production in certain countries they are being made for replacement use only. Only in certain specialised applications, mainly in high power service where no suitable solid-state devices have yet been developed, are valves being used as original equipment.

SOME LANDMARKS
IN RECEIVER DEVELOPMENT

1922-23 Battery-operated regenerative receivers in general use. Radio-frequency (signal) amplification first came into use using triode valves.

1924 Horn-loaded moving-iron speakers came into general use.

1926 Power output tubes first used in conjunction with moving-iron (magnetic) cone speakers.

1927 Screen-grid valves were developed for greatly increased and stable radio-frequency amplification.

1926-27 Special types of tubes developed for use in AC mains operated receivers. Single-dial control achieved by the ganging of individual tuning condensers.

1928 Invention of the pentode valve in Holland, originally for use in output stages only.

1929 Moving-coil (dynamic) speakers came into general use in the U.S. AC operated screen-grid tubes became available in the U.S.

1930 First use of diode detection and automatic volume control (originally in TRF receivers). Indirectly-heated pentode output valves produced in England for use in AC receivers.

1931 Introduction in the U.S. of AC operated superheterodyne receivers. Production of 'variable-mu' screen-grid tubes in the U.S. First use of pentode output tubes in the U.S.

1932 First radio-frequency pentodes and first combination duodiode-triode tubes produced in the U.S. Permanent-magnet moving-coil speakers first used in Holland and the U.K.

1933 Production of special combination tubes for use as frequency changers in superheterodynes. Automatic volume control (AVC) came into general use. Production of specialised tubes for use in combination AC/DC receivers.

1934 Inclusion of one or more shortwave bands became commonplace in better class receivers.

1937 Introduction of beam tetrode output tubes in the U.S.

It may be remarked, apropos to the above, that there are some people, and the author is one of them, who believe that little of real value has occurred in domestic receiver development since 1934. It is a fact that by this time receivers incorporated all the features which were to remain in use thereafter for as long as valve-operated radios continued to be produced. The superheterodyne circuit with pentode RF and IF amplifying stages, diode detection with automatic gain control, combination frequency-changer valves featuring multiplicative mixing, pentode or beam tetrode output valves and moving-coil speakers were never superseded. Even when transistorised receivers appeared they still used the same basic circuitry.

FADA 6 Model 460-A

In cases where outside aerials could not be used an indoor type, known as a 'frame aerial' in Britian, and 'loop antenna' in the U.S., could often provide satisfactory reception. This 1926 Fada Battery set had an aerial which could be folded down inside the lid when not in use.

CHAPTER THREE

What they looked like

In 1977 London's Victoria and Albert Museum, in conjunction with the British Vintage Wireless Society, mounted an exhibition of 'classic' radio receivers produced in the U.K. between 1922 and 1957, a 35-year period which spanned the years from the establishment of broadcasting to the cessation of the manufacture of valve-operated radios and saw tremendous progress in the technological development of receivers and also continuing changes in their appearance. Known as 'The Wireless Show', this exhibition was unique in that it was concerned only with the latter aspect of this development, that is the changes in physical appearance which took place during the period. Allowing for the fact that the Victoria and Albert Museum is not a technological museum it was nevertheless somewhat disconcerting to a technical person to find numerous exhibits described in the Exhibition catalogue as being "Designed by . . . ", when what was really meant was—"Cabinets designed by . . . ".

Naturally the 'Wireless Show' could be concerned only with examples of British-made receivers, though as early as 1928 the Dutch firm of Philips had set up a British factory, and by 1932 the American firm of Philco had done likewise. Although examples of both these makes were included it would be difficult to judge what effect, if any, they had on the overall development of cabinet styling in Great Britain.

Although the period during which the domestic radio receiver occupied pride of place in family living rooms around the world lasted for

little more than 30 years (depending upon how soon the Cyclopean monster of television invaded those same living rooms), by the end of the 1950s the development of valve technology was nearing its limits, and similarly, or seemingly, so was cabinet styling.

Because the first cabinets were no more than plain wooden boxes intended to keep dust out of the works there was no thought given to making their appearance attractive, any more than there would have been in the case of a radio transmitter, for example. It was only when radio broadcasting had been accepted as a means of family entertainment, and receivers had been allowed into family living rooms, that the matter of their appearance began to take on a new significance and receivers started to look less like pieces of scientific apparatus and more like pieces of furniture.

When in June 1922 the Radio Corporation of America (RCA) issued their first catalogue of household radio equipment it was appropriately entitled 'Radio Enters the Home'. While most of the apparatus offered consisted of small two and three-tube sets for use with earphones, a 4-tube de-luxe model known as the 'Aeriola Grand' was housed in a free-standing cabinet complete with inbuilt speaker and self-contained batteries. It was probably the first time that any radio manufacturer had deliberately set out to dress up his product so that it could take its place alongside living-room furniture of the period; thus was born the so-called 'furniture' cabinet.

By the end of 1924 several American manufacturers were offering similar models, some examples being: De Forest, Fada, Magnavox, Michigan, Operadio and WorkRite. However, it should be emphasised that such models were very much in the minority, because speakers and batteries continued to be regarded as 'accessories' for several more years, and the majority of receivers continued to be housed in horizontal boxes; in fact some manufacturers continued to make their sets in this form until the advent of all-electric receivers in 1927 eventually sounded the death-knell of battery sets.

The development of the completely enclosed set was somewhat slower in Great Britain,

Freshman 'Masterpiece' 5-v TRF 1925.
A typical American battery set.

De Forest model W6, 6-v battery set 1925.
It featured a "hand-wrought, hand-carved" cabinet designed by a "renowned sculptor, architect and painter".

Atwater Kent model 37 1928.
A typical example of an early all-electric receiver housed in a metal box.

although by 1924 at least two manufacturers, Cosmos and Gecophone, had marketed free-standing models in which speaker and batteries were enclosed within the cabinet. But, as in the U.S., it was not until mains-operated models appeared that 'one-piece' radios became commonplace. For a few years, in both countries, the first AC sets were often housed in metal cabinets and provided with separate speakers, the use of metal as a cabinet material being for technical reasons. A British trade catalogue issued for the 1931-32 season listed no less than ten manufacturers of AC sets with a total of 16 models intended for use with separate speakers, though by that time nearly all makers had at least one self-contained model on the market.

So it may be said that, apart from the few exceptions mentioned earlier, it was not until mains-driven radios became commonplace that much attempt was made to produce receivers in which the cabinet work could be described as ornamental.

The year 1929 in the U.S. saw the production of a new generation of AC receivers housed in massive and often ornate 'console' cabinets, the word console in this context being used to describe the free-standing type of cabinet. Console cabinets were available in either 'lowboy' or 'highboy' style, depending largely on whether the speaker was placed above or below the chassis. Cabinet styling was often advertised as being Early English, Jacobean and so on, but regardless of how true to style they actually were most American cabinets

of the 1929-32 period were solidly built from high quality timber and in addition were extremely well finished.

Following the onset of the Great Depression at the end of 1929, however, the production of console models tapered off sharply and by 1930 a completely new breed of diminutive low-priced receivers had largely taken over the market. The introduction of these 'midget' radios, as they were called, enabled sets to be produced at prices suited to the depressed economic conditions, thus putting them within the reach of purchasers who would otherwise have been unable to afford to buy a radio.

So it was that after little more than a year an abrupt change in the size and shape of radio cabinets occurred for, while console models never completely disappeared, by far the greatest number of sets produced during the years 1930 to 1933 were of the so-called 'midget' variety. Midget receivers required midget cabinets which were usually of lightweight construction to assist in keeping the price of the set as low as possible. Speakers were invariably mounted above chassis resulting in the cabinets being comparatively tall in relation to their width. A distinguishing feature was the use of shaped cabinet tops which were curved, arched, pointed, stepped or angled, in fact anything but flat. When it came to describing the overall styling the term 'Gothic' or 'cathredral' was often used. As applied to architecture this term is defined as a style having a predominance of vertical lines and pointed arches, a description which fitted many, but not all, of the cabinets used on American midget receivers.

In spite of its popularity in the U.S., Gothic styling never became popular in the U.K., or on the Continent for that matter, though at least one British manufacturer is known to have produced a set housed in a cathedral-style cabinet. British receivers made between the years 1932 and 1935 were usually provided with rather plain squarish cabinets, though by 1935 many makers were

Philomel radio (U.K.) 1932. Described as "modernistic" at the time of its debut, this styling would now be known as art deco.

Bush (U.K.) 4-v TRF 1932. A rare example of British use of American Gothic cabinet styling.

Stewart Warner model R105 1933. This six-legged console is an example of an American 'furniture' cabinet of the period.

changing over to placing the speaker alongside the chassis thus allowing the use of a horizontal style cabinet.

Apart from what may be called 'mainstream' cabinet styling a completely different development, known at the time as 'modernistic', and in later years as 'art deco' styling achieved a limited degree of popularity, mainly in the U.K. It was characterised by a 'jazzy' and sometimes asymmetrical appearance and often incorporated a chromium trim. This style lent itself well to the use of moulded bakelite cabinets which could be easily made in any desired shape.

As an indication of the growing importance being attached to cabinet styling in the early 1930s a *Wireless World* review dated July 1931 and referring to the Murphy model A3 receiver commenced not with the usual technical description but with a discussion of the cabinet styling, describing it as "challenging" and "provocative". The review goes on to mention the maker's view that as the household radio is essentially a modern development then its cabinet should be equally modern in concept. In other words a radio should look like a radio and not be disguised in a 'period' cabinet of quite inappropriate style. A completely logical argument, yet there were still people who preferred something which was more in keeping with the type of furniture they were likely to have in the house at the time. Anyway, who was to say what a radio was supposed to look like?

Sooner or later in the development of the domestic radio it was inevitable that more and more attention would be paid to cabinet styling and from about 1933 some of the larger manufacturers on both sides of the Atlantic began to retain the services of well-known architects and furniture designers to take care of that very aspect. But it is on record that even earlier than this at least one American radio manufacturer,

RCA-Victor, had considered the matter of cabinet appearance sufficiently important to make use of a then new concept in artistic design known as 'dynamic symmetry'.*

Throughout the entire period during which pre-transistorised receivers were in production wood was always the most common material used in cabinet construction, and in the case of large console models, the only material, but after about 1933 the use of plastics became increasingly common. Initially a phenolic resin compound known in the U.K. and the U.S. under its tradename of 'Bakelite' was used, but by the late 1930s other types of plastics became increasingly used.

Bakelite had been invented in 1919 by a Belgian scientist, L. H. Baekeland, and it was in Europe that it was first used for the manufacture of moulded plastic radio cabinets. By comparison with wood bakelite had the advantage of cheapness, provided production levels could be made sufficiently high to justify the heavy cost of the dies needed for the moulding process; it was

---

* Dynamic Symmetry was the name given to principles used in ancient Greek art, rediscovered in the U.S. about 1917. Though based on mathematical concepts the end result had, nevertheless, to be visually attractive.

Kadette (U.S.A.) 4-v TRF 1933. Example of early use of bakelite cabinet.

Fada model 1256W, 6-v DW 1936. An example of a set using a bakelite cabinet.

Two early bakelite-cased radios—Silvertone, 4500 (1934) Columbia (1933).

also a very durable material and needed no hand finishing. At first the use of bakelite was limited to the production of small radio and electrical components and not until the late 1930s had moulding techniques reached the stage where full-sized radio cabinets could be produced.

The Dutch firm of Philips were pioneers in the use of bakelite (which they termed 'Philite'), due probably to the almost complete absence of any indigenous timber supplies in Holland By 1928 they had produced, among other things, a large cone speaker measuring 46 cm (18 in) in diameter, and by 1930 had marketed a receiver, their model 2601, housed in a bakelite console cabinet which stood 81 cm (30 in) high, while the following year, 1931, saw the release of their first bakelite table model, the 2634.

Apart from using moulded bakelite Philips also made use of laminated paper-based bakelite in sheet form known as 'Arborlite' which, as its name suggests, had an appearance resembling wood. In this case the thinness of the material necessitated using metal reinforced edges to provide sufficient rigidity. The model 930 of 1931 was an example of a set housed in a cabinet of this type. Yet another form of construction was the use of heavier bakelised panels (the equivalent of early Formica) fitted into a skeletal metal framework, as exemplified in the models 2514 and 2510.

In Great Britain moulded bakelite cabinets were first seen in 1931 when the firm of E. K. Cole Ltd (EKCO) produced their model RS2. As well as pioneering the use of bakelite cabinets

Ekco were also the first to offer them in a choice of colours, initially jade green in addition to the usual wood-grain finish.

By 1936 bakelite cabinets had attained a fair degree of popularity on the British market, with such other well-known firms as Ferranti, Philco and GEC offering a selection of models.

In spite of the fact that American manufacturers, notably Atwater Kent and Gilfillan Bros, had pioneered the use of moulded bakelite for the production of small electrical and radio components in the early 1920s bakelite cabinets were not seen in the United States before 1932, and then only to a very limited degree. Furthermore, they never attained the same degree of popularity that they did in Europe.

The first American receiver to be housed in a plastic cabinet seems to have been the International Radio Co.'s 'Kadette', a diminutive 3-tube AC/DC model produced early in 1932. One of the first manufacturers to produce a standard sized table model set housed in a moulded bakelite cabinet was Pilot who in 1933 marketed their model 12.

By 1936 a few other American manufacturers, for example Fada and Arvin, had made occasional use of bakelite cabinets, but these firms were very much in the minority. Not until 1940 did the use of plastic cabinets become commonplace on smaller AC and AC/DC receivers in the U.S. and by then several manufacturers were offering a choice of colours in addition to the usual black or brown.

It may come as a surprise to some readers to learn that bakelite cabinets were made in Australia as early as 1932. In December of that year Amalgamated Wireless A/sia Ltd (AWA) advertised their first 'Radiolette' model which had a cathedral-style bakelite cabinet.

Some other Australian manufacturers who used bakelite cabinets in pre-war days were Airzone, Astor, Philips and Mullard.

On the local scene New Zealand-made receivers using bakelite cabinets were not seen until after the war, some early examples being Philco's model 200 and Philips' model 525 'Philette', both of which appeared in 1947. As in England and the Continent, Philips produced a bigger range of bakelite-cased sets, including some quite large sized ones such as the model 465 of 1948 which measured 16½ x 10½ x 7½ inches (43 x 27 x 19 cms). Another firm, Radio (1936) Ltd, produced a similar sized set, their model RU, in a cabinet which was marginally larger. However, the use of bakelite for cabinets of such a size was not common in this country.

A variation in cabinet finishes, seen on one early model 'Kadette' AC/DC midget, consisted of a thin layer of plastic known as 'Celluloid' applied

Empire 5-v DW (Made in N.Z.) 1950. An example of a cabinet moulded from 'Perspex' (Plexiglass) plastic.

over a wooden cabinet in place of veneer. Celluloid was the same material as used for dial scales in the early 1930s; it often had a rippled or mother-of-pearl finish. One N.Z. manufacturer who used such cabinets (c.1937) was World Radio Industries Ltd.

A development which may well have been unique to New Zealand was the use of cabinets moulded from 'Perspex' sheet plastic (known in the U.S. as 'Plexiglass'). This enabled small runs of cabinets to be produced quite cheaply, making it well suited to the needs of smaller set makers whose production levels did not warrant the high initial cost of moulded bakelite. Perspex cabinets were used briefly in the early 1950s by such firms

as Webb's Radios and Westco Products. Other firms, such as Antone and Sheffield, used a hybrid-style cabinet having a wooden carcass fitted with Perspex front and back sections.

Inevitably the introduction of plastic cabinets met with criticism from some quarters in the early days; there were those who held that bakelite was an *Ersatz* material—a poor substitute for wood—which had a cold appearance and adversely affected the tone of the receiver. But these criticisms did not appear to have much, if any, effect on the increasing use of plastic cabinets on small receivers, a class of set which could never have been produced as cheaply and thus never have achieved such large sales volumes, if wooden cabinets had been used.

Although polished or fabric covered wood, and even solid leather, was sometimes used for the cabinets of the earliest transistor radios it was not long before moulded plastic cabinets became universally used; in fact it would be fair to say that the subsequent enormous production of such sets would have been impossible without its use.

CHAPTER FOUR

New Zealand radio manufacturing

Nowadays it may not be generally realised that, prior to the introduction of import restrictions in 1938, the establishment of a radio manufacturing industry in this country was accomplished in the face of unrestricted competition from imported receivers, in itself an indication of the determination and confidence of those pioneering firms who were responsible for starting things off in the early days.

In those days the word 'multinational' had not been heard of and radio manufacturing in this country was entirely in the hands of New Zealand firms which were completely free of any form of overseas control. Two minor exceptions may be cited—His Master's Voice (N.Z.) Ltd and Philips Lamps (N.Z.) Ltd, both mainly importers whose manufacturing activities were not large in pre-war days. Thus, apart from having access to the world's patents in the same way as did the manufacturers of any other country, New Zealand was completely on its own when it came to matters of technical knowhow and production expertise.

Yet, in spite of being both a young and small country with no history of manufacturing, there were by 1938 New Zealand-made radios which could compare favourably with, and in some cases even surpass, the products of such countries as Australia, England and the United States.

Although the bulk of radio manufacturing was in the hands of the 'big three' companies—Collier & Beale Ltd, Radio Corporation of N.Z. Ltd and Radio Ltd, it was surprising how many small manufacturers came into existence in the pre-war years. It is estimated that over 50 different firms came and went between 1927 and 1940, some of them lasting no more than a couple of years. Most of these 'manufacturers' were really only assemblers who bought in everything from outside suppliers, although in one or two cases the extent of true manufacture was quite large.

Of the smaller firms only about seven remained in existence at the end of World War II, while the larger ones all remained intact. The industry total was supplemented by the establishment of 14 new firms in the post-war years, chief among whom were Allied Industries

Ltd, Autocrat Radio Ltd and Thorn Radio Industries Ltd. Sadly, not one of the original big three firms now remains in existence.

The last valve radios made in New Zealand were produced in 1975 by a small Christchurch manufacturer, Stewart Radio Ltd, who had previously made only portable record players. These particular sets were 6-valve models produced in response to a demand for a radio which would provide good daylight reception in areas where transistor sets were inadequate.

NEW ZEALAND RADIO MANUFACTURERS

The following listing contains the names of all known N.Z. manufacturers of household and car radios. The dates indicate the period during which manufacturing actually took place, not the total years the companies were in existence. Unless otherwise stated, all firms were located in the Auckland city area.

*Akrad Radio Corporation Ltd (Waihi)	1934-82
†Allied Industries Ltd	1955-
Ambassador Radio Co.	1935-36
†Antone Ltd	1947-49
Atlanta Radio Co.	1934-37
†Autocrat Radio Ltd	1946-
†Bell Radio-Television Corp.	1949-80
Preston Billing Ltd (Wellington)	?
Challenge Radio Co.	1933-35
R. Chaston (Wellington)	1948-50
*Collier & Beale Ltd (Wellington)	1927-73
A. Cunningham	1933-36
A. J. Daycome Ltd (Christchurch)	1927-28
*Dominion Radio & Electrical Corp. Ltd	1939-80
Ellis & Co. Ltd	1933-34
Ellison Radio Labs (no details)	
Electric Service Co. (Wellington)	1937-40
Fisher Radio Co.	1933-38
General Radio Co. Ltd	1933-34
Hartle & Gray Ltd	1927-30
Heath Electronics	
*His Master's Voice (N.Z.) Ltd (Wellington)	1940-55
Harley Mfg Co. (Christchurch)	c. 1935
Imperial Radio Mfg Co. Ltd	1935-40
*International Traders Ltd	1937-52

K. S. Irvine (Wellington)	c. 1936	
Johns Ltd	1926-27	
†Keith's Radio Service	1949-52	
†La Wood Television Ltd	1960-	
L. J. Lawrence	1950-51	
†Lincoln & Fletcher Ltd	1947-53	
*S. D. Mandeno & Co. Ltd	1935-40	
McMillan Radio Supplies	1938-40	
W. Marks (Wellington)	1930-33	
T. Megann (Wellington)	1947-48	
*F. W. Mountjoy & Sons Ltd	1934-54	
†Mowat Radio Industries Ltd	1950-60	
Natcla Radio Ltd (Wellington)	1927-28	
N.Z. Radio Mfg Co. Ltd (Christchurch)	1933-35	
Philips Lamps (N.Z.) Ltd (Wellington)		
(later became Philips Elec. Ind. of N.Z.)	1938-	
Parsons & Drury	1934-36	
Probert & Hunt (Wellington)	c. 1937	
*Radio Corporation of		
New Zealand Ltd (Wellington)	1934-59	
Radio & Electric Service Co.	1947-49	
*Radio Ltd		
(became Ultimate-Ekco Ltd)	1923-67	
†Radio Products Ltd	1947-49	
Radio Service Ltd (Dunedin)	1927-28	
Ross & Ramsden Ltd (Hastings)	c. 1937	
Royal Engineering Co. (Hamilton)	c. 1936	
Selectra Radio Ltd	1929-31	
Sexton Radio Co.	1927-35	
*Sheffield Radio Ltd	1934-70	
D. H. Shipperd	c. 1932	
†Stella Industries Ltd	1959-69	
†Stewart Radio Ltd (Christchurch)	1959-79	
†Swan Electric Co. Ltd (Wellington)	1948-49	
†Swinburne Radios Ltd	1946-60	
†Thorn Radio Industries Ltd	1970-	
Turnbull & Jones Ltd	1932-34	
*Universal Radio Co.	1934-48	
*Webbs Radios Ltd	1939-65	
*Wellmade Ltd	1928-57	
*Westco Products Ltd	1934-55	
J. Wiseman & Sons Ltd	1927-31	
*World Radio Industries Ltd	1933-55	

* Pre-war firms still manufacturing after the war.
† Firms established after the end of World War II.

EXPLANATORY NOTES

This listing applies only to valve-operated household and car radios manufactured in New Zealand. Although the large number of brand names may occasion some surprise it should be realised that many of the 'companies', whether listed as manufacturers or brand name owners, were sometimes no more than one or two-man businesses which existed for quite short periods, in some cases lasting for only a couple of years. In cases where overseas names appear it indicates that local manufacture took place under licence, except where piracy of such names occurred.

Regarding the word 'piracy' which appears in the listing, it is the author's belief that the use of such a word to describe the actions of certain firms or individuals is fully justified, as at various times one or two N.Z. manufacturers have used well-known overseas names on their products in a manner which can only be viewed as an attempt to cash in on the publicity value attached to those names.

The first known example of this deceitful practice occurred in 1933 when a small Auckland firm, General Radio Ltd, used the 'GR' trademark belonging to the world-famous General Radio Co., U.S.A. Not content with this they also pirated A. F. Bulgin's slogan 'The Choice of Critics', together with the Bulgin trade-mark of a bewigged aristocrat peeping through a lorgnette. Another pre-war example occurred when a Wellington retailer used the name 'ARC-Victor', reproduced in exactly the same style of script as the world-famous RCA-Victor name.

The last example occurred in the early post-war years when the Wellington firm of T. Megann Ltd made use of at least two well-known American names—Atwater Kent and Zenith. The name Atwater Kent was again used, this time about 1955 on sets made by the Akrad Radio Corp. In this case it is understood that the name was used at the behest of an Auckland retailer—Atwaters Ltd, and that the name Atwaters itself was made up from the firm's one-time slogan—"Get It At Waters".

BRAND NAMES OF NEW ZEALAND RADIOS

Brand	Distributor	Manufacturer
Ace (c. 1927)	Johns Ltd	Wellmade Ltd
Ace (c. 1949)		T. Megann Ltd
Acme		W. Marks
Aerola	Dominion Radio Co.	(no connection Creco)
Air King	Warwick Smeeton Ltd	Imperial Radio Mfg Co.
Airmasta		Antone Ltd
Airmaster	McCabes Radios	?
Air Ranger	General Motors N.Z. Ltd	Akrad Radio Corp.
Alsec		Alan Seccome

Brand	Distributor	Manufacturer
Altona	Johns Ltd	Wellmade Ltd
Ambassador		Ambassador Radio Co.
Antone		Antone Ltd
Ariel (1932-40)	Warwick Smeeton Ltd	Imperial Radio Mfg Co.
Ariel (1940-65)		Webb's Radios Ltd
ARC-Victor	(imitation of U.S. name)	Collier & Beale Ltd
Aristocrat	Todd Motors Ltd	Collier & Beale Ltd
Arnrite	Arnold & Wright Ltd	Chaston Ltd
Argosy		Probert & Hunt Ltd
Atlas	Hamilton Nimmo Ltd	?
Atomic	Atomic Radio Ltd	Sheffield Radio Ltd
Atwater Kent (1949)	(piracy of U.S. name)	T. Megann
Atwater Kent (1955)	(piracy of U.S. name)	Akrad Radio Corp.
Autocrat		Autocrat Radio Ltd
Avalon		Swinburne Radio Ltd
Astor	G. A. Wooller Ltd	Akrad Radio Corp.
Austin	Radio Warehouse (ChCh)	?
Bell		Bell Radio-TV Corp.
Bellbird		W. Marks Ltd
Briton	Briton Trading Co.	General Radio Ltd
Bulle B	Wingate & Co. Ltd	Akrad Radio Corp.
Bush (after 1940)		International Traders Ltd
Cambridge		Webb's Radios Ltd
Cardinal	Smith & Brown Ltd	various
Carlton	V.B. Climo	Westonhouse Radio Ltd
Carillon	John Burns & Co. Ltd	Sheffield/Sexton
Chappel		Sheffield Radio Ltd
Climax		W. Marks Ltd
Courier (early)		J. Wiseman & Sons Ltd
Courier		Radio (1936) Ltd
Centurion		?
Challen	Challen-Rad Dist.	Challenge Radio Co.
Champion		?
Clivic	Johns Ltd	Wellmade Ltd
Columbus	Radio Centre Ltd	Radio Corporation of N.Z.
Commodore	La Gloria Gramophones	D. H. Shipperd
Companion	Johns Ltd	Wellmade Ltd
C-Q	Hope Gibbons Ltd	Radio Corporation of N.Z.
Courtella	John Court Ltd	Westco Products Ltd
Courtenay (1931-34)	Stewart Hardware Ltd	W. Marks Ltd
Courtenay (1934-56)	Turnbull & Jones Ltd	Radio Corporation of N.Z.
Cromwell	H. W. Clarke Ltd	Collier & Beale Ltd
CRS	Cash Radio Stores	?
Crusader	Bond & Bond Ltd	various
Disco	Direct Supply Co. (ChCh)	?
Daventry	E. R. Cooper & Co.	Wellmade Ltd/Westco
Denco	(use of English name)	Westco Products Ltd
Dominion	Dominion Motors Ltd	General Radio Ltd
Daycoma		A. J. Daycombe & Co. (ChCh)
EIL	Electric Industries Ltd	International Traders Ltd
Elco	E. D. Ellingam & Co.	World Radio Industries Ltd
Elgar		Westonhouse Radio Co.
Elgin		Rees & Ramsden (Hastings)
Ellison		Ellison Radio Labs
Empire Concertone	Thos Ballinger & Co.	?
Empire		Westco and World Radio Ind.
Ensign	Electric Lamphouse Ltd	Collier & Beale Ltd
Escort	McKay & Wills	Akrad Radio Corp.

Brand	Distributor	Manufacturer
Essex		Westonhouse Radio Co.
Everest	Max Gunn Radios	Akrad Radio Corp. Ltd
Explorer		Patterson(U.S.A.)
Fisher		Fisher Radio Service
Fideles		L. J. Lawrence
Fidelity	Johns Ltd	Wellmade Ltd
Fleetwood	C. & A. Odlin Ltd	Philips Elec. Ind. of N.Z. Ltd
Forest Junior		Westonhouse Radio Co.
Franklin		Preston Billings Ltd
Fountain		Fountain Mfg Ltd
Futura		Akrad Radio Corp. Ltd
Galleon		
General		Bell Radio-TV Corp. Ltd
Gen Rad	General Radio Ltd	
Gloradio	La Gloria Gramophones	?
Gloucester		Collier & Beale Ltd
Golden Bell	Lewis Eady Ltd	Sheffield Radio Ltd
Golden Knight	Farmers/Calder McKay	various
Goldentone	Lewis Eady Ltd	Collier & Beale and Fisher
Gordon		(made in Wanganui)
Gulbransen (N.Z.)	H. W. Clarke Ltd	Collier & Beale Ltd
Hamilton	Hamilton Nimmo Ltd	Radio (1936) Ltd
Harley		Harley Mfg Co. (ChCh)
Haywin	Hays Ltd (ChCh)	?
Hagra		Hartle & Gray
Heath		Heath Radio Ltd
HMV	His Master's Voice N.Z. Ltd	various
Hy-Line	Waldo Hunter Ltd	Keith's Radio Service
Imperial		
Invincible	Wingate & Co. Ltd	Akrad Radio Corp. Ltd
K	Kodak (N.Z.) Ltd	Westonhouse Radio Co.
Kiwi	Johns Ltd	Wellmade Ltd
La Gloria		Dominion Radio & Elec. Corp.
Larsen		Larsen's Radio
Lewis Eady	Lewis Eady Ltd	Radio (1936) Ltd
La Wood	La Wood Wholesalers	La Wood Television Ltd
Lincoln-Fletcher	Lincoln & Fletcher Ltd	Westco Products Ltd
Luxor		Radio (1936) Ltd
Lynks		Chaston Ltd
Lyric	Ripley's Radios	Ellis & Co. Ltd
McCabe	McCabe's Radios	Radio Ltd
McMillan	McMillan Radio Supplies	World Radio Industries
Madison	Garnett Keene Ltd	Radio (1936) Ltd
Maestro	La Gloria Gramophones	?
Magic Notes		His Master's Voice N.Z. Ltd
Magness	R. J. Magness Ltd	Westco Products Ltd
Majestic (N.Z.)		Dominion Radio & Elec. Corp.
Marsden		Imperial Radio Mfg Co. Ltd
Melodia	McCabe's Radios	?
Melton Mastiff		Sexton Radio Co.
Micromatic	F. J. W. Fear & Co. Ltd	?
Minstrel	A. W. McCarthy Ltd	?
Minitone		Radio & Elec Service Co.
Moderne		The Electric Service Co.
Monitor	Farmers Trading Co.	various
Motorola (N.Z.)		International Traders Ltd
Mullard	C. & A. Odlin Ltd	Philips Elec. Ind. of N.Z. Ltd
Murphy (early N.Z.)	Westco Distributors Ltd	Westco Products Ltd

Brand	Distributor	Manufacturer
Murphy (later N.Z.)	Fisher & Paykel Ltd	Allied Industries Ltd
Natcla		Natcla Radio Ltd (Wgtn)
National (N.Z.)	John Burns Ltd	various
Neeco	National Elec. & Eng. Co.	Collier & Beale/World
New Century		?
Oxford		Webb's Radios Ltd
Ozarka (N.Z.)	Challen Rad. Dist. Ltd	Challenge Radio Co.
Pacific (c. 1935)	Pacific Radio Co.	Radio Corp. of N.Z. Ltd
Pacific (c. 1945)	A. H. Nathan Ltd	Akrad Radio Corp. Ltd
Paragon		A. Cunningham
Pacemaker	H. W. Clarke Ltd	Collier & Beale Ltd
Paramount	Electric Const. Co. Ltd	Radio (1936) Ltd
Pathfinder		Westco Products Ltd
Peerless		T. Megann Ltd
Philips		Philips Elec. Ind. of N.Z. Ltd
Philco (N.Z.)	Chas Begg & Co. Ltd	Dominion Radio & Elec Corp.
Planet		Planet Radios Ltd
Plymouth Aeroplayer		Parsons & Drury Ltd
Premier		T. Megann Ltd
Pye (N.Z.)	G. A. Wooller & Co. Ltd	Akrad Radio Corp. Ltd
Radiojoy		F. W. Mountjoy & Sons Ltd
Radiola (N.Z.)	AWA (N.Z.) Ltd	Allied Industries Ltd
Radion	Todd Motors Ltd	Collier & Beale Ltd
Regent	G. A. Wooller & Co. Ltd	Akrad Radio Corp. Ltd
Regal		
RES		Radio & Elec. Services Ltd
Robertson	Robertson Sewing Machines	Westonhouse Radio Co.
Rolax	Saddeley, Wells Ltd	?
Rolls	Rolls Radio Ltd	Radio (1936) Ltd
Royal		Royal Engineering Co.
RSL		Radio Service Co. (Dunedin)
Sandison		K. S. Irvine (Wellington)
Saxon		Westonhouse Radio Co.
Seven Seas		S. D. Mandeno & Co. Ltd
Sheffield		Sheffield Radio Ltd
Silvertone (c. 1932)	S. E. Moe & Co.	Sexton Radio Co.
Silvertone (c. 1947)	Radio Specialities Ltd	Sheffield Radio Ltd
Skyscraper	Bond & Bond Ltd	various
Skymaster	Bond & Bond Ltd	Bell Radio-Television Corp.
Sonomatic		Radio (1936) Ltd
SOS	S.O.S. Radio Ltd	Westco Products Ltd
Southern Cross		Westonhouse Radio Co.
Sovereign (c. 1934)		?
State	Wright Stephenson Ltd	Collier & Beale Ltd
Stella (early)	Cory, Wright & Salmon Ltd	Radio Corp./Collier & Beale
Stella (c. 1959)		Stella Industries Ltd
Sterling	Sterling Stores Ltd	Collier & Beale Ltd
Strohmeyer		Collier & Beale Ltd
Strola		Radio Products Ltd
Superdyne	Frank Wiseman Ltd	World Radio Industries Ltd
Supola		Universal Radio Co.
Supreme		?
Swan		Swan Electric Co. Ltd
Sylvia	L. D. Nathan Ltd	Collier & Beale Ltd
Tasman	Tasman Traders Ltd	Westonhouse Radio Co.
Temple (c. 1932)	Ellis & Co. Ltd	General Radio Ltd
Temple (later)	Ripley's Radios	World Radio Industries Ltd
Thorn		Thorn Radio Industries Ltd

Brand	Distributor	Manufacturer
Trav-Ler		Collier & Beale Ltd
Trojan		Ambassador Radio Co.
Troubadour		Turnbull & Jones Ltd
Universal		Universal Radio Co.
Ultimate		Radio Ltd
Victory	Farmers Trading Co. Ltd	?
Viking		N.Z. Radio Mfg Co. Ltd (ChCh)
Vocalion		Sexton Radio Co.
Wavemaster		?
Wayfarer	Waldo Hunter Ltd	Keith's Radio Service
Wiseman's Winner	Frank Wiseman Ltd	Bell Radio-Television Corp.
World		World Radio Industries Ltd
Victory	Farmers Trading Co. Ltd	?
Yale		Westonhouse Radio Co.
Zenith	(piracy of U.S. name)	T. Megann Ltd
Wellmade	Johns Ltd	Wellmade Ltd

New Zealand Names Used On Overseas Radios

Brand	Distributor	Manufacturer
Aeolian	Briton Radio	? (made in Australia)
Oxford	N.Z. Express Co. Ltd	? (made in U.S.A.
Lyratone	Crawford & Finlayson	Gilfillan Bros (U.S.A.)
Minuette	Radio Equipment Ltd	Radio Products Co. (U.S.A.)
Stannage	Stannage Radio Co.	Thom & Smith Ltd (Australia)
Viking	N.Z. Express Co. Ltd	? (U.S.A.)

CHAPTER FIVE

Some New Zealand radio manufacturers

AKRAD RADIO CORP. and PYE LTD

The firm which eventually became Pye (N.Z.) Ltd, and grew to be one of the largest of its kind in the country, had extremely humble beginnings back in 1932. In that year an 18-year old, Keith M. Wrigley, opened a one-man radio repair shop in the small country town of Waihi. By 1933 the staff numbered two.

Waihi, a former gold-mining centre, was a place that had seen better days and was not a spot where much money was likely to be made, one imagines. Furthermore, it must be remembered that those were the days of the Great Depression. Together these two factors made it highly likely that Keith Wrigley's tiny business could have easily sunk without a trace. That this did not happen is now a matter of history and was due to two things—the outbreak of World War II and, later, the appearance on the post-war scene of an energetic and ambitious young man by the name of George Wooller.

But back in 1932 all this was in the future. At that time Keith Wrigley, in order to supplement what can only have been a meagre income from his small repair shop, decided to embark on the manufacture of a few radios. The initial production was only 12 sets but they sold well and were more profitable to handle than similar ones bought through normal wholesale channels. The name chosen was 'Futura', and this name remained in use for the next seven years.

In 1934 the name of the business was changed to Akrad Radio Corporation, from which it may be inferred that Mr Wrigley's choice of such a grandiose title revealed his ideas on the future of the business. It may be remarked that, then as now, the use of the American term 'Corporation' was quite foreign to New Zealand commercial practice and Wrigley's choice could possibly have been influenced by the slightly earlier emergence of another firm which used the same word—William Marks' Radio Corporation (N.Z.) Ltd. Be that as it may, the word remained in the company title until the end of its days.

Progress during the pre-war years was slow but steady and as time went on other lines were introduced. From the manufacture of complete receivers it was but a step to the marketing of kitsets and components, as no change in production schedules was required. Later on the production of small electrical appliances such as heaters, battery chargers, electric poker-work machines and electric fence controllers was commenced in addition.

In 1941, or thereabouts, the brand name 'Pacific' was introduced to supersede Futura, although it is not clear just why this was done. The Pacific name had formerly been owned by a company named Pacific Radio Ltd which had been active between 1934 and 1937 when it had marketed a line of receivers made by Radio Corporation (N.Z.) Ltd. Wrigley took over the Pacific name together with the associated slogan "In a Sphere of its Own" which remained in use until 1952.

In common with certain other manufacturers Akrad was not as adversely affected by wartime conditions as might have been expected when the ban on the manufacture of domestic radios came into force in 1942. For one thing the ban did not prohibit the manufacture or sale of radio parts or kitsets. Amongst the company's contributions to the war effort was the production of Morse keys and high-note buzzers, Morse code practice sets and Morse oscillators as well as certain parts for the ZC1 military transceiver. By 1943 the staff had increased to 51.

An event which was to have profound significance in the future of the company occurred shortly after the end of the war when a partnership was formed with the previously mentioned G. A. Wooller which resulted in Akrad becoming a limited liability company with a capital of £30,000. However, shortly after this in 1947, Keith Wrigley died suddenly, which left George Wooller in full control of the company.

By coincidence Wooller had been born in Waihi but had left there in 1932 to seek his fortune in Auckland. As it happened this was also the same year as Wrigley had started up in business. Wooller obtained a job on the production line at the Ultimate factory in Rocklands Avenue, Balmoral and within three years had risen to the position of production manager. During the war he was co-opted by the Ministry of Supply to co-

All "Pacific" radios employ iron core litz I.F.s and Broadcast Coils

PACIFIC

BAND EXPANSION RADIO

IN A SPHERE OF ITS OWN.

Model 95 (as illustrated) incorporates 9 tubes and 5 bands, including broadcast. Dial is a 12in. slide tune with spinner action, printed in shaded colours.

Features of note are:
☆ TWELVE - INCH SPEAKER.
☆ PUSH - PULL OUTPUT.

Price £39/10/-.

Model 85. Identical to model 95, but does not include push pull.

Price £37/10/-.

Model 65. A 6-tube band-expansion model, using 8in. speaker, but same dial as in 95.

Price £29/10/-.

Model 65V. 6-tube band-expansion vibrator model, incorporating 10in. p.m. speaker.

Price £38/10/-.

Illustration: Models 95 and 85.

BAND EXPANSION has come to stay. Pacific offer three splendid models in A.C. and one in battery. Attractive illustrated pamphlets and window cards are available to dealers.

Models are available in low-boy style consoles and in radio-gramophone.

All models—band-expansion and others—are guaranteed by the manufacturer for 12 months.

From Akrad Radio Corp's 1941 Price List.

SELECT FROM THE WORLD'S BEST

Model "YRG"
N.I. £69/19/6
S.I. £72/15/0

Model "G"
£31/10/0

Model "H"
£55/12/6

5 valve, 5 waveband, BAND-SPREAD Superhet for A.C. Operation. Cabinet in Sapele Mahogany with contrasting grille and dial colours. Fully tropicalised.

for only **29'15'0**

Pye Perfection in the '71'

Short-wave BANDSPREADING and a "magic-eye" (for easier, better tuning on short-wave or Broadcast bands); a cabinet of gleaming, rich mahogany; five valves for superb reproduction. These are a few of the features of the outstanding "71"—another Pye contribution to better listening. See the "71" at your Pye dealer today.

PYE Radio and Television

Look for the distinctive PYE trademark at better radio dealers everywhere, or for your nearest PYE Agent, write to:

PYE (NEW ZEALAND) LIMITED.

P.O. Box 2839, Auckland

October 1953.

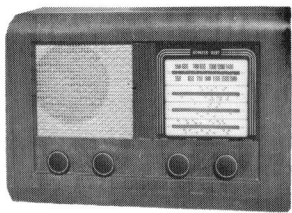

The 5W3A was a standard model normally sold under the name of Clipper. Note that the name Atwater-Kent is spelt in hyphenated form (see text).

The Pye 'Black Box' record player 1957.

THE PACIFIC AND REGENT **CLOCK-RADIOS**

There has long been room in New Zealand for a **really superlative** clock-radio at a practical price. G. A. Wooller with their Regent and Pacific Models 4CR fulfil this need to perfection. The Regent and Pacific Clock-Radios combine a quality 4-valve radio (with one dual-purpose valve to give genuine 5-valve performance) with a most reliable electric alarm-type clock. All this at a retail price of only £25 10s.

Model 4CR alarm-clock radio 1948.

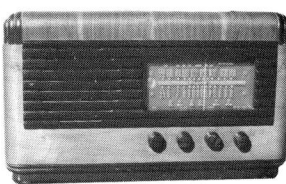

Regent model 727 1949. Also sold under the Pacific brand.

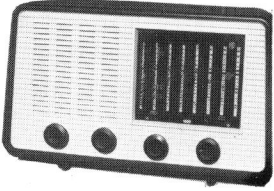

Pye PZ39 model 'G' was the first to appear on the N.Z. market and remained in production for several years. 1953-57.

Clipper 5-valve 1954 model 5M4.

PYE "MESSENGER"
6 multi-purpose valves give superb performance on broadcast, shipping and 3 shortwave bands. Piano key frequency switches. American Walnut Cabinet.
£43/15/0

PYE "RICARDO"
A 5-valve Mantel Radio manner. Bandspread styled in the modern fully tropicalised chassis. Available in Blonde Oak or Mahogany.
£35/19/6 Blonde Oak
£37/19/6 Mahogany

PYE "PENTETE"
Attractive moulded cabinet 5-valve Broadcast, printed circuit chassis. 4-inch High Flux speaker
£18/10/0

PYE "RANCHERO"
6-transistor 1 diode printed circuit chassis. Durable 2-tone Plastic Cabinet makes it a perfect all-round set. Operates for months on 4 torch batteries.

PYE "INTERCONTINENTAL"
7-valve Bandspread Radio in an attractive Mahogany Cabinet. Banjo-key band switches, adjustable aerial. One 6" x 8" speaker and two 3-inch tweeters.
£59/17 6

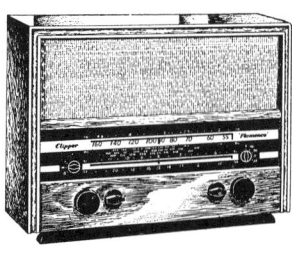

Model 6TR2 1958.

The Pye model 222 used a printed circuit board in place of the normal metal chassis. 1960.

The model PZ302 used three speakers.

The Astor model FEU was made in the Radio Corp. factory and was identical to the Columbus model 525A. 1960.

Pye model PZ108 'Ricardo' 1960-61.

ordinate wartime radio production and it was then that he had first come in contact with Keith Wrigley. In 1946 the firm of G. A. Wooller & Co. Ltd was formed as an importer and wholesaler of radio components and accessories. In the following year the brand name 'Fivestar' was introduced to be used on radios made by Akrad for distribution by Woollers.

At this time, too, another brand name, 'Regent', was also introduced, presumably for the usual reason of securing increased market coverage. Up till then the receivers produced were of quite conventional design, although by comparison with pre-war models the quality had been considerably improved.

It was not long before George Wooller conceived the idea of linking up with a British firm, largely in order to secure access to overseas research and developments, particularly in the area of television, which was then but a tiny speck on the local horizon. So it was that in 1953 the first New Zealand-made 'Pye' radios appeared. Initially they were almost identical to British models minus the long-wave band, but as time went by the Waihi factory developed other models of their own design, particularly in the case of radiograms. Here the company claimed to have originated radiogram styles which were accepted by Pye companies in other countries. Car radio production was commenced in 1956, sets being sold under the names Pye and 'Clipper' and in addition the name 'Air Ranger' was used on sets made for General Motors (N.Z.) Ltd.

In 1962 Pye acquired a majority shareholding

in the N.Z. company which then became Pye (N.Z.) Ltd. By that time the brand names 'Astor' and 'Clipper' had been added to the company's repertoire, presumably, in the jargon of the day, to increase market penetration because access to the Pye brand was limited to franchised dealers only.

Pye was one of the earliest New Zealand television manufacturers, having marketed their first sets in 1960. The first model was a 21-inch console using a 90-degree picture tube requiring the use of an ion-trap magnet. This same model was also made for HMV (N.Z.) Ltd who marketed it through their existing HMV dealer network.

By 1964 the N.Z. TV boom was at its height and to cope with increasing demands the factory production had to be increased enormously. At that time the company employed 500 people, quite a large staff by N.Z. standards. By 1971 the number of employees had reached 1,100 which represented a peak in Pye's manufacturing activities.

During the 1960s changes were in the wind in the British electronics industry, changes which were to have a profound effect on the local scene. The first of these events was the takeover of E. K. Cole (Ekco) by Pye of Cambridge in 1960 which in turn gave Pye (N.Z.) Ltd control of Ultimate-Ekco (N.Z.) Co. Ltd. In spite of assurances that U-E would continue to operate as before, the company was soon being dismembered. The Quay Street factory was the first casualty and by 1968 all operations there had ceased. The manufacture of Ultimate electrical appliances continued at the Glen Innes factory until 1972 when this operation was acquired by Sunbeam (N.Z.) Ltd.

In 1967 Philips of Holland acquired a controlling (60%) interest in Pye of Cambridge. Ten years later, in 1977, Philips acquired full control of Pye Ltd, then a subsidiary of Pye Holdings Ltd. This move thus gave Philips in N.Z. full control of N.Z. Pye and eventually led to the winding up, in December 1982, of all nine N.Z. companies then owned by Pye. Included in the casualties were Pye Electronics Corporation of New Zealand Ltd and the Akrad Radio Corporation Ltd, an event which marked the end of a chapter in the history of electronics manufacturing in this country.

BELL RADIO-TELEVISION CORPORATION

Of the New Zealand manufacturers who came into existence after the end of the Second World War the Bell Radio-Television Corporation became, and remained the largest and fastest growing. The origins of the company go back to 1947 when two young returned servicemen,

O'Brien and Stewart, went into business with the idea of making hearing aids. However, this idea was abandoned before any production had commenced and, instead, the two decided to manufacture a then new type of portable radio, one that would work on both mains and batteries. The design of this set was quite unique in that it had separate interchangeable battery and mains power units which plugged into a recess in its base resulting in a set of extremely small dimensions and light weight.

By 1948 production of the 'Antone' portable, as it was known, was underway at 347 Queen Street, Auckland, the factory at that time being an upstairs room. A modified and slightly larger version superseded the original model in 1950 and in the same year a small 4-valve AC set known as the Antone 'Cadet' was produced.

At about this time a third person, Mr A. Bell, joined Antone Ltd. Al Bell was a man with considerable business acumen and an ambition to be first in the field in the production of television receivers. Not long after his appearance on the scene the two original members of the group pulled out of the company leaving Al Bell in control. In 1950 the Bell Radio-Television Corp. was formed, the inclusion of the word 'television' in the company title at this early date being an indication of Bell's intentions.

Production of the Cadet radio was continued until 1951 when it was superseded by a completely different model known as the 'Colt', a 5-valve set and the first to carry the Bell name. At the time of its release no one could have foreseen how successful it would become or how long it would remain in production. Although most familiar in its plastic-cased form the Colt was also available in a solid oak cabinet. The use of solid timber was an innovation quite out of keeping with contemporary practice where wooden cabinets were invariably constructed of veneered plywood. Although the use of solid timber resulted in the set having a rather 'chunky' appearance it allowed a lower selling price than would otherwise have been the case.

With various changes in circuitry along the way, the Colt remained in production for the next 20 years, a quite incredible lifespan for any single model and very likely unsurpassed anywhere in the world. At the time of its introduction the Colt sold for £13-9-6 (roughly $28), at which figure it remained for the next 15 years! By 1962 over 160,000 had been sold, but in spite of this record Bell decided to discontinue production in favour of a line of Japanese-designed valve and transistor radios which were made under licence using the name 'General'.

In spite of their smart appearance the General valve-operated models were of an

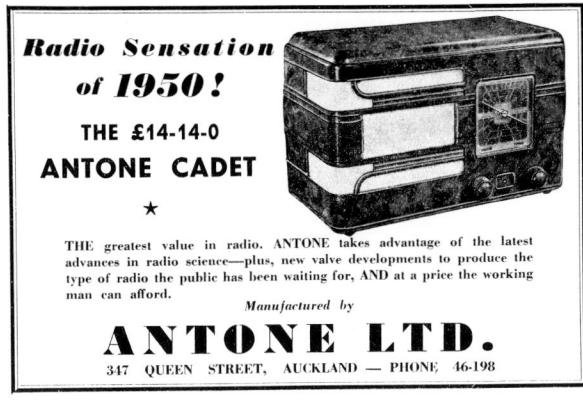
The first 'Antone' 4-valve Battery-Electric portable 1948-50.

Antone 'Cadet', a 4-valve AC model introduced in 1950.

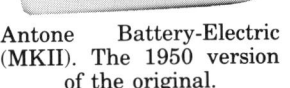
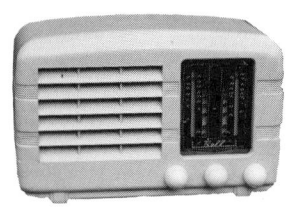

Antone Battery-Electric (MKII). The 1950 version of the original.

The famous 'Colt' 1951-71.

Model 1, the first Bell portable, successor to the Antone 1952.

Bell 'Colt' in solid oak cabinet.

RADIO AND ELECTRICAL REVIEW
July 1957.

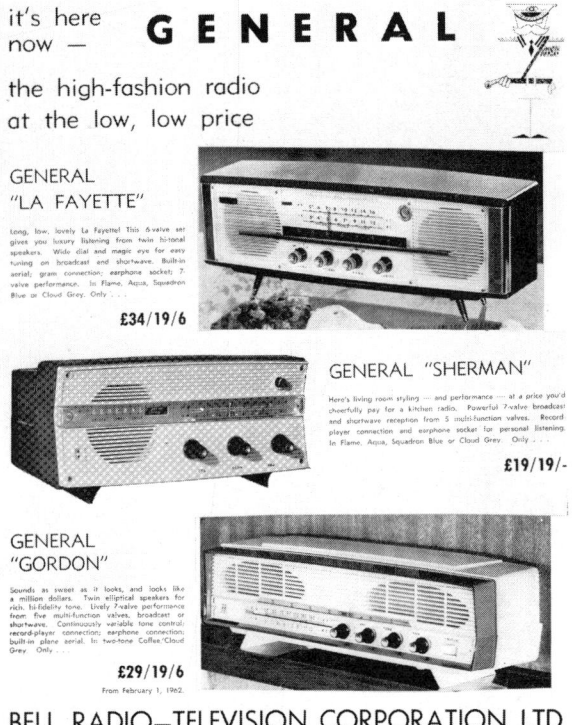
Introduced by Bell to the N.Z. market in 1962, 'General' radios were made under licence to the General Co. of Japan.

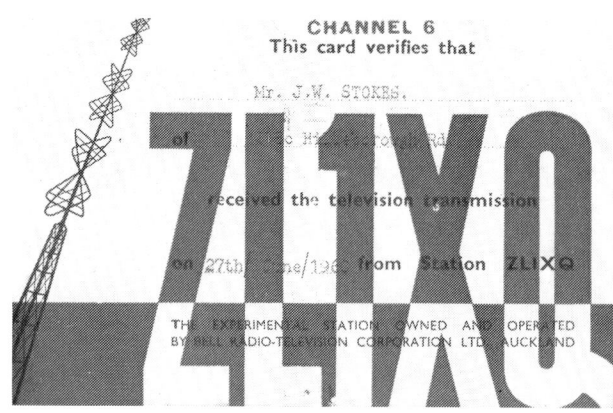

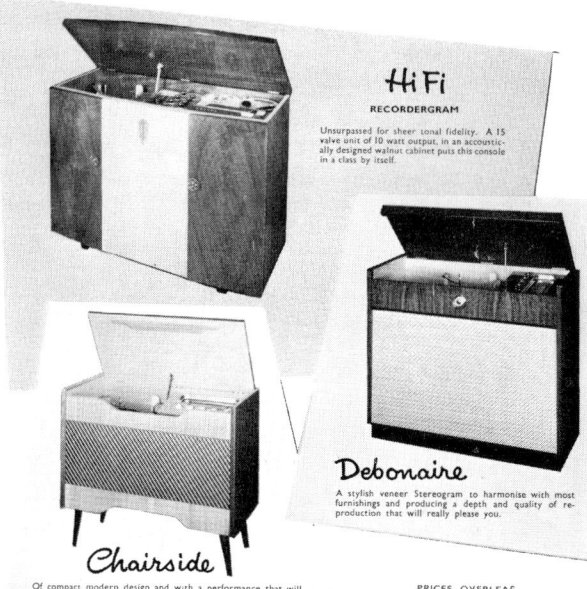

Verification card received by the author three months before the Station closed in September 1960. Experimental television broadcasts were first made in 1957 using the British 405-line system.

Right: 1960

Two views of TV set production at the Bell factory in 1963.

outmoded design using AC/DC circuitry and Japanese miniature 7-pin (B7G) valves which proved unreliable in service. By comparison, the Colt was then using the latest European noval-based valves and was an extremely reliable set. In view of the impending transistor revolution, which had already started to make its effect felt, it seems surprising that the production of a new line of valve radios should have been contemplated at this late hour; perhaps the Japs had made it part of a package deal. Although Bell pushed the General line hard, somehow it never really caught on and production of both valve and transistor models was soon dropped.

Probably because the Colt had been New Zealand's top selling radio at the time (over 6,500 were sold in 1961) another firm was quick to take over their manufacture and in 1962 Tee Vee Radio Ltd produced and marketed 'Tee Rad' Colts. But never again were such sales figures achieved, for by this time the combined effect of the two 'Ts', transistors and television, were playing havoc with the sale of valve radios and within the next two years Tee Vee Radio discontinued manufacture.

This was not the end of the Colt, however, for Bell again took up manufacture, continuing production until 1972. Even then the name Colt did not disappear for in March 1973 a transistorised version in the same old cabinet was produced which remained in production until the closure of the Dominion Road plant in 1980.

Another product which did much to put the name Bell on the map in the early days was a line of low-priced radiograms. Whilst still at the Queen Street premises the first of these, known as the 'Truetone', was released in 1953 and sold at the incredibly low price of £69-10. It became an instant success and its production caused at least one other manufacturer to emulate Bell's example. The cabinet of the Truetone was of solid oak timber, a type of construction, it will be remembered, which had earlier been used successfully on the Colt. At the time of its introduction the trade was sceptical as to whether the buying public would accept the plain timber cabinet after having been used to walnut veneer, but to a large number of buyers the low price proved irresistible.

By 1953 production facilities at Queen Street had become quite inadequate and a move was made to larger premises at 247 Dominion Road, Mt Eden, a suburb which already had a history of radio manufacturing, though this was obviously coincidental. Here the production of Colts and radiograms proceeded apace. This was the post-war period of the boom in record playing and with the advent of long-playing records the future looked bright. Such was the demand for radiograms that Bell opened a South Island factory in Christchurch which remained in operation for several years.

Although Bell's production figures were soaring at this time, the company's profits were not keeping pace, perhaps not surprising in view of the degree to which price cutting had been carried on. The writer recalls being informed by Al Bell on one occasion that the company made only 1/6 (15 cents) profit on each Colt sold!

To Al Bell, more than to any other single person must go the credit, if that is the right word, for hastening the introduction of television in New Zealand; even though he jumped the gun in doing so. In 1957 the Bell Corp. commenced experimental TV transmissions using the British 405-line standard and, rashly, even produced some 405-line receivers until the government of the day decided on the 625-line standard for this country. After being forced to cease transmitting for a period Bell returned to the air in 1960 with 625-line transmissions using the call sign ZL1XQ. At that time regular Sunday night programmes were being broadcast using a home-made transmitter installed at the company's No. 2 factory at 67 Dominion Road, which by a quirk of fate, was the old Wellmade Ltd building. It was from Bell's station that Aucklanders got their first taste of television, for although a few manufacturers had receivers on the market, the NZBS had not yet commenced transmitting regular programmes. Bell's early 'telecasts' undoubtedly did much to accelerate the advent of television in New Zealand and at the same time provided much useful publicity for the company.

It was the commencement of a regular television broadcasting service throughout the country with the accompanying large initial demand for receivers which really put Bell on its feet. From a nett loss in 1960 the company's tax-paid profits rose from £13,833 in 1962 to £127,000 in 1963. In the next few years production figures reached record heights, but following the death of Al Bell the company seemed to lose something of its vitality. In April 1973 Bell was reorganised as "An All New Company", according to a sales brochure of the period. This event coincided with the advent of colour television and Bell were obviously hoping to repeat the success they had had with monochrome TV.

With the introduction of CTV Bell were faced with the problem, common to all manufacturers of the period, of having to combine with others or perish. Some companies who had previously made black and white sets individually, now amalgamated with others to produce colour sets. In Bell's case the company combined with the Dominion Radio & Electrical Corp. to form a new firm known as Consolidated Industries Ltd. For a time production of colour sets was carried on at Dominion Road but after the initial demand for receivers had subsided production was concentrated at Otahuhu and in 1980 the Dominion Road premises were finally vacated, thus ending Bell's 32-year history.

COLLIER & BEALE

It was in 1926 that two young electricians, P. C. Collier and G. H. Beale, who had previously been employed by the Wellington City Council, decided to form a partnership and go into business on their own account. Thus it was that the firm of Collier & Beale, Electrical & Radio Engineers, came into being. Percy Collier was one of New Zealand's first amateur radio operators (he was licensed as 2AP in 1923) and he retained a life-long interest in the technical side of radio.

The manufacture of radio sets soon became an important part of the firm's business and by 1927 a staff of five was engaged in the assembly of battery sets. These were sold locally in the Wellington area, one of the first customers being the then well-known firm of Thomas Ballinger & Sons Ltd.

Another early activity was the manufacture of cinema sound systems in association with De Forest Phonofilms Ltd. Collier & Beale also became and remained active in the field of transmitter construction and in later years this side of the business became quite important.

Steadily increasing business soon necessitated larger premises and in 1934 a move was made to Ghuznee Street, at which time the staff numbered 34. Just prior to this the partnership was changed to a limited liability company with a capital of £4,000 with P. C. Collier holding two-thirds of the shares. An interesting sidelight on the operations of the company is that for nearly 30 years no dividends were paid on shares, all profits being ploughed back into the business.

Initially the distribution of radios had been limited to the Wellington area but in 1932 an association was formed with the firm of H. W. Clarke Ltd who became national distributors for 'Radion' receivers. H. W. Clarke had been established in 1928 as importers of Gulbransen player pianos from America and 'Mastertouch' player piano rolls from Australia. It was as a result of the decline of the piano business, consequent upon the rise of broadcasting, that the Gulbransen Co. went into the radio business and in 1929 Clarke's commenced to import Gulbransen radios. Imported sets were sold along with locally made ones but the latter seem to have been very much overshadowed by the American Gulbransen. Clarke's gave up handling Radion in 1933 after which time the agency was

taken up by Todd Motors Ltd. However this firm gave up handling radios after a little over three years and the name Radion then disappeared.

The introduction of import restrictions in 1936 caused Clarke's to once again turn to Collier & Beale for supplies of radios and in 1937 a new arrangement was entered into whereby C. & B. contracted to supply chassis to be fitted into cabinets by Clarke's. At this time a new brand name, 'Cromwell', was introduced to replace the former Radion. The drying up of imported sets from the U.S. also resulted in the name Gulbransen eventually being used on locally made receivers. After all, the *mana* attaching to the name Gulbransen was too good to lose!

Import restrictions also had the effect of sending others running to Collier & Beale to secure a source of locally made sets to replace previously imported ones. The brand names under which radios made by C. & B. were sold included: Ensign, HMV, Neeco, Stella, Sterling, Strohmeyer and also "ARC-Victor", the last-named being virtual piracy of the world famous RCA-Victor name, done at the behest of a certain Wellington retailer.

In 1939 a new brand name, 'Pacemaker', was introduced for a line of small, low-priced sets to be sold by non-franchised dealers. Unlike most of the other brand names, which disappeared with the cessation of production in the early years of World War II, the Pacemaker name continued in use after the war and as time went by was expanded to include larger sets and even radiograms.

During the war Collier & Beale's experience in the design and construction of transmitters was put to good use, as in addition to being responsible for the design of the ZC1 military transceiver they also designed and built other military and marine radio equipment as well as radar sets and communications receivers. The latter was a N.Z. version of the famous American 'National' and used some American components including the plug-in coil assembly.

The resumption of civilian radio production at the war's end seemed to mark a turning point for the company which changed from being a somewhat conservative manufacturer to a quite innovative one. In 1947 Collier & Beale were the first manufacturer to produce receivers using the new American miniature tubes. Another 'first' for the company was the introduction of the mains/battery portable in the same year. This was followed in 1951 by the model 5150 'Leader', an AC/Batt portable which became an instant success and remained in production for over six years, this in itself being something of a record. Even though the cabinet styling with its trick flip-up dial had come via Tecnico-Pacemaker in Australia (who had copied it from the original

1928

1932

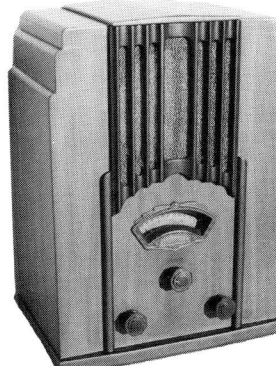

Cromwell 7-valve BC 1933.

Radion 5-valve superhet 1933.

This picture was used in a window display by a Wellington retailer in August 1932.

The first Collier & Beale receiver to incorporate a short-wave band May 1933.

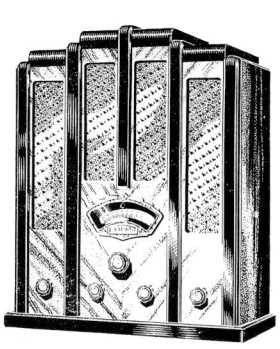

Radion 'Daventry', 7-valve AW 1934.

Cromwell 7-valve BC 1934.

Cromwell 6-valve BC 1935.

Radion 'Rugby' 5-valve
DW 1936.

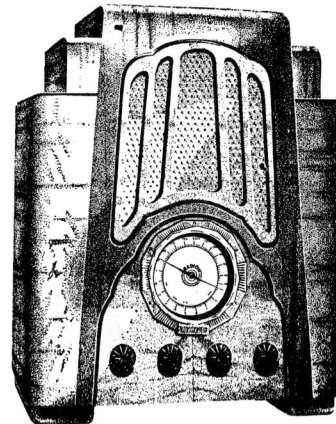

January 1936.

American Zenith!), the Pacemaker Leader was a real winner and was one of the most successful models ever produced.

On the occasion of the company's 25th anniversary in 1951 a commemorative brochure was issued outlining a quarter of a century's progress. At the time Collier & Beale was an entirely New Zealand owned company and remained so for the next few years. By the end of 1954, however, the General Electric Co. of England (GEC) had acquired a majority shareholding and this marked the beginning of the end for Collier & Beale as a purely N.Z. company.

In 1957 the firm of Collier & Beale was the first manufacturer to design and market a New Zealand-made transistor portable. Known as the Pacemaker 'Transportable', it used 7 RCA transistors and was claimed to be the only set in the world at that time to use an RF stage. The set was of robust construction using a metal chassis and a solid oak cabinet. A later version, using one less transistor and known as the 'Transportable 58', was produced in the following year.

Shortly after this, mainly to supply a demand for small, plastic-cased models, Collier & Beale made arrangements with the Sony Corp. to enable certain Japanese models to be made locally under licence. These sets were sold under the namestyle 'Sony Pacemaker' and production was continued until 1966.

With the advent of televison in New Zealand an arrangement was entered into with the Admiral Corp., U.S.A. to allow manufacture of Admiral television sets under licence. For some reason the name Admiral never became well known in this country and local production ceased after less than seven years.

After nearly 50 years service with the company he founded, P. C. Collier retired. It might be said that his departure marked the end of the line for what had once been a wholly New Zealand owned company. By 1973 the firm of Collier & Beale had ceased to exist, having been taken over by GEC (N.Z.) Ltd. For a short time transistor radios were made and marketed under the GEC brand but, as in the case of other N.Z. manufacturers, the rising flood of Japanese sets soon made continuing production uneconomical.

DOMINION RADIO
& ELECTRICAL CORP. LTD

The name Philco has been known in New Zealand since the beginning of the 'all-electric' era when the first Philcos were imported by Chas Begg & Co. in 1929. Over the years Philco became one of the best known American receivers

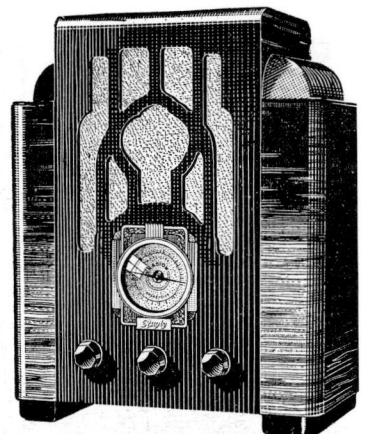

Four years ago the first RADION was introduced to New Zealanders. To-day there are thousands of not merely satisfied but EN-THUSIASTIC owners throughout the country—and an ever-growing number of people are buying RADION — definite proof that RADION **must** be the greatest Radio Value in the Dominion. Every Radion is carefully made of the highest quality components, rigorously tested to give outstanding service.

ALL-WAVE 'Rugby' Model

—the lowest priced ALL-WAVE Radio in New Zealand. Brings in London, France, America, Japan, on an INDOOR aerial as clear as a bell.

£16/10/-
Cash.

5-VALVE Broadcast

RADION "Little Aristocrat" Model—the finest 5-valve receiver at anywhere near its price, and actually the most popular 5-valve SUPER-HETERODYNE receiver in the Dominion!

£11/19/-
Cash.

See the DAVENTRY 'iSOmatic' ALL-WAVE

With Cathode Ray Tuning. All Radions sold are covered by the most comprehensive written guarantee issued in New Zealand.

All Radions are obtainable on extremely easy terms.

(All prices plus Royalty—all prices include Sales Tax.)

RADION
~ the Aristocrat
TODD MOTORS, LTD.
HOME UTILITIES DIVISION, WELLINGTON, N.Z.

July 1936

Gulbransen 628, 6-valve DW 1948.

Gulbransen 628 6-valve DW 1948.

Model 4154 in plastic cabinet 1954.

Codeword: "Petit". Model 5155 in bakelite cabinet 1955.

Robertson 5-valve BC 1939. Made for the Robertson Reversible Sewing Machine Co.

Stella 6-valve model S1 1940. For use on 230 V AC or 6-volt battery. A vibrator unit is fastened inside the cabinet.

The first Collier & Beale portable 1940. It sold for £18-10 complete with batteries.

Pacemaker 5-valve 1940. First of the long line of sets issued under this name.

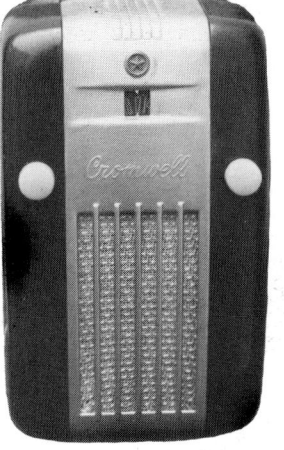

Cromwell 5-valve model 518N 1949. The cabinet design was a deliberate 'steal' from U.S. Westinghouse model H127.

Model 5151 in bakelite cabinet 1951.

"Buffalo" 1957.

Pacemaker "Atlanta" 1957.

47

For the Radio Enthusiast

The new 1941 11-Valve PHILCO

WITH AMAZING
SPREAD-BAND TUNING

Total World reception becomes an accomplished fact for the first time with this sensational new 11-Valve PHILCO. The top quarter of the short-wave spectrum has been split into 5 separate tuning bands, each 20 times the length of the conventional tuning scale. Stations previously too close together for reception can now be tuned-in with ease—the stretching of the 11-metre band alone giving you 26 world-wide stations that previously have remained a confused tangle of tongues. See and hear this revolutionary new PHILCO at your nearest Begg's branch today.

Model 888 1941.

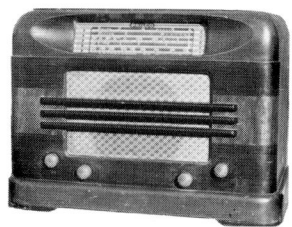

Philco 155, 6-valve, 3-band 1941.

Model 733 1948.

Model 730, 6-valve bandspread 1949.

Model 611 6-valve BC 1949.

Model 353 AC-DC-Battery Roll-top portable 1953.

Philco 203A, 5-valve 1949.

Model 860, 8-valve de luxe bandspread 1950.

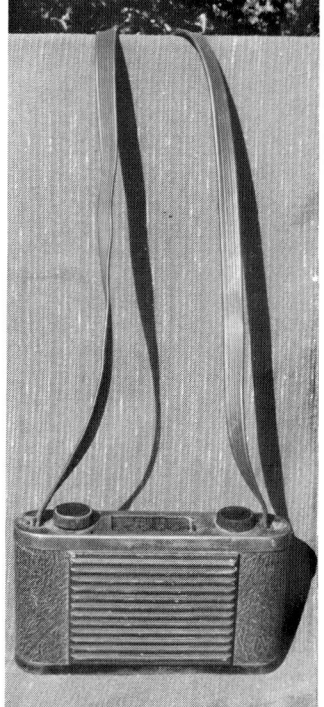

Philco model 89C battery portable 1949. The loop aerial was moulded into the plastic shoulder strap.

Model 521B, 5-valve DW 1954.

Below: 1954

MANUFACTURED UNDER LICENCE FROM PHILCO PHILCO CORPORATION U. S. A.

The World's largest Radio and Television Manufacturers.

PHILCO MODEL 401

Philco's famous midget with power and punch capable of receiving in most remote localities. Available in Walnut or Ivory Plastic. £16/16/-.

PHILCO MODEL 501

A powerful 5-valve Broadcast radio in a larger sized Walnut Plastic cabinet. Variable Tone Control, Local Distance Switch. Oversize Speaker. £24/10/-.

PHILCO MODEL 501RN

As above with the addition of Philco's Famous Radio Nurse feature. £27.

PHILCO MODEL 521

Philco's amazing 5-valve Dual Wave receiver. All Philco features. £29/15/-.

PHILCO MODEL 612

A dignified 6-valve Broadcast receiver in a Walnut veneered wooden cabinet. Large speaker with superlative tone. £35/10/-.

PHILCO MODEL 735

Philco's super powerful All-wave Bandspread 7-valve receiver. World wide range with ease of tuning. For world wide listening Model 735 cannot be bettered. £53/10/-.

PHILCO MODEL 1255

An amazingly low-priced 3-speed Radiogram which plays all records. Five powerful Loctal Valves for broadcast reception. £43/10/-.

PHILCO MODEL 1224

A 6-valve de luxe Dual Wave Table Radiogram with 3-speed Automatic Record Changer and world wide reception. £69/10/-.

PHILCO MODEL 555

Philco's sensational Swedish style furniture Broadcast Radiogram. 3-speed Record Player and full broadcast reception. £69/10/-.

PHILCO MODEL 555ARC

As above with Automatic Record Changer. £74/10/-.

PHILCO MODEL 852

Philco's super de luxe 8-valve All wave Bandspread Auto Record Changer Console. For those discriminating listeners for whom only the best will do. £134/10/-.

48

Model 804 Alarm-clock
radio 1954.

Philco 4-valve model 806
1955.

Philco 614 6-valve BC
1956.

The first La Gloria radiograms introduced in February
1956 featured cabinet styling which proved unpopular.

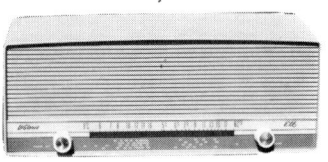

Model 523, 5-valve, 3-band
1957.

La Gloria 'ELF" 4-valve
1958.

La Gloria 'Imp'
A 5-valve model produced
between 1956 and 1966.

The name Majestic was
introduced in 1962 for use
in place of Philco.

sold in this country. However, the advent of import restrictions in 1937 affected their importation and led to the establishment of local production. In 1938 a company known as Dominion Radio & Electrical Corp. Ltd (Dreco) was formed which, because of the lateness of the day, turned out to be the last pre-war radio manufacturer to be established in this country.

Initial production was on an extremely small scale, the first 'factory' being no more than a dilapidated old house situated in Wellesley Street, Auckland. The size of the enterprise can be judged from the fact that initially just eight people were employed. At that time some receivers continued to be imported in the form of chassis and speakers, which were fitted into locally made cabinets.

Eventually local production was able to satisfy the N.Z. market, but before this could be accomplished the manufacturing operation had to be considerably expanded, so, within a couple of years a move was made to larger premises located at the corner of Broadway and Great South Road, Newmarket. Here production began in earnest.

The New Zealand-made Philcos differed somewhat from the American, although most were based on American designs. Right from the

start the local content was quite high, though as in the case of all other local manufacturers, certain items such as valves, tuning condensers, controls (potentiometers) and capacitors had to be imported. An obvious difference between the American and N.Z. chassis was the use of a chromium-plated finish on the latter, though Dreco was not the only local manufacturer to adopt this practice.

As they had done in the United States, Philco also introduced lock-in (Loktal) tubes to the local scene, Dreco being the only pre-war manufacturer to use this series of valves.

After the war Dreco continued to occupy the Newmarket premises until 1955 when a move was made to a new location at Otahuhu. Here a large, modern factory had been erected and here production of Philco radios was continued. At the same time a new line of radios and radiograms was produced under a newly introduced name— La Gloria.*

The changed post-war conditions, which affected the importation of components from the U.S. and forced local manufacturers to turn to the

* This name had originated many years earlier when Charles H. Pearson, father of Dreco's managing director, Charles A. Pearson, owned a shop in Karangahape Road named La Gloria Gramophones.

U.K. for supplies, led in Dreco's case to the weakening of links with American Philco. It was not long before the production under the La Gloria brand name exceeded that under Philco; in fact by 1958 the name Philco had all but disappeared from the local scene. Furthermore, the last Philcos produced were almost indistinguishable from La Glorias.

This state of affairs was probably brought about by the declining fortunes of American Philco where the company had been steadily losing ground since 1956. In 1961 the American company was sold to the Ford Motor Co., Philco having long been the sole supplier of car radios to Ford. In turn Ford sold Philco to General Telephone Co., the company which, incidentally, bought the tube making firm of Sylvania in 1963.

With the reorganisation of American Philco, consequent upon its sale to the Ford Motor Company in 1961, the former manufacturing arrangement with Dreco ceased, leaving the N.Z. company without a 'franchised' brand. Because the time of this event more or less coincided with the introduction of television in New Zealand the name Philco thus did not appear on TV sets made by Dreco.

To replace the loss of the Philco name Dreco, in 1962, introduced the name 'Majestic' for use on their higher priced lines of radio and television receivers. At the time this name was introduced there must have been many people who, remembering the original Majestic name belonging to the American firm Grigsby-Grunow, wondered at its use by Dreco.

Two other new names were also introduced at this time—'Dreco' for use on portable record players, tape recorders and transistor radios, and 'Picturama' for use on low-priced 'private brand' TV receivers.

The coming of colour television in 1974 led to many mergers and amalgamations within the industry by firms who had previously individually produced monochrome receivers. In Dreco's case a merger with the Bell Radio-Television Corp. resulted in the formation of Consolidated Electronic Industries Ltd.

JOHNS LTD—WELLMADE LTD

Shortly after the end of World War I, in December 1920 actually, two young returned soldiers, the brothers Clive and Victor Johns, set up in partnership as importers of wireless components and accessories. A few years later they registered a private company, Johns Ltd, and adopted the slogan—"Auckland's Oldest Radio Firm".

As was usual in those days, a large part of any radio dealer's business was in kitsets and

Johns Ltd was no exception. The firm secured the agency for Hammarlund, a well-known American manufacturer of coils and tuning condensers, and in addition to selling Hammarlund-Roberts kitsets also offered them in made-up form to customers who were not inclined to undertake the assembly themselves. This may be regarded as the start of Johns Ltd's manufacturing activities.

By 1928 they were offering sets of their own design under the names 'Altona', 'Ace' and 'Meniwave', the latter being a short-wave model. It was this constructional work, as distinct from repair work, which led to the establishment of a separate factory in January 1928, located at 75 Dominion Road in suburban Mt Eden.

Under the name Wellmade Ltd the factory was run as a separate entity using the trade-name "Well Mayde" for its products. The reason for the difference in the spelling of the two names was that under N.Z. law a company name cannot be used as a registered trade-mark. Used in conjunction with the name was a pictorial trade-mark in the form of a girl drawing water from a well—a well maid, no less! After two years of operation Wellmade Ltd was claimed to be—"The Best Equipped Factory in New Zealand".

The coming of AC mains operation brought about a decline in the popularity of battery sets and as mains-operated sets were initially considered too complicated or dangerous for home assembly this also meant a decline in kitset sales. The first AC sets produced by the Wellmade factory were small 3 and 4-valve models using separate speakers which were sold under the name 'Ace Electric'. First marketed in 1929, the Ace models were notable for the use of a British Westinghouse 'metal' (copper oxide) HT rectifier in the power supply. Another model, the 'Altona Prince' was a 5-valve plus rectifier using two stages of neutralised RF. The first screen-grid model, the 'Triumph' used battery valves with the filaments supplied with DC obtained from a Westinghouse rectifier whilst another Westinghouse rectifier supplied the HT.

The name Well Mayde was not used on complete radio sets, apart from the Well Mayde crystal sets produced between 1929 and 1935, but it was used on such items as amplifiers, battery chargers and battery elminators. Although battery eliminators were 'eliminated' in 1935 the remaining Well Mayde items continued to be produced until 1940.

Johns' Ltd, like many other radio dealers of the day, established their own private broadcasting station and in 1930 1ZJ first came on the air. The station provided more than just publicity value as it also came in handy when sets had to be demonstrated during times when the local YA station was off the air. In those days the

WELL - MAYDE.

IN FUTURE, THE RADIOS MANUFACTURED BY OUR FACTORY, WITH

OVER TEN YEARS' EXPERIENCE

IN THE PRODUCTION OF

SETS SPECIALLY SUITED TO NEW ZEALAND CONDITIONS

WILL BEAR THE NAME

Well—Mayde Radio.

Already, the high quality of WELL-MAYDE APPARATUS is well known throughout New Zealand. This standard of excellence will, of course, be fully Maintained
in the future.

WELL-MAYDE MEANS:—

1. DESIGN to suit local New Zealand conditions.
2. High Quality, and Efficiency.
3. Prompt Factory Service.
4. The GUARANTEE that IS a guarantee.
5. Employment for fellow New Zealanders.

MAKE YOUR SET THE
NEW ZEALAND BUILT WELL-MAYDE.

ELECTRIC MODELS from £14/10/–. BATTERY MODELS from £13/10/–.

This announcement was made in May 1931, some three
years after the establishment of Wellmade Ltd in 1928.

HAMMARLUND ROBERTS FOUR VALVE
REGENERATIVE SET.

This set used a well-known American circuit. It was
available with or without the meter shown, which cost £2
extra. The basic price, less accessories, was £24 in 1927.

'Hinemoa' 5-valve Neutrodyne using Hammarlund
components 1928.

Hammarlund-Roberts 'Junior' assembled by Johns Ltd
1928.

Johns Ltd 'ACE 3' regenerative model 1928.

ALTONA GRAND (For Accumulator Valves).

[Our experience has proved that neutrodynes do not operate satisfactorily on dry cell
valves. Therefore, if accumulators cannot readily be charged, we strongly recommend
the Hammarlund-Roberts set, which gives excellent results, either with accumulator or
dry cell valves.]

The ALTONA GRAND is a highly efficient five-valve set of the neutrodyne type.
It cannot cause interference.

1927

Left: Well
Mayde
'Screen
Grid 6'
Model 61
1931.

Right:
R. E.
Marett,
Service
Manager,
Johns Ltd
in 1931.

Johns Ltd service van outside Roy Marett's house in 1931.

Oxford Console

1933

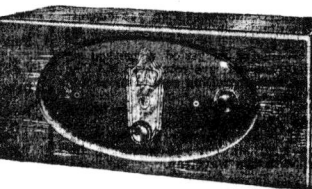
1933

Oxford Mantel

1933

From Johns Ltd catalogue 1933.

Right: 'Companion' plastic loop aerials were also used for a short time by Radio (1936) Ltd.

Left: Model 65 BC 1935.

Built to Last :: Honourably Guaranteed

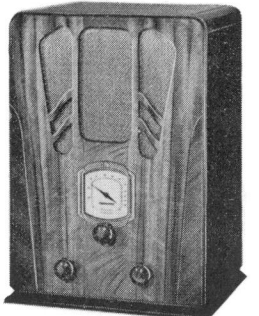
" BRIGHTON "

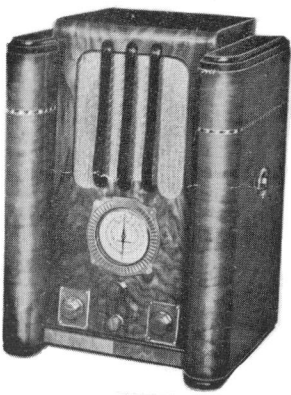
" DERBY "

" REGENT "

" CAMBRIDGE "

'Companion' radios using metal valves 1937.

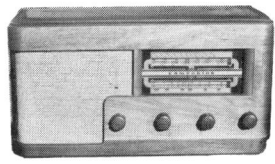

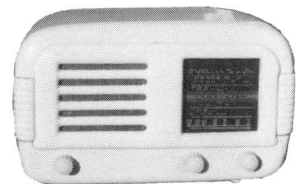

Companion RAAR 5-valve BC 1948. Assembled by Service Dept of Johns Ltd. Also available in kitset form.

Companion 5-valve BC c. 1950. Not built at Wellmade Ltd factory. Probably assembled by Johns Ltd Service Department.

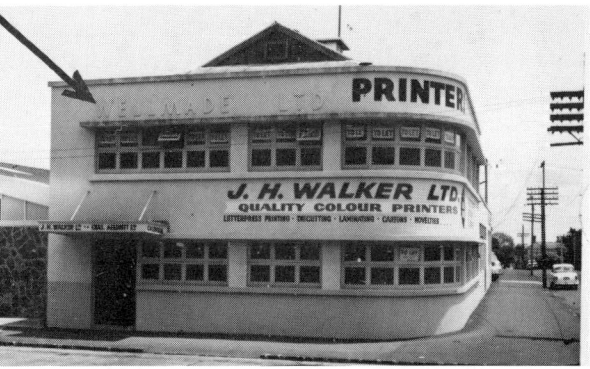

The old Wellmade Ltd building, vacant in 1968 before the front was cut back for road widening.

hours of broadcasting were extremely limited, there being no morning programmes for example. Like other private 'B' class stations, 1ZJ was closed down in 1935 by government order.

By 1931 several models of AC TRF receivers having self-contained dynamic speakers were being offered and most were available with a choice of either mantel or console cabinets. To emphasise their New Zealand-made aspect these sets were given model identification by the use of Maori names such as Ariki, Rangatira, Kiwi and Tui, but this policy was dropped after 1932.

In September 1933 an event of some significance was the introduction of the first superhet models. At the same time a new brand name, 'Companion',* was also introduced to supersede all formerly used names except Well Mayde which remained in use for items other than radios. Companion radios remained in production until 1951 when Johns Ltd sold out to the Swan Electric Co. which continued to operate both the city premises and the Dominion Road factory, but not for radio production. This made Companion the first post-war casualty in the field of radio manufacture though it did not mean the end of the Johns family's activities. For a short while the Dominion Road factory was leased by Swan Electric and used by them for the manufacture of Rola speakers after the transfer of operations from Wellington to Auckland.

After the closure of Johns Ltd a son of Victor Johns established a new firm, Graham Johns Ltd, carrying on the family tradition as radio and sports goods retailers. Graham Johns also established a sizeable service department which remained in existence until the early 1960s. Today the firm of Johns & Long Ltd perpetuates the Johns' name.

PHILIPS

When in May 1927, Philips opened a New Zealand sales office in Wellington, the "Concern" as they later referred to themselves, were then known as Philips Lamps (N.Z.) Ltd. At that time lamps was the name of the game and no radio products, apart from valves were being manufactured. Before 1927 Philips' lamps had been jointly distributed in this country by two companies, Turnbull & Jones Ltd and Lawrence & Hanson Ltd. The former was an all-New Zealand company, the latter being a branch of an Australian firm which closed down its N.Z. operation in 1931.

When Philips in Holland entered the radio manufacturing field in earnest their first products

were not complete receivers but components and accessories such as battery chargers, HT battery eliminators, cone speakers and interstage audio transformers. To achieve success in what was then a highly competitive retail market these items had to be not only of high quality but also attractively finished. As an indication of how far Philips were prepared to go in this direction it may be mentioned that their audio transformers were wound with silver wire on the primary and nickel wire on the secondary.

Their first radio, produced at the end of 1927, was a small 4-valve mains-operated model, type 2501. Its only claim to fame was that it was the world's first commercially produced receiver to use a pentode output valve.

Towards the end of 1928, seeking to expand their export markets, Philips established a small radio factory in England where they were already in existence through the acquisition of the Mullard Radio Valve Co. in 1926. This later move enabled them to supply not only the British market but also to export to other British countries, thereby taking advantage of the duty-free entrance accorded to British-made goods. During the 1930s Philips were in the process of establishing factories in many European countries, a move which led eventually to their becoming one of world's largest multinational electronics companies.

The first Philips sets seen in New Zealand were the models 2515, (also known as the AC-QP), and the 2802. Both were marketed here in 1929-30. The former was a 3-valve regenerative set encased in a metal box which in appearance closely resembled a Philips HT battery eliminator; the latter was a 4-valve battery set using a screen-grid RF stage and a set of plug-in coils giving a wavelength coverage of 10 to 2,400 metres.

Following the QP came the 2510, a much larger set using two stages of screen-grid amplification. This set appears to have been a special export model as, unlike all other European ones, it covered only the broadcast (MW) band. Although somewhat lacking in selectivity due to the aerial being coupled directly to the top end of the grid coil the 2510 was an extremely well made set of pleasing appearance. The cabinet was of uniquely Philips design consisting of a metal frame carrying five handsome Formica panels, and was provided with a hinged lockable lid. It was claimed that the purpose of the lock was to prevent unauthorised use of the receiver, but actually the set could be operated whether or not the lid was locked! The only function of the lock was to prevent the lid being opened without a key, hardly sufficient justification for the extra trouble and expense involved in fitting it. Like its

---

* Like the earlier Altona name, the Companion name was also revived and used by Dennis C. Green Ltd, though never on radios.

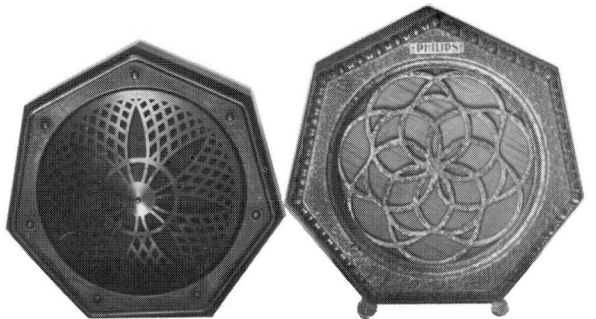

The well-known 'Sevenette' is on the left but the speaker on the right cannot be identified.

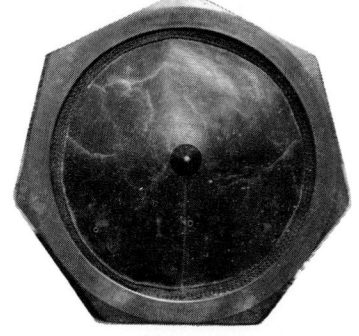

Philips 2515 with 'Sevenette' speaker.
Also known as the AC-QP, this was a 3-valve regenerative model using a triode detector and pentode output valve.

Philips H.T. Battery Eliminators types 3009, 3002, 372.

Type 450 battery charger.   Type 1016 trickle charger.   Type 3003 H.T. battery eliminator.

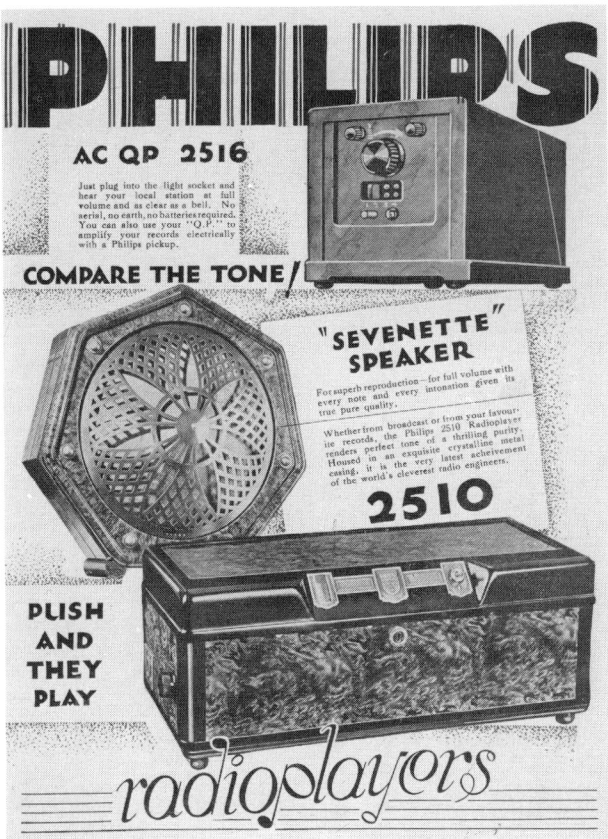

'La Boite a Jambon' 1931.
The model 930A is sometimes referred to by present-day collectors as the "ham tin".

HEAR a new Philips 1203 and realise what 1931 radio really is. The 1203 is the result of many years research by Philips in Australia, and in presenting this model it is felt that a new standard has been achieved.

Tone, volume, and selectivity are all such that the 1203 is the ideal entertainer for the home. And as a thing of beauty the piano-finished cabinet represents the ultimate in consoles, "at home in any home."

(Registered Cabinet Design 9031)

£24 10 0 COMPLETE

Although housed in an expensive-looking cabinet this Australian-made model 1203 was only a 2-valve (detector and audio) set. Selectivity was inadequate.

Here it is !
PHILIPS
BRITISH
Radioplayer

THE NEW PHILIPS

THIS is the Set New Zealand has been waiting for! A Set created with two ideals in view. A low price and a quality performance. Both have been achieved. The price is the lowest at which quality radio can be produced, and the performance is such that even experts are amazed at its remarkable fidelity. There is only one way to discover for yourself just what an advance the new 930A is on other Sets—and that is to hear it! Arrange for a demonstration today and remember—IT IS BRITISH MADE.

AT THE LOW PRICE OF

£15

See the name PHILIPS on Every Radio Set.

ASK TO HEAR THE NEW 930A

N.Z. Radio Record, May 1932.

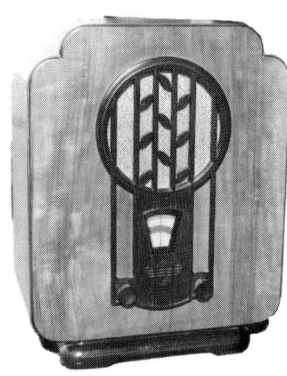

The 1932 model 630A Super Inductance was sold in New Zealand in 1933.

The 1933 model 630A Super Inductance featured a round-top cabinet and was the first model to have A.V.C. fitted.

Model 588 September 1934.

351A, 6-valve, 2-band.   352A, 9-valve, 3 band.

Shown side by side for size comparison, these two sets were both 1937 models and were the first to use the "Magic Star" turning indicators.

Model 730A, the first of the "Super Inductance" series July 1932.

A 6-valve all-wave model of 1935 vintage.

Model 516P, made in N.Z. by Radio Corporation in 1935.

The unique V7A 'Theatrette' had no chassis. In 1937 this model sold for 6 gns in the U.K. and 13 gns in N.Z.

Mallard 'Westminster', the equivalent of the Philips 'Theatrette' 1937.

predecessors, the 2510 was designed for use with a separate speaker, normally a moving-iron type, though provision was also made for using a moving-coil type. A console version encased in a 'Philite' (bakelite) cabinet standing only 30 inches high was marketed in 1931. Also in 1931 the first Philips radiogram, type 2910, was marketed. It used an EM speaker requiring a separate field exitation unit. A feature of this model was the use of the then new E443N pentode, a valve capable of an unprecedented 5.4 watts output.

The first table-model Philips sets to have built-in speakers were the 930A and 932A. Both were 1931 models, although they were not sold in New Zealand until the following year. The use of magnetic (moving-iron) speakers at a time when all American and locally made receivers were using moving-coil speakers made their design considerably outdated. The 930A was a 4-valve regenerative model using a triode detector resistance-coupled to another triode which was similarly coupled to an output pentode; the 932A used a similar circuit but with the addition of a screen-gird RF stage.

Towards the end of 1932 came the first of the famous 'Super Inductance' TRF models, a series claimed to have the same degree of selectivity as a superheterodyne. The first of these, the model 730A, was released here in July 1932. It was a 5-valve set using two stages of S.G. amplification and an inbuilt moving-coil speaker and was contained in a highly polished, wooden cabinet. A little later in the same year came the 630A, a set of similar design though having quite a different chassis and cabinet. In 1933 an improved version known as the 634A was released. It, too, was of similar basic design and appearance though the cabinet was distinguished by having a rounded top where the previous year's model had a flat top. This difference in styling was in complete reversal of what was happening elsewhere in the world at that time and seems to have been a purely Philips' idiosyncrasy. The last Super Inductance model seen in New Zealand was the 472A released in 1934. It had a square open-faced dial, and as if to emphasise Holland's procilivity for cycling, its chassis, which was of fairly light gauge metal, was cross-braced with two ordinary bicycle spokes to give increased rigidity!

Good as the Super Inductance design was it just did not have the all round performance of the superhet, and with American and locally made sets of this type dominating the market in 1934 Philips in N.Z. were obviously concerned about their inability to offer competitive models. Due to the slower acceptance of the superheterodyne in Europe, none had been developed by Philips by the time they were needed here. As a result Philips arranged to have supplies of suitable

receivers made right here in New Zealand and this is where Radio Corporation of New Zealand came into the picture. The first New Zealand-made superhets sold under the Philips name were the models 5H, 5V and 6V, the suffix H or V denoted the cabinet style—horizontal or vertical. They were standard Radio Corp. designs, marketed also by Courtenay Radio Ltd under the Courtenay brand and by Turnbull & Jones Ltd under their Troubadour brand. A fourth brand, Pacific, was marketed by Pacific Radio Ltd. The only difference between them was that the Philips and Troubadour used Philips 'Golden Series' valves, except for the frequency converter. In this position an American type 2A7 was used for the very good reason that Philips had no suitable valve available in New Zealand at that time. The Courtenay and Pacific sets, on the other hand, used American valves throughout.

The year 1934 saw the production of the last of the Super Inductance models and the introduction of the first superhets. This year was also notable for the introduction of side-contact (Cap P) valves, used for the first time in the new models. Two of the first superhets were the 522A and the 531A. A British model, the 588A, using English (Cap M) valves was also produced. The model 531A, seen here early in 1935, was the first Philips AC set be fitted with a short-wave band.

During 1935 there appeared to be some difficulty in obtaining a continuity of supplies of suitable receivers from either Holland or the U.K. and although a few were imported from Australia, e.g. the model 715, once again a local source of supply was sought. This time Radio Corp. produced the models P516 and P636. As in the earlier case, these two sets contained no Philips parts except the valves. Their chassis were 'disguised' by having the Philips emblem stamped into the tops of the IF coil cans.

It was in 1936 that Philips made their first move towards manufacturing in this country by setting up a small factory close to their Wellington office. In spite of claims made, there was little real production before 1939. Examples of the first sets actually made in New Zealand by Philips were the models 042 and 152.

To cater for the growing U.K. market, and also to supply 'British-made' receivers to British Empire countries, Philips established a new factory in Mitcham, Surrey, in 1938 capable of large-scale production of all types of radios. With this factory in operation Philips then claimed to be "the world's largest radio manufacturers".* It was here that the so-called 'New Listening' series

---

* It must be borne in mind that by this time Philips had factories in several European countries and also that the word "radio" did not necessarily mean only radio receivers.

was produced, a line of receivers which clearly showed that Philips were taking the export market seriously. All but the cheapest models in the range had altered band coverages to suit export conditions. Except in the cases of the models V7A and 470A the long-wave band, as fitted to sets intended for the European market, was replaced by an extra short-wave band. Prior to this time Philips did not make special export models, although admittedly the 1930 model 2510 was an exception.

Even so, certain type of battery sets, particularly vibrator operated types, were not then available from the U.K. and this led to the importation of such models from Australia; examples were the 517V and 528V. These particular sets, as in the case of earlier Australian imports were manufactured by Thom & Smith Ltd, Sydney.

Following the introduction of import restrictions in 1938 some firms took advantage of the lower rate of duty applicable to the importing of receivers in chassis form for fitting into New Zealand-made cabinets. Owing to their peculiar type of construction, Philips receivers did not lend themselves to this procedure, though at least two models, the 361 and 362, were fitted into locally made console cabinets.

In common with other N.Z. firms, Philips were able to import car radios because this class of receiver was not then made in New Zealand and so was exempt from import restrictions.

By 1940 Philips were able to supply the local market from their Wellington factory, although the range of models was necessarily limited. Local production continued until 1942 when wartime regulations prohibited further manufacture. During the war Philips made certain components such as microphones and headsets for the ZC1 military transceiver, as well as undertaking 'hush hush' work on radar equipment for the government.

After the war one of the first receivers was the little bakelite-cased 'Philette', first marketed in 1947. Other early post-war models were the 593, 596 and 648, all of which used octal-based valves. By comparison with pre-war locally produced models, these sets showed a strong American influence in their design and construction which is explained as follows. With the occupation of Holland by Nazi Germany during World War II, Philips in New Zealand in common with other countries, was cut off from contact with the 'fountainhead'. As a result of this the N.Z. company turned to Philips, Argentina, for the supply of components and design data, and this is where the American influence originated. En passant, the author cannot refrain from mentioning that at least one post-war model,

e.g. the 461, made use of the ubiquitous bicycle spoke, this time as a dial pointer slide!

As the reconstruction of war damaged Europe, including Holland, was gradually accomplished, Philips in Eindhoven were once again able to resume leadership of the concern. From 1948 onwards locally produced receivers grew to be more European in design and construction.

The first receiver to use the newly developed 'Rimlock' series of miniature valves was the model 209, a small bakelite-cased set released towards the end of 1948.

By 1950 all vestiges of Americanisation had disappeared when at this time a change to the use of metric screw threads was made to supersede the formerly used Whitworth and U.S.A types.

As time went on it became obvious that import restrictions were not going to be lifted and thus Philips were faced with the task of completely reorganising their production facilities to cope with the ever-increasing post-war demands. As early as 1951 plans were made for the construction of a new factory to be situated at Naenae, about 12 miles north of Wellington City. In 1956 the first stage was completed, but not until 1958 was the work finished and the official opening ceremony held.

By this time television was in the offing and for the next few years TV receiver production accounted for a large part of the new factory's output. In addition certain electrical appliances, notably the 'Philishave' electric shaver, were manufactured.

An aspect of the post-war radios made in this country was that they were almost identical to those of British and Dutch origin, the only difference being in the omission of the long-wave band. From 1955 the smaller models were of transformerless (AC/DC) construction, which was in marked contrast to the position in Australia where similar models were largely of Australian design and were never transformerless.

A peculiarly Philips contribution to post-war radio design was the introduction in 1958 of the so-called 'Hi-Z' series of radios and radiograms featuring speakers having high-impedance voice coils in the order of 400 or 800 ohms. Special circuitry using single-ended, push-pull output stages allowed the speaker to be capacitance coupled without the need for an output transformer. Incidentally, this same circuitry was also used in Philips monochrome TV sets.

The last Philips valve radio produced in this country was the model B2Z56U marketed during 1968-70. It was not the same as an earlier model, the BZ256U. By this time, of course, transistorised receivers had long since captured the market and it is interesting to speculate on

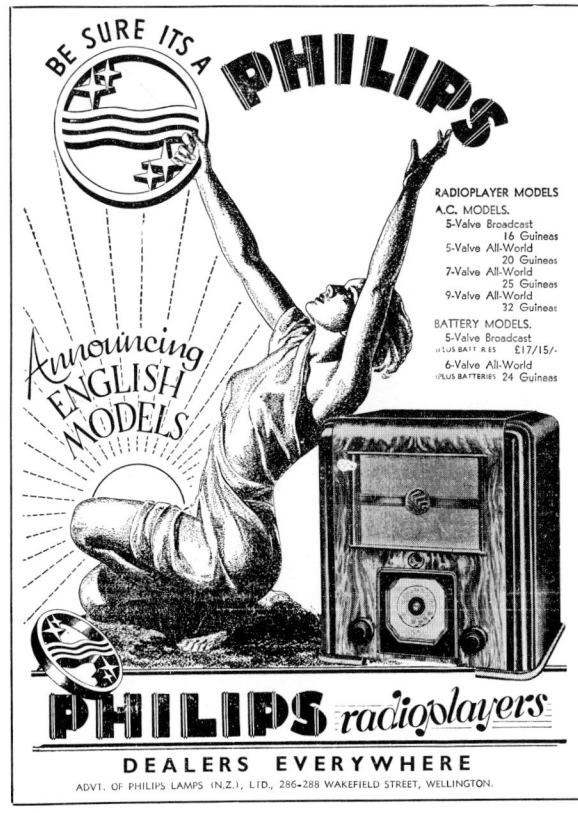
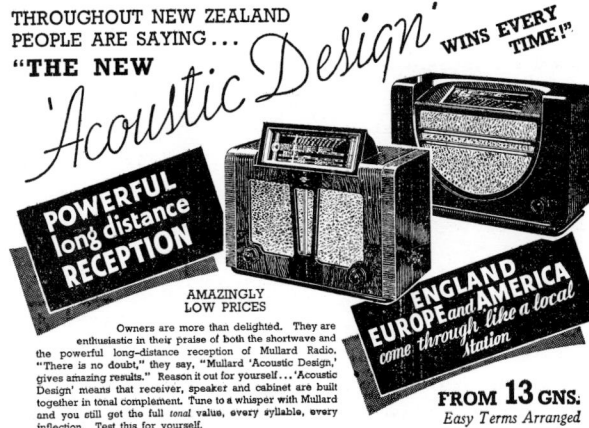
N.Z. Radio Record, July 1938.

753   650

470   660

361A   362

771

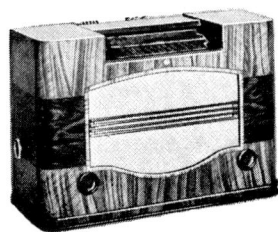   

463A   518/v

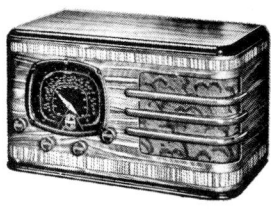   

628/v   528/v

Some Mullard Radios.

Model 12, 4-valve.

Model 15, 6-valve.

Model 45, 6-valve.

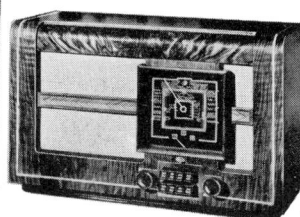

Model 24, 6-valve.

Model 30, 7-valve.

Model 17, 8-valve.

Model 55 V.B., 5-valve.

Mullard 558.

Model 31C

Model 540

"Philette", is proving one of the most popular radios ever produced by the Philips organisation. The performance of the tiny set amazes many purchasers, and hundreds of tributes have been paid to the smartness of the coloured plastic cabinets. The compactness of "Philette" has been a strong selling point. Many of these receivers have been purchased by flat dwellers to whom space is a vital consideration.

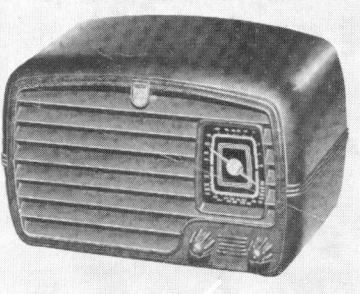

The model 540 was marketed in N.Z. in 1947. It was the first Philips 'midget' model.

An early post-war set, the model 648 was released in August 1947.

The model 461 was released in 1948. The removable dial scale was all too easily broken.

MAINS MANTEL RADIO

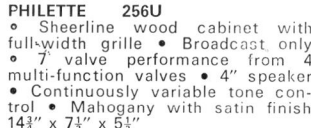

PHILETTE   256U
● Sheerline wood cabinet with full-width grille ● Broadcast only ● 7 valve performance from 4 multi-function valves ● 4" speaker ● Continuously variable tone control ● Mahogany with satin finish 14¾" x 7½" x 5½"

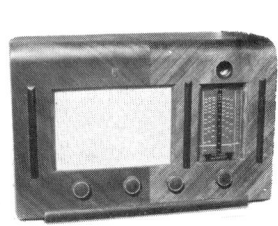

One of the first N.Z. made Philips, the model 153 of 1941.

Philips 209

Right: First issued in 1968, this was the last valve radio produced by Philips. It was not the same as the earlier BZ 256U of 1952.

Philips Made in N.Z.

the reason for the production of a valve operated model at this late hour.

MULLARD

Because Mullard Ltd has since 1927 been owned by Philips the story of the two companies in the U.K. has been more or less interwoven as a result. Although Mullard has always remained a valve manufacturer, from time to time there were other items marketed under the Mullard name. For example, late in 1927 three types of the then current range of Philips cone speakers were, in somewhat altered form, sold under the Mullard name. Similarly, in 1929 Philips HT battery eliminators, filament transformers and audio transformers were also marketed under the Mullard name.

In the early days Mullard also sponsored the building of various kitsets with the idea of promoting the use of their valves. Examples of these were the Mullard 'Master Three' and 'Master Five' of 1928, and the 'Orgola' of 1931.

The first factory-built receiver to bear the Mullard name, type MU35, was a 6-valve AC/DC model marketed in 1935, but this model was not seen in New Zealand. In fact no Mullard receivers were imported until 1938 when Mullard counterparts of the Philips 1938 'New Listening' range appeared.

The Mullard agency had originally been held by Spedding Ltd of Auckland, but at the end of 1937 it was taken over by C. & A. Odlin Ltd of Wellington and henceforth this firm distributed both Mullard sets and valves. When, in 1938, Philips imported vibrator-type battery sets from Australia Odlins did likewise. These particular receivers were obtained from the Sydney firm of Thom & Smith Ltd as Philips in Australia were not then making vibrator sets. Incidentally, Mullard receivers sold in Australia at that time were made by yet another firm, Airzone Ltd.

Following the end of World War II Odlins continued to distribute the full range of New Zealand-made Philips receivers under the Mullard name until 1957 when the name 'Fleetwood' was introduced in its place. Using this brand name Odlins continued to market both radio and television receivers until the 1970s. The Mullard name continued to be used on valves and picture tubes, however.

RADIO CORPORATION OF NEW ZEALAND

Not long after the end of the First World War a refugee from Russia arrived in New Zealand and settled in Wellington. Before long he had obtained a job as a meter repairer in the Wellington City Council's Municipal Electricity Department. The year was 1926 and the man's name was William Markoff (later changed to Marks). Four years later, in 1930, he left the job to commence business on his own account. Premises were obtained in Cornhill Street, Wellington, where the work of winding transformers and making amplifiers was undertaken. From this small beginning grew one of the country's largest radio manufacturers.

At the time there was no shortage of transformer work as many American radios were still coming into the country with 110-volt transformers, due either to their manufacturers not making export models or (dare it be whispered?) to many importers not realising the need to specify 230-volt operation when ordering.

Initially Marks did not manufacture radios, but by 1931 the first sets were being produced. Later in the year a private company under the name W. Marks Ltd was formed. It was at this time that Marks became associated with Stewart Hardware Ltd of Courtenay Place who acted as distributor for his radios which were sold under the brand name 'Courtenay', the name rather obviously being derived from the name of the street.

The first Courtenay produced was of most unconventional design, being no more than a crystal set with an audio amplifier and AC power supply added. Even though having the convenience of mains operation it is difficult to see how such a receiver could have had any chance of being successful, bearing in mind that by this time multi-valve screen-grid sets were in general use. It is the writer's belief that the production of this first model reflected Marks' lack of experience in radio design, particularly in the area of RF amplification, which led to the production of such an unorthodox receiver. Be that as it may, however, the first 'proper' radios were not long following and by the end of 1931 a range of 3, 4 and 6-valve models was being advertised.

Indicative of Marks' plans for the future was the change of company name to Radio Corporation (N.Z.) Ltd in 1932. Not surprisingly growth was slow during that year, it being in the depth of the Great Depression. By 1933, however, business had increased to the point where larger premises were needed and a move was made to a new location in nearby Courtenay Place. This same year, 1933, also saw the formation of a new company, Courtenay Radio Ltd, to handle distribution following the demise of Stewart Hardware Ltd.

Besides continuing production under the Courtenay name, Radio Corp. commenced to manufacture 'private brand' sets for distribution by certain wholesalers. These were: 'Stella' by

This 1931 advertisement lists 3, 4 and 6-valve models which must obviously all be TRF sets. These were the first 'modern' receivers produced, the previous year's model being a crystal detector and amplifier.

This advertisement from the *Radio Record* for 31 March 1933 shows the continuing use of 'peephole' dials which by then were quite outdated.

Pacific 5-valves 1934.
The art-deco style speaker grille is chromium-plated. Similar cabinet shapes were used on Courtenay, Philips and Troubadour brands but were minus the chrome grille.

The first Courtenay superheterodyne was produced in 1933. This was the last advertisement to appear in the name of Stewart Hardware Ltd. For the next two years distribution was made by a firm called Courtenay Radio Ltd.

Pacific 6-valves 1933-34. (Same as Courtenay model 106)

Courtenay model 106 1934.

Courtenay model 108 6-valve DW 1934. This was the first dual-wave model and the first to use an 'aeroplane' dial.

Pacific 5-valve dual-wave 1934. Note speaker opening in top of cabinet.

Cory, Wright & Salmon Ltd, 'C-Q' by Hope Gibbons Ltd, 'Pacific' by Pacific Radio Ltd. For the record, even Philips Lamps (N.Z.) Ltd had some sets made by Radio Corp. during 1934-36.

Because these firms often insisted on special models being made to their own requirements it resulted in the factory having to put through small uneconomic runs which increased costs and lowered profitability. This, coupled with under-utilisation of existing plant and machinery led to a complete reorganisation of the company in 1936.

Another change occurred in 1935 when the old-established electrical firm of Turnbull & Jones Ltd came into the picture as a large supplier of imported components to Radio Corp. Incidentally, Turnbull & Jones had previously manufactured radios on a small scale in their Auckland workshops using the name 'Troubadour', but production ceased in 1934. For a short time afterwards this same brand name was used on sets made by Radio Corp. for Turnbull & Jones but after 1934 the latter firm took over the distribution of Courtenay. At the same time they arranged to have a line of coils and transformers, and (in 1935) kitsets, made for them which were sold under the name 'Exelrad'. For the most part these were standard factory items as used in receiver production but some additional lines such as push-pull audio transformers and universal output transformers were included in the range. Production of Exelrad components continued until 1940 when wartime shortage of raw materials caused cessation of manufacture. Exelrad components sold by Turnbull & Jones after the war were no longer made by Radio Corp.

Rapid growth during the immediate pre-war years called for an increase in the company's working capital and in December 1936 a new company known as Radio Corporation of New Zealand Ltd was formed having a capital of £80,000. The directors were a group of business and professional men which included the managing directors of Cory, Wright & Salmon Ltd and Turnbull & Jones Ltd.

Early in 1937 a decision was made to phase out the previous uneconomic production of 'private brand' receivers, though the existing arrangement with Turnbull & Jones was (perforce?) continued. In this case an exception was made for "commercial reasons" having to do with T. & J.'s position as a parts supplier.

Another significant event of 1937 was the setting up of a subsidiary company, Radio Centre Ltd, which established a nation-wide chain of retail outlets to handle distribution directly using a newly introduced house brand, 'Columbus'. Under the new set-up Radio Corp. went from strength to strength, the sales figures climbing from £52,425 in 1935 to £107,716 in 1938. By 1939 the buoyant state of business called for another increase in capital which went from £80,000 to £180,000.

On the technical side the company had early displayed a progressive outlook and had introduced such innovations as the use of cadmium plating (1934), one-piece pressed chassis (1936) and the manufacture of loudspeakers (1937). The production of small components such as valve sockets, wave-change switches, paper and mica capacitors were all New Zealand 'firsts', as was the manufacture of bakelite moulded parts such as knobs. Radio Corp. was also one of the first to use iron-core coils and IF transformers and to introduce edge-lit glass dial scales.

By this time the factory was turning out a well-engineered and well-finished product which could compete in both performance and appearance with most imported receivers. Here it is interesting to note that between 1937 and 1940 Radio Corp. was one of two N.Z. firms which established an export trade to Australia.

Another pioneering effort was the introduction of band-spread short-wave tuning but unfortunately the company in publicising its work made two false claims, which were: " . . . the first domestic radio of its type in the world", and " . . . a full 17 months before any others, in October 1939, our own Columbus engineers put into production the first domestic calibrated band-spread radios in the world's history". The facts are that Radio Corp's first band-spread set, the model 75, was not on the market until 1940 by which time it was two years after RCA's HF2 and HF4 had been marketed in the U.S. It was true that the model 75 was well ahead of AWA's first band-spread set, the model 276 which was not released until March 1941, and Radio Corp's claim was apparently based on the later Australian release.

In the early days of World War II before the manufacture of domestic receivers was prohibited, and when there was an extreme shortage of imported loudspeakers, other manufacturers had reason to be grateful for Radio Corp's ability to supply them with speakers and thus enable receiver production to be maintained.

Since the earliest days Radio Corp. maintained its own printing press which was used in the production of dial scales, sales literature and service manuals. As a long-time user, the writer wishes to draw attention to the comprehensive nature of Radio Corp's service data sheets which included stage-by-stage figures for receiver sensitivity, information not published by any other manufacturer in New Zealand or Australia, or even in the United States, at least not until the post-war years.

Admittedly not many privately-owned service

STYLED for every TASTE

A full range of models in table and console cabinets is available for power mains or battery use.

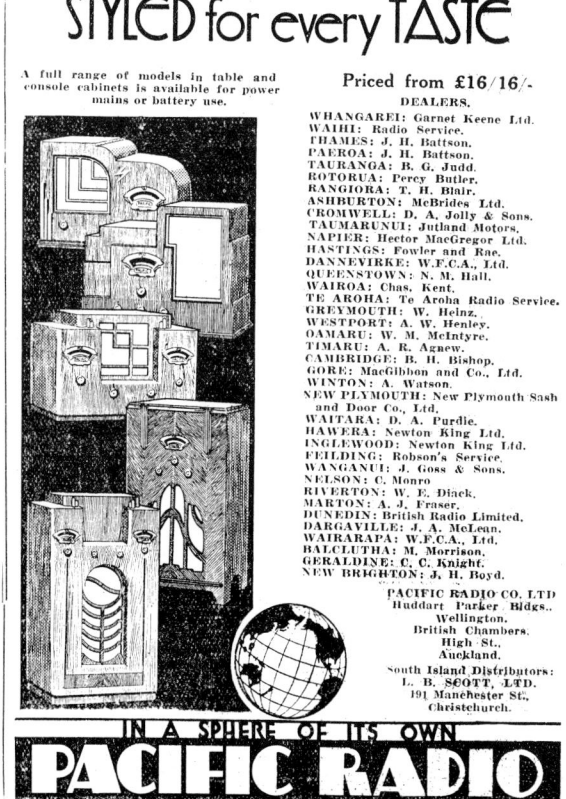

Priced from £16/16/-

DEALERS.

WHANGAREI: Garnet Keene Ltd.
WAIHI: Radio Service.
THAMES: J. H. Battson.
PAEROA: J. H. Battson.
TAURANGA: B. G. Judd.
ROTORUA: Percy Butler.
RANGIORA: T. H. Butler.
ASHBURTON: McBrides Ltd.
CROMWELL: D. A. Jolly & Sons.
TAUMARUNUI: Jutland Motors.
NAPIER: Hector MacGregor Ltd.
HASTINGS: Fowler and Rae.
DANNEVIRKE: W.F.C.A., Ltd.
QUEENSTOWN: N. M. Hall.
WAIROA: Chas. Kent.
TE AROHA: Te Aroha Radio Service.
GREYMOUTH: W. Heinz.
WESTPORT: A. W. Henley.
OAMARU: W. M. McIntyre.
TIMARU: A. R. Agnew.
CAMBRIDGE: B. H. Bishop.
GORE: MacGibbon and Co., Ltd.
WINTON: A. Watson.
NEW PLYMOUTH: New Plymouth Sash
    and Door Co., Ltd.
WAITARA: D. A. Purdie.
HAWERA: Newton King Ltd.
INGLEWOOD: Newton King Ltd.
FEILDING: Robson's Service.
WANGANUI: J. Goss & Sons.
NELSON: C. Monro
RIVERTON: W. E. Dinck.
MARTON: A. J. Fraser.
DUNEDIN: British Radio Limited.
DARGAVILLE: J. A. McLean.
WAIRARAPA: W.F.C.A., Ltd.
BALCLUTHA: M. Morrison.
GERALDINE: C. C. Knight.
NEW BRIGHTON: J. H. Boyd.

PACIFIC RADIO CO. LTD
Huddart Parker Bldgs.,
Wellington.
British Chambers,
High St.,
Auckland.

South Island Distributors:
L. B. SCOTT, LTD.
191 Manchester St.,
Christchurch.

IN A SPHERE OF ITS OWN
PACIFIC RADIO

Advertisement appearing in *N.Z. Radio Record* 23-11-34.

Friday, July 12, 1935.   N.Z. RADIO RECORD   15

--the Key to the World's Treasure House of Music

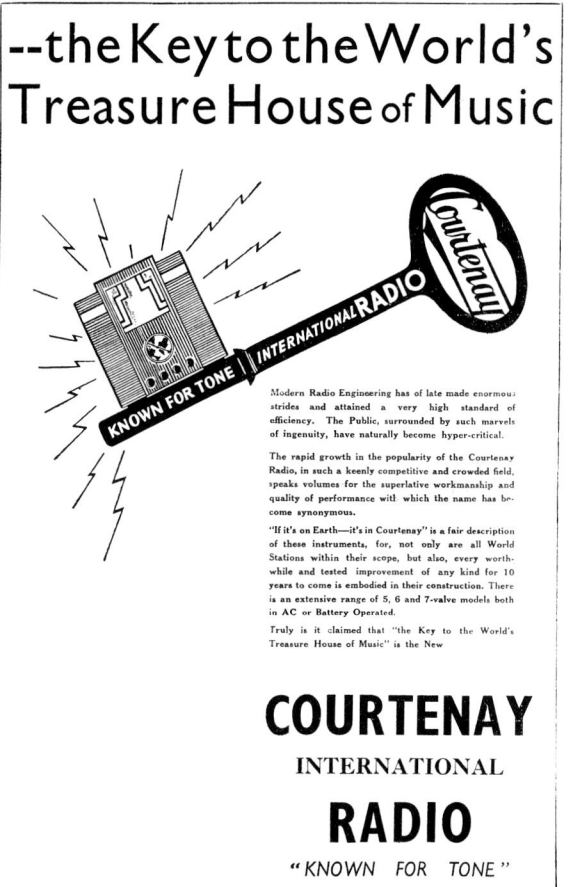

KNOWN FOR TONE INTERNATIONAL RADIO

Modern Radio Engineering has of late made enormous strides and attained a very high standard of efficiency. The Public, surrounded by such marvels of ingenuity, have naturally become hyper-critical.

The rapid growth in the popularity of the Courtenay Radio, in such a keenly competitive and crowded field, speaks volumes for the superlative workmanship and quality of performance with which the name has become synonymous.

"If it's on Earth—it's in Courtenay" is a fair description of these instruments, for, not only are all World Stations within their scope, but also, every worthwhile and tested improvement of any kind for 10 years to come is embodied in their construction. There is an extensive range of 5, 6 and 7-valve models both in AC or Battery Operated.

Truly is it claimed that "the Key to the World's Treasure House of Music" is the New

COURTENAY
INTERNATIONAL
RADIO

"KNOWN FOR TONE"

ONGARUE No. 1
1st Sept 1933

The Manager,
The Courtenay Radio
WELLINGTON

Dear Sir

    In reply to your enquiries I am glad to say that I am receiving wonderful results from the "COURTENAY TABLE MODEL," which I may add is a little short of marvellous.

    The Log I am forwarding you is interesting and gives the Stations that I receive.

So far I have logged:

109 American Stations   58 Australian Stations
15 Japanese Stations   14 V.K Amateurs
11 European Stations   6 Eastern Stations
          36 New Zealand Stations

Of these 250 Stations I have identified all except 33. I have received distant verifications from several away avaiting verification. I have several CXRM Manilla and WSAI Cincinnati from KLS Salt Lake City, KGFW CFCN Calgary. KGU Villa Acuna, WEWVA Wheeling, we in the morning and WHO Des Moines. Almost every evening we get 7 European Stations at good volume recep. Stations are able to receive approximately 25 American tion from the KOMB. Honolulu great volume recep. KGU, in fact that two nicely the smaller of the two to be turned down

My "Courtenay" has great selectivity, and I easily separate stations only 10 kilocycles apart. The volume is equal to almost any stat. ions in New Zealand from 9.30 p.m. I receive quite a few Australian Stations during daylight hours. I also near from Australia 14 short-wave amateurs who work on the Broadcast Band

Apart from the great distant reception of my "Courtenay" it has a beautiful tone, and my friends often remark how nicely the set brings out the bass notes

You may use this letter if you desire

Yours faithfully,
D. Hoskin

There is a "COURTENAY" Dealer in your own district.

The Incomparable
Courtenay

Courtenay Radio Ltd., Stewart Building,
82 Courtenay Place - - - Wellington.

Some More of the "COURTENAY" Dealers.

LEVIN .... F. MacIntosh
SHANNON .... H. D. Richards
WANGANUI ...... Tyre Supply Co.

BULLS .... Meads Bros.
FEILDING ... Wackrill & Stewart
PALMERSTON NORTH
              A. J. Berrymans Ltd.

NEW PLYMOUTH ...... Lightband & Wann.

MADE IN NEW ZEALAND!

This is the new 1934 CATHEDRAL Model. Rich in tone, wide in far-reaching selectivity and stately in appearance. Ring 54-341 for demonstration in your home or hear it at your local distributors.

Note the description of this model as the new 1934 Cathedral.

Saturday, August 10, 1935. **THE N.Z. RADIO TIMES** 11

H ERE'S a simpler and cheaper Kit, but the "punch" is there just the same . . .

PUNCH & PEP POWER

. . because the Coils are . . "EXELRAD"

The Comet Dual-Wave Five

The Comet Dual-Wave Five Kit is a winner in its class. Simple to construct and much lower in price—yet it has the PUNCH —POWER and PEP of a much bigger set, because the coils are "EXELRAD." Don't take chances—always use Individually Matched "Exelrad" Components and play safe. Their efficiency is absolutely dependable.

Master Distributors:
TURNBULL & JONES, LTD.,
AUCKLAND, WELLINGTON, CHRISTCHURCH,
DUNEDIN.
Wellington Distributors: FEAR AND CO., Willis Street.
Stockists:
ELECTRICAL & GENERAL IMPORT CO.
Christchurch.

shops were well enough equipped to take advantage of published sensitivity data, but Radio Centre shops certainly were. And this brings up another facet of Radio Corp's activities—the manufacture of test equipment.

To adequately equip the service departments of their Radio Centre shops the company produced copies of the world-famous General Radio standard signal generators and vacuum-tube voltmeters, as well as other items of test equipment which they designed themselves. So the words: "Connect the output from the standard signal generator . . ." appearing in the alignment instructions in Radio Corp's Service Bulletins could be taken literally, at least by some people.

As with other major radio factories, Radio Corp. became deeply involved in the manufacture of the famous ZC1 military transceiver during World War II.

PRECISION TESTS AND LABORATORY EQUIPMENT

When the development of a radio chassis which is to be used in a Majestic receiver is being carried on, it is done by long experienced radio engineers and technicians who have at their disposal thousands of dollars worth of the latest type of laboratory equipment. After an experimental chassis is constructed, it is carefully tested by elaborate instruments and meters for hum, sensitivity, selectivity, fidelity, etc., to make sure that it meets all the necessary requirements of a Majestic radio.

Copyright 1933
Grigsby-Grunow Co.
Chicago

Copycat!
"Imitation is the sincerest form of flattery", or plagiarism is the name of the game. Note the small differences in the drawing.

With the resumption of normal production after the war's end Radio Corporation continued along established lines, most of the Radio Centre shops having somehow managed to remain open during the war. A range of post-war models was in production by 1946, though quantities were restricted due to shortages of imported parts and material. It must be said, however, that the first post-war models differed very little from their pre-war counterparts, in fact by comparison with the products of other manufacturers they were outmoded as Radio Corp. remained the only firm to continue using EM speakers. Even after the company had produced PM speakers these were initially used only in battery sets and car radios and not until 1954 did production of EM types cease.

Mention of car radios recalls the fact that Radio Corp. did produce a solitary model, the MC7 of 1946, about which it might be kinder to say nothing at all! But having had firsthand experience with this set the writer claims the right to say this much: If any manufacturer had tried to make every mistake possible in the design of a car radio, then Radio Corp. did just that! The disastrous MC7 represented the company's only venture into the car radio field, a great blessing for all concerned.

Another much bolder, and happily more successful, venture was the production of a 78 rpm record-playing unit in 1951. In this unit, which featured a needle-armature pickup, every part was New Zealand designed and made, a quite remarkable achievement. These units were used in Columbus and Courtenay radiograms and gave good service until rendered obsolete by the introduction of long-playing records in 1955.

What might be called the beginning of the end occurred in 1956 when Turnbull & Jones Ltd gave up handling radios and withdrew the name Courtenay from the market. The last set sold under the Courtenay name was the model 45 which had been introduced in 1954 and remained current for the next two years.

It was at this time that the first definite changes in receiver construction became apparent when two Australian designed models were issued in 1955 under the 'Radiola' name, as well as the Columbus brand. They were both small 5-valve sets housed in Perspex cabinets, one model incorporating an electric alarm clock.

From this time onwards the fortunes of the company steadily declined and by 1961 the name Columbus was no longer on the market. During the preceding two years a few transistorised portables had been produced, in addition to a few radiograms, but the company seemed to have lost heart and in 1958 sold out to Pye Ltd. For a short time afterwards some radios were made under the

STELLA

is still
supreme among
modern receivers

For quality of workmanship, tone and performance, STELLA continues to forge ahead. Examine the many STELLA models and see for yourself why STELLA is the favourite choice. More features . . . more value! Why pay more?

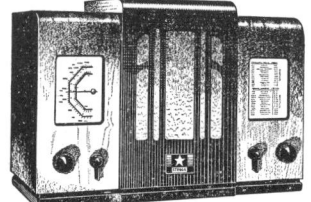

STELLA "Orion 18"
(Illustrated above) is a Dual-wave, 7-valve set with magic eye. Outstanding performer on both broadcast and shortwave bands. Latest circuit. Delightful cabinet.

STELLA "Argo 57B"
(Illustrated on left) is a broadcast BATTERY model with 5 valves. Powerful, yet economical to operate from 2 volts to 90 volts. Battery triumph of 1937.

HEAR STELLA !
DEALERS THROUGHOUT NEW ZEALAND.

New Zealand Distributors: CORY-WRIGHT & SALMON, LIMITED,
P.O. Box 1230, Wellington. P.O. Box 1650, Auckland. Ashby Bergh and Co., Ltd., Christchurch and Dunedin.

An advertisement from *Radio Record* 9 July 1937.

Pacific 6-valve dual-wave 1936.

Courtenay model 35 1939.

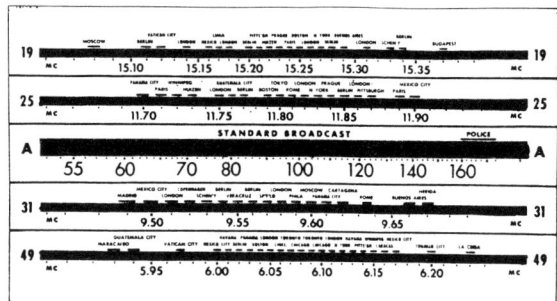

Facsimile of dial scale of 1938 RCA Radiola models HF2 and HF4 showing the use of band-spread short-wave tuning two years before Radio Corporation of New Zealand.

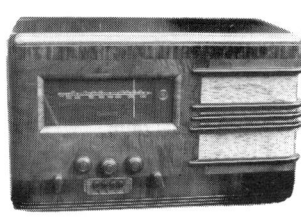 

Courtenay model 173 6-valve DW 1940. It was the first N.Z. made set to feature permeability-tuned I.F.s and the first Radio Corp. set to use a slide-rule dial.

Courtenay model 94 5-valve 1940. This was an updated version of the 1939 model.

STELLA "AQUILA 38"
★ All-wave, 7-valve glass tubes including magic eye with automatic low level bass compensation, iron-cored I.F. transformers. Improved automatic volume control and tone control, new spiral dial, and mechanical eyes on volume and tone control. A remarkable performer, delightful cabinet design with particularly fine finish. On and off switch on set.

STELLA "ORION 18"
★ Dual-wave, 7-valve glass tubes, including magic eye. Performs outstandingly on both broadcast and short-wave bands. Glass edge-lit dial, unsurpassed tonal qualities. A particularly popular model incorporating latest circuit developments, in a delightfully finished cabinet. You'll be amazed at radio progress when you hear and see "Orion 18."

The models 38 and 18 were also issued under the Columbus and Courtenay brands, which had very similar cabinets. The complicated spiral dial was also used on the model 43. 1937.

Columbus model 39, 5-valve DW 1937. This was the first set issued under the Columbus brand name.

Pacific 5-valve (plus eye) 1937. It featured a list of stations in the right-hand opening.

 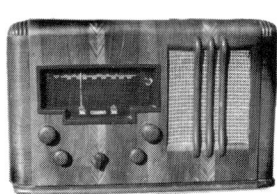

Courtenay model 94, 5-valve 1939.

Columbus model 75 7-valve 1940. The first of Radio Corporation's band-spread models. It featured permeability-tuned I.F.s and had a somewhat higher cabinet than later models.

Courtenay model 75 7-valve B.S. 1940. This was the Mark II version which quickly followed the original one.

Columbus model 12 5-valve 1940.

Columbus model 14R 5-valve BC 1947.

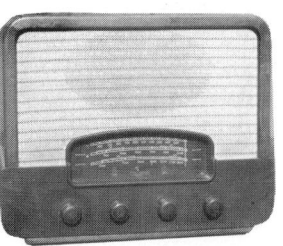

Columbus model 34 6-valve AW 1947. An uncommon model and the first Radio Corp. set to use an oval speaker.

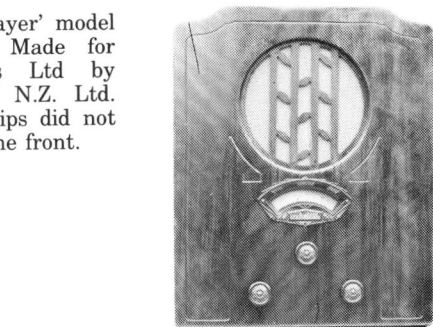

Right: 'Radioplayer' model 5-valve 1933. Made for Philips Lamps Ltd by Radio Corp. of N.Z. Ltd. The name Philips did not appear on the front.

Courtenay model 61.

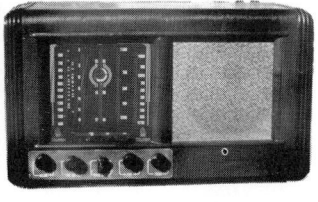

Columbus model 92 9-valve 1949. "The Last of the Big Ones." This model had a push-pull output stage.

Courtenay model 5M 5-valve 1952. The last small set sold under the Courtenay name.

Courtenay model 45 5-valve 1954 to 1956. The last receiver issued under the Courtenay brand name.

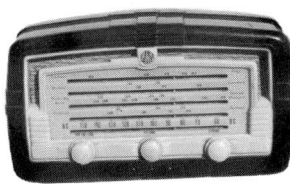

'Radiola' model 565B 5-valve 1955. This model was also sold under the Columbus name. It was almost identical to a similar Australian Radiola model.

Columbus model 525A 5-valve 1960. This model was also sold under the 'Astor' brand name and was the last of the smaller sets produced by Radio Corporation.

Tanza Record No. 1.

78 rpm motor and pickup 1949-52. It featured a needle-armature pickup and a 12-inch turntable.

'Astor' brand, but the Courtenay Place factory was used mainly to fabricate metal chassis for use at Pye's Waihi factory, as well as for the manufacture of insulated wire and cable under the 'Raycol' brand.

In turn Pye Ltd was taken over by Philips in 1977 and finally, in December 1982, nine of Pye's subsidiary companies were voluntarily wound up. Included in the casualties were: Radio Corporation of N.Z. Ltd, Pye Electronics Ltd and Akrad Radio Corp. Truly the end of an era in the history of radio manufacturing in New Zealand.

Date coding used on Radio Corp. Receivers*

For the benefit of those interested, a description of the method of chassis date coding used by Radio Corp. is given here.

The code was introduced in 1934 and ran through a series of 10-year periods, the first decade running from 1934 to 1943. To determine the year of issue of a particular chassis it is necessary to note the *first numeral* of the serial number, as this is the key to the year of production. This number corresponds to the *last numeral* of the year of issue within a particular decade. For example, a chassis having a serial number commencing with '4' could have been made in 1934 or 1954 (none were made in 1944); one starting with '6' in 1936, 1946 or 1956, and so on. A chassis having a number starting with '2' could only have been made in 1942 or 1952 as production had ceased by 1962. To determine in which particular decade a set was made it is necessary to look for 'signposts' such as the types of valves used, constructional features, type of ARTS & P decal on the chassis, and so on.

A facet of Radio Corp's activities, nowadays all but forgotten, was the production of what were then, in 1949, still called 'gramophone' records. Although the purely technical aspect of cutting and pressing 78 rpm shellac records did not present much difficulty, the launching of the finished product was a different matter altogether. There were two factors which weighed heavily against the success of the enterprise, one being the record buying public's initial reluctance to spend money on unknown records made by

* This information was supplied by Murray Stevenson, a former employee of the company.

unknown artists, and secondly the difficulty faced by Radio Corp. in breaking into the gramophone record market.

To appreciate just how difficult the latter task was it is necessary to know something of the conditions existing at the time. In those early post-war years His Master's Voice (N.Z.) Ltd held a complete monopoly of the local market, for in addition to their own products, which included British pressings of the main American companies Bunswick, Decca, Columbia and Victor, they also had sole distribution rights for the products of their only British competitor, Decca. Thus armed HMV did not welcome competition from any upstart local company, even going to the extent of covertly dissuading retailers from handling labels other than their own.

All this happened a long time ago but has been related here to indicate one of the difficulties Radio Corp. was facing when in February 1949 they launched their first, and *the* first, all-New Zealand record under the name TANZA. The name itself was made up from the initial letters of the words To Assist New Zealand Artists.

Fittingly it was a Maori singer, Pixie Williams, whose name appeared on Tanza record No. 1, the two items she sang being 'Blue Smoke' and 'Senorita'. The issuance of this record can be regarded as the start of a New Zealand industry as it was not long afterwards that HMV followed suit by issuing N.Z. pressings of overseas records, and a few years later similarly made recordings of New Zealand artists.

An undoubted factor in Radio Corp's success was that they had a ready-made national distribution set-up in the form of their Columbus Radio Centre shops, and had it not been for this the enterprise might well have never got off the ground.

ULTIMATE RADIO

The company which became New Zealand's largest radio manufacturer had its beginnings back in 1922, following the return of the representative of an Auckland firm of importers from Canada. Whilst there he had heard a radio broadcast and was sufficiently impressed with the commercial possibilities of the new medium of entertainment to suggest to his company, after his return home, that they should add radio apparatus to their range of imports. So it was that in October 1922 the firm of Radio Ltd was formed as a separate company to handle this new side of the business. But early as it was, they just missed being Auckland's first radio importers for the Johns brothers had started in business during the previous year (1921).

Radio Ltd's first act was to place an order for 300 crystal sets with the Canadian Independent Telephone Co. of Toronto. In an attempt to steal a march on the competition it was arranged to have the order forwarded by express transit to Vancouver for direct shipment to Auckland, but in placing the order a small trifle had been overlooked. There was no broadcasting station in Auckland! And without any station there was no hope of selling those 300 crystal sets, so Radio Ltd had no option but to establish one. A cable was hurriedly sent off to the Canadian De Forest Co. requesting the urgent despatch of a suitable transmitter. Pending its arrival a tiny 15-watt De Forest Radiophone was pressed into use. Radio Ltd thus became, albeit somewhat unwillingly, the owner of Auckland's first broadcasting station—1YA.

Fourteen years later it was revealed by the then managing director of the company, W. J. Trustcott, that the crystal sets had cost £3-9-0 to land, which made the retail price rather too high, so much so that a sizeable quantity remained unsold at the end of two years.

However, this initial setback in no way deterred the fledgling company who went on to become the country's largest importer of radio parts and receivers. For many years Radio Ltd's main business remained that of an importer, the company securing many choice agencies for both components and receivers. By 1929 the company had a nation-wide network of dealers throughout both islands.

The name 'Ultimate' was introduced in 1923 when a decision was made to commence manufacturing receivers. The first Ultimate was actually no more that a 2-valve Gilfillan kitset, model RA-1. It goes without saying that it did not need much capital outlay or require a great deal of technical knowledge or manufacturing expertise to 'make' a radio in those days—home constructors were doing it all the time!

Over the next three years 4 and 5-valve sets were produced until in 1927 the first all-wave model appeared. It was a 4-valve regenerative set of up-to-date design using a screen-grid RF stage and ganged tuning condensers. A set of 8 plug-in coils provided coverage down to 19 metres. It was housed in an attractive aluminium cabinet finished in black lacquer, although other colours were available to order.

During 1928-29 the same model continued to be produced, though with minor variations, including the use of a pentode output valve. It was one of these sets which was used by the company's chief engineer, R. J. Orbell, when he accompanied Admiral Richard E. Bird's first Antarctic expedition in 1929 as assistant radio operator. This event represented quite a feather in Radio Ltd's cap and provided much useful publicity for the Ultimate name.

An AC version of almost identical construction was introduced in 1929. It was housed in the same metal cabinet and was connected to its separate power pack by a 4 ft long 'umbilical cord'. The extreme length of cable was considered necessary to allow placement of the power pack at a sufficient distance to prevent hum pickup by the audio transformers in the set.

THE NEW SCREEN - GRID "4"

THIS wonderful new Screen-Grid 4-Valve Receiver is one of the most remarkable sets ever offered to the radio-loving public.

Wherever it has been tried, results have been little short of marvellous. Beginners have picked up stations in Siberia, America, Holland, England, Australia, etc., at tremendous loudspeaker volume, with the utmost ease.

Incorporates the new screen-grid that will, it is predicted, revolutionise radio reception. Single dial control; all aluminium duco-finished cabinet. Wave-length 20 to 550 metres Full Particulars from—

RADIO LTD.
Commerce Buildings,
Cnr. Anzac Avenue and Beach Road, 1928
AUCKLAND.

Assembled and sold by Radio Ltd in 1923, this Gilfillan RA-1 kitset was later claimed to be "the first Ultimate".

The first set sold by Radio Ltd was made by the Canadian Independent Telephone Co. In this picture the crystal detector is not original. 1923.

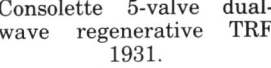

The power pack used on the AC version of the Ultimate Screen-Grid 4 was made by the Sexton Radio Co. 1929.

First AC version of the Screen-Grid 4 1929.

Right: The cabinet of the SG4 was normally finished in maroon lacquer but other colours were available to order. 1928.

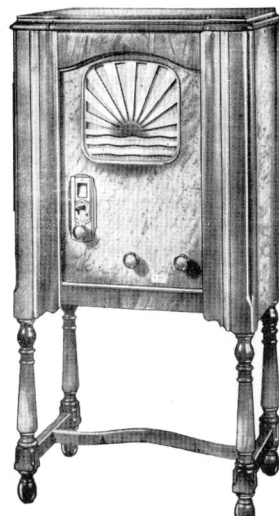 

Consolette 5-valve dual-wave regenerative TRF 1931.

Consolette 7-valve BC superhet 1931.

Model 856, 8-valve all-wave superheterodyne 1931. It used plug-in coils.

Model 524, chassis 'L' 1932. The first Ultimate superhet.

Ultimate 4-valve TRF, chassis 'S' 1932.

Model 5LN, 5-valve BC 1933.

Metal nameplate as fitted to cabinet backs, 1932-33. (Slightly larger than full size.)

Right: Ultimate logo used in connection with all-wave models during 1931-33.

ULTIMATE Model 627
(All-Electric)

Mantel Cabinet of Matched Burl Walnut

Specification

6 ARCTURUS Valves Multi-Mu and Pentode Superheterodyne circuit.
Highest quality Dynamic Speaker.
Tone Control and Static Modifier.
Extra Stage of Tuned Radio Frequency preceding the Detector-Oscillator.

Effco 180 degree full-vision dials were first used by Radio Ltd in 1932.

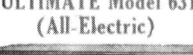

ULTIMATE Model 631
(All-Electric)

CONSOLETTE CABINET
Chassis specification same as described in Model 627

This cabinet was also used on the 5-valve model 527 in 1932.

Skyscraper model 5NR, 5-valve BC 1933.

Model 5LA, 5-valve BC 1934.

Courier model 7LAW 1935.

Ultimate 6-valve AW 1936.

A point of interest is that the power pack was not made by Radio Ltd but by another early Auckland manufacturer, W. J. Sexton.

Receiver production continued to grow steadily and in 1930 Radio Ltd could claim to have made and sold over 1,000 console models, a quite respectable figure considering the fierce competition from imported receivers, including those imported by the company itself, one might say. Although there were no import restrictions in those days there was one factor which favoured local production, the not inconsiderable "Be British, Buy British" sentiment in existence at the time. Radio Ltd was not slow to take advantage of the situation and for several years made a point of advertising Ultimate receivers as being of "British Construction"; in fact these words were actually embossed on the dial escutcheons of some 1932-33 models. After all, New Zealand was a British country and this fact was justification for the claim, even if some of the components used were not of British manufacture.

Another factor favouring local production was that because most imported receivers were of American origin they incurred a fairly high rate of duty while, on the other hand, New Zealand-made sets could incorporate English raw material and components which could be imported duty free. In 1932 an Ultimate 5-valve superhet in a floor-model cabinet was being advertised as— "This Beautiful Console at the Price of the Imported Midget".

During 1931 Radio Ltd continued their pioneering tradition by producing this country's first AC superheterodynes, one of which was an all-wave model. When it is realised that, even in the U.S., only one company, RCA, had marketed superhets before this, Radio Ltd's accomplishment was all the more noteworthy.

New models, both broadcast and all-wave, followed in 1932, the total for that year amounting to 12, including a 3-valve short-wave converter.

By 1933 there were 16 different models in production, ranging from a 5-valve chest to a 10-valve de luxe all-wave radiogram.

In spite of the prevailing depressed economic conditions of the early 1930s, Radio Ltd continued to flourish and in 1932 could claim to have accounted for over 20% of the country's radio sales for that year, having sold 1,800 sets in the months of May, June and July alone.

By 1935 the company had two Mt Eden factories in operation, No. 1 in Rocklands Avenue and No. 2 in Porters Avenue. Production figures for that year exceeded 9,000 sets. However, so rapidly was business increasing that larger premises were soon required and at the end of

1935 a move was made to a large four-storey building in Quay Street. Here the company was reorganised as Radio (1936) Ltd, under which name it was to remain for the next 20 years.

Although by this time the firm was no longer stressing the 'British' aspect of its products, they were nevertheless sufficiently aware of the still extant public preference for British goods, and this led to what can only be described as a dirty trick on their part. Even after all these years a description of it will bear repeating. Since about 1934 Rola speakers had been used exclusively in the manufacture of Radio Ltd's products, supplies being obtained from America, Australia or England. However, when using American-made speakers the firm stooped to the deceitful practice of painting out the words "Cleveland, Ohio, U.S.A." which would otherwise have been only too readily apparent to any prospective purchaser who happened to look inside the back of the set. This was a deliberate deception intended to conceal the fact that the speakers were not of British manufacture.

But is only fair to say that, in spite of this minor lapse, the name Ultimate earned for itself a well-deserved reputation for quality of workmanship among technicians and sales people alike. In any case the continuing need for subterfuge was removed by the introduction of New Zealand-made Rola speakers towards the end of 1939.

By 1934 production had increased to the extent that there were no less than 18 different models available in that year. From this time onwards a policy of issuing sets under different brand names was put into effect and within the next few years the number had increased to 12. Initially, in 1931, only one additional brand name, that of Courier, was used, but by about 1938 the following were in existence: Courier, Crusader, Hamilton, Golden Knight, Lewis Eady, Luxor, Madison, National, Paramount, Rolls, Skyscraper and, of course, Ultimate. With the exception of Courier, these brand names belonged to various distributors or retailers who, in many cases, also had radios made for them by firms other than Radio (1936) Ltd.

Originally, in the case of the Courier brand, although the same dials were used, the cabinet styles differed considerably from those used on the Ultimate brand. Later, with the advent of the so-called 'aero' dials in 1935, the Ultimate brand sets used square escutcheons while others used round escutcheons. When glass dial scales came into use from 1938 onwards all brands used the same dials. Up until 1940 there were minor differences in cabinet styles between the various brands but after that they were virtually indistinguishable. By that time, however, there

"The World's Finest Radio for 1938."
How about that? But it really was a good set.

Skyscraper NS, 5-valve BC 1935.

Skyscraper BAU, one of Radio Ltd's first 4-valve reflexed models. 1936.

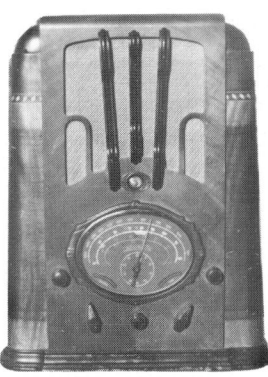

National BCU, 7-valve all-wave 1937.

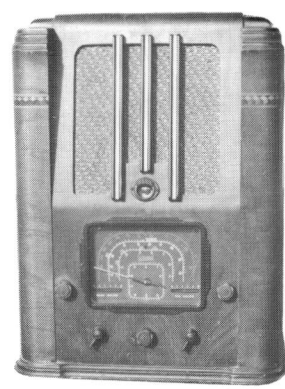

Ultimate BCU, 8-valve all-wave using metal valves. 1937.

Ultimate BXU, 8-valve AW 1938.

Skyscraper model EA 6-valve DW 1940. Note similarity in appearance to British Bush PB63, even to the inclusion of push-buttons and "Teleflic" tuning.

Ultimate model FA, 7-valve bandspread 1940. It had a cabinet styling almost identical to that of the Bush PB63.

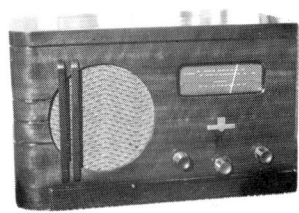

Skyscraper 4-valve reflex 1941.

Ultimate model RU, 5-valve BC 1947. The bakelite cabinet was the largest made in N.Z. at that time.

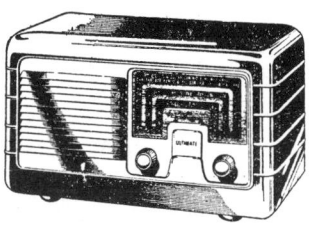
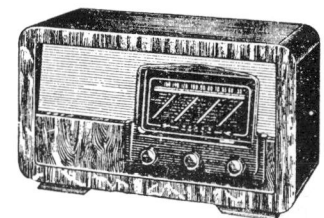
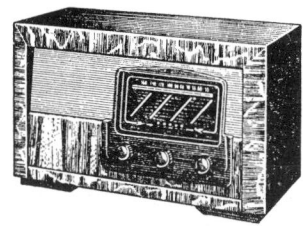
73

Ultimate Quality

MANTEL RADIOS & TABLEGRAMS

When you sell an Ultimate Radio or Tablegram you are selling the BEST. You can be confident of QUALITY that will outlast all others—PERFORMANCE that is perfect and a rich, clear TONE that will give true-to-life reproduction.

ULTIMATE "STUART"

Oak cabinet with new type inclined dial fitted with 6 - 9H speaker with provision for gramophone input and extension speaker.

Retail £27 19 6

A few selections from the great range of ULTIMATE-EKCO Radios

ULTIMATE "WINDSOR"

Solid oak cabinet — new crystal dial. Full volume 5-7 elliptical speaker, B.S.R. automatic record player.

Retail £49 19 6

Ultimate RBP, 4-valve BC 1952. This model was supplied with a base which could convert it to table mounting. When wall mounted it was not unknown for the string to break. This set earned for itself the name 'The Hanging Horror'.

EKCO "SPRITE"

Modern design moulded cabinet. 5 valve broadcast mantel with outstanding performance.

Retail £19 18 6

EKCO "CORONET"

6 valve bandspread with sensitive and selective circuit giving brilliant reception. Streamlined walnut veneer cabinet with wide, easy-to-read dial.

Retail £42 10 /-

EKCO "AIRLIE"

5 valve, 5 bandspread in grained walnut moulded cabinet. Provision for gramophone input and extension speaker.

Retail £36/-/-

ULTIMATE "CYGNET"

Occupies a minimum of space — gives maximum performance. 5 valve broadcast. Moulded cabinet in range of 5 pastel colours.

Retail £18/10/-

Ekco 'Ekcosprite' model RCX, 5-valve BC 1957. An English model originally AC/DC modified locally by the addition of an auto transformer. In 1961 it was redesigned as model REI using a full AC circuit.

Quality products of ULTIMATE-EKCO (N.Z.) CO. LTD., Quay Street, Auckland. **1957**

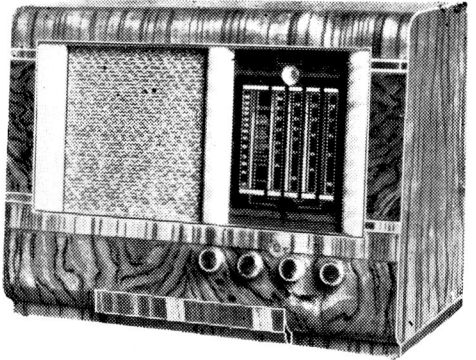

The 'box' illustrated houses National's latest 9-Valve All Wave Band Spread job. Its a wow —and so is the 7. Try one soon!

NATIONAL ALL-WAVE BAND SPREAD 7 VALVE MODEL £33/10/0

9 Valve Model as Illustrated £42/0/0

JOHN BURNS & CO. LTD.

Radio Department, Ground Floor, Customs Street East
AUCKLAND :: Phone 32-685

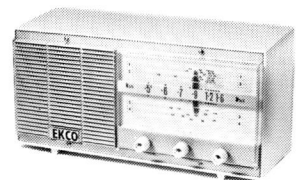

Ekco 'Embassy' 5-valve BC 1964. Nearing the end of the line.

Left: Model FC, 9-valve bandspread 1941.

74

remained only about four different brand names, apart from Ultimate, still in use.

A little known fact, worth recording here, is that between 1938 and 1941 Ultimate radios were exported in sizeable quantities. Although Australia provided the main market some sets went as far a field as India. Unfortunately, full exploitation of the export market was prevented by wartime conditions and after the war this side of the business was not proceeded with.

After many years of using American cabinet styling a sudden switch was made in 1940 when a contemporary British Bush receiver became the model for Radio (1936) Ltd. In fact, so similar was the outward appearance of the Ultimate model EA to the Bush model 71 that the two could be taken for twins; even the Bush 'Teleflic' dial was transplanted.

After a notable wartime effort in the production of military radio equipment, which is a story in itself, Radio (1936) Ltd continued to hold the position of New Zealand's leading manufacturer. It was at this time that the production of a range of electrical appliances, first commenced in 1937, became firmly established.

One of the first post-war sets, released early in 1946, was the model RB. It was notable for being housed in a metal cabinet, finished in baked white enamel which was lined inside with Pinex softboard. The use of such a cabinet probably reflected the early post-war difficulties in obtaining supplies of veneered plywood for wooden cabinets and, as yet, bakelite cabinets were not in production. By 1947 however, the first bakelite cased sets appeared, the model RV being an early example.

The first post-war radiograms, such as the model RY, appeared in 1948, but production was dependent entirely on the availability of record playing units from England which were then in extremely short supply.

As with other local manufacturers, Radio Ltd's post-war receiver production levels were greatly affected by the availability of certain imported components, a situation that remained for several years.

With the advent of television looming large on the horizon in the late 1950s, the need for technical assistance and production knowhow called for overseas connections and led to an association being formed with the old-established British firm of E. K. Cole Ltd. In 1955 the company was reorganised as Ultimate-Ecko (N.Z.) Co. Ltd and not long afterwards selected models of Ecko radios were put into production and marketed alongside existing locally designed Ultimates.

Although not among the first manufacturers of television receivers, Ultimate-Ecko produced one of the highest quality sets until 1965, when E. K. Cole Ltd was taken over by Pye Ltd. It was this takeover which eventually resulted in Ultimate-Ekco coming under the control of N.Z. Pye, and in 1967 the Quay Street premises were finally vacated after being the home of Ultimate radio for 31 years.

The closure of the factory represented the end of an era in New Zealand radio manufacturing and the start of the domination of this country's electronics industry by overseas interests. Although the Ultimate name was carried on for the next 15 years or so, it was by then only one of the brand names used by Pye.

CHAPTER SIX

Brief biographies of some other New Zealand manufacturers

Ariel

This name was originally owned by Abel, Smeeton Ltd who started making sets on a small scale in 1932. In 1936 the business became Warwick Smeeton Ltd and at this time a separate factory, known as Imperial Radio Mfg Co., was set up, radio production continuing until 1938. In that year the business was taken over by Webb's Radio Ltd who carried on small-scale production in the basement of the retail premises until 1942. After the war Webbs specialised in the production of kitsets, offering portables and car radios in addition to household models. Production ceased in 1970.

Carillon

Radios were manufactured for a short period in the early 1930s by the Sexton Radio Co. and distributed by John Burns & Co. Ltd.

Genrad and Briton

This brand was manufactured for a brief period during 1933 by a firm called General Radio Ltd. Its short existence may have had something to do with its unethical and flagrant copying of other firms' trade-marks. Both the well-known 'GR' trade-mark of the world-famous General Radio Co., U.S.A. and the slogan of the British company A. F. Bulgin Ltd—"The Choice of Critics" were pirated by this "rat bag" N.Z. firm.

Courier

This name was originally owned by the firm J. Wiseman & Sons (saddlery manufacturers) which had been founded in 1861. In turn the business passed to a son of the founder, Mr J. W. Wiseman, and in 1927 the manufacture of radios was commenced as a sideline. This was a rather surprising move for a saddlery manufacturer, to say the least, as at that time there were only two or three radio manufacturers in the whole of the country. By 1928 there were four different models on the market. The first electric models were produced in 1929 and newer models were introduced in 1930. But then something went

wrong; just what happened all those years ago is now a matter of conjecture, but radio production suddenly ceased. In 1931 the name was taken over by Radio Ltd who produced their first Courier in that same year. Thereafter the name continued in use until 1955 as an additional brand name on receivers made by the company.

Murphy

A British name originally used in New Zealand by Westco Products Ltd as licensees for Murphy Radio Ltd, England. After the demise of Westco in 1957 the agency was acquired by Allied Industries Ltd, an associate company of Fisher & Paykel Ltd. The latter firm had previously imported 'Pilot' radios in pre-war days but had not handled radios since. Allied Industries commenced radio manufacturing in the old Westco factory in Lorne Street but soon after moved to a new factory at Mt Wellington. In 1967 Amalgamated Wireless Valve Co. of Australia became a fifth partner in Allied Industries and for a time 'Radiola' radios were made at the Mt Wellington factory.

Peerless

The trade-name of a small Wellington firm, Megann Ltd, who had started in business in pre-war days as Megann's Radio Service. Radio manufacturing was commenced in 1947 when a line of portables and household sets was marketed. The receivers themselves were unremarkable but the firm was known for its piracy of such well-known American names as Atwater Kent and Zenith.

Radiojoy

Made by F. W. Mountjoy & Sons Ltd, a family concern founded in 1933, the first Radiojoys were assembled using parts bought in from Radio Ltd. A separate factory was established in 1939 and production continued to 1950. Today, as a home appliance retailer, the firm is still carried on under its original name by a grandson of the founder, Noel Mountjoy.

Manufactured by
SEXTON MOTORS,
6, Lower Albert St., Auckland
Telephone 42-367

Courier model 4, Serial No. 1040 1928. This set was a dual-wave model using a patented method of bandswitching. (N.Z. Patent No. 50508)

Selectra 3-valve regenerative, Serial No. 0313, dated 20-9-29.

MACK'S FAMOUS RADIO SET

76 KENT TERRACE, WELLINGTON

THIS set is made in New Zealand, for New Zealand, by a New Zealander, therefore it deserves your special consideration. There are features in it that are not found in any similar kind of set on the market to-day. Some of its advantages are:—It will tune from the lowest known wave-length on Broadcast—below 12 metres and up. It has coil for local Broadcast, rendering music and speech distinct and clear. At rear of set is a Gramophone Pick-up plug. No volume control is required for Pick-up—simply plug in. By withdrawing Pick-up plug the set is ready for Radio.

Mack's Famous Radio Set

is made from the highest known quality of Radio parts on the market. Finished in black, with Crystaline surface, the cabinet is entirely of metal, conforming to the latest in radio engineering design. It is designed to take any kind of *power tube in last stage* and will work comfortably on "B" Battery Eliminators or Batteries. In every way the set has been designed to meet the requirements of New Zealand. It can honestly be deemed to be the only set in the world designed to suit our New Zealand conditions. Calibrated, and stations all checked *from the air* ensures to you a safe proposition, especially when it is backed by our guarantee of money back if you are not satisfied.

The Set You Have Been Waiting for——
MACK'S FAMOUS RADIO SET!

Mack's 3-valve AW battery set 1929.

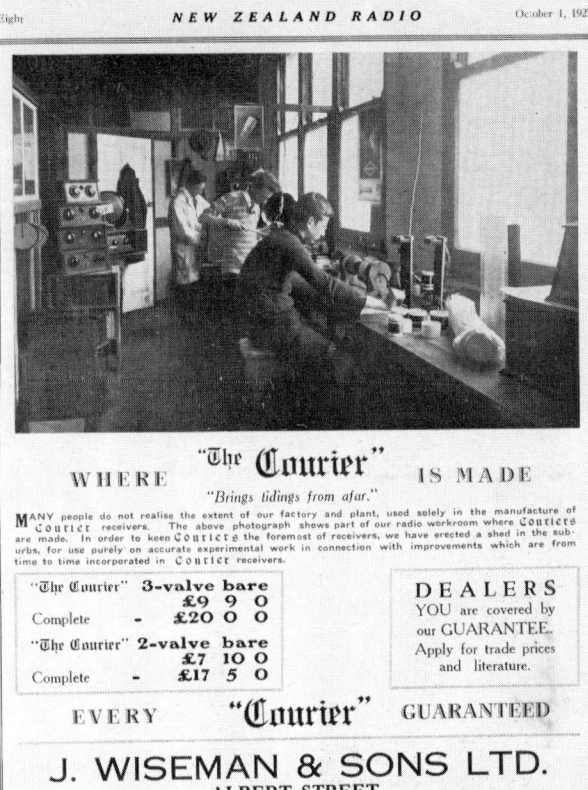
The Courier radio factory going full blast. Note the hand-cranked coil winder.

Mack's 4-valve AW battery set 1929. Manufactured by Mack's Radio Co., Wellington.

Silvertone 6-valve 1932. Manufactured by Sexton Radio Co.

Silvertone superhet 6-valve 1932. Manufactured by Sexton Radio Co.

Paragon 6-valve BC 1932.

Carillon 5-valve superhet 1932. Made by Sexton Radio Co.

Carillon 5-valve chassis 1933.

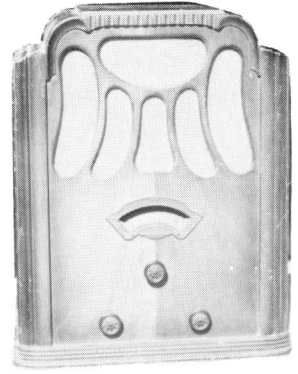

Commodore 5-valve TRF 1932.

Ariel 7-valve 1933.

Sadly, this Ariel radio had to be advertised as British-built rather than New Zealand-made. 1933.

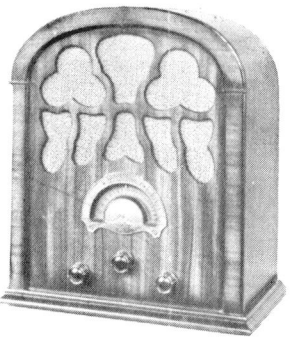

Viking, made by the N.Z. Radio Mfg Co. Ltd, Christchurch. No details available. 1933.

Temple 5-valve BC 1933. Manufactured by Ellis & Co. Ltd.

Troubadour superhet 6-valve 1933. Manufactured by Turnbull & Jones Ltd, Auckland.

Royal 6-valve BC 1933. Manufactured by the Royal Engineering Co., Hamilton.

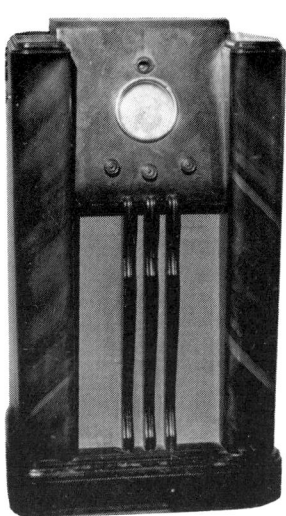

Radiojoy chassis 'A' 7-valve dual-wave 1936.

Haywin 'Broadcaster' 5-valve 1936. Made for Hays Ltd, Christchurch.

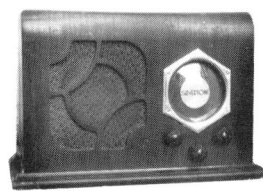

Silvertone 5-valve BC 1936. Manufactured by S. D. Mandeno & Co.

Lyric 5-valve 1934. Manufactured by Ellis & Co. Ltd.

Austin 5-valve BC 1936.

The Grandfather Clock Model "ARIEL"

6-VALVE CHASSIS, with either Electric or Mechanical Clock.

The glorious tone of this Radio is a feature directly resultant from the unique shape of the Cabinet.

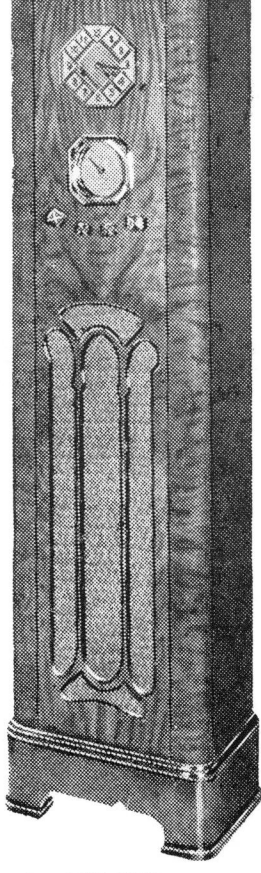

Ariel 6-valve DW 1936.
One of only two known makes of radios made as grandfather clock models.

Ariel 12-valve AW 1937.

Yale 5-valve BC 1937. Manufactured by Westonhouse Radio Ltd.

Ariel 5-valve BC AC/DC 1937.

Elgin 6-valve DW 1936. Manufactured by Rees & Ramsden, Hastings.

Moderne 7-valve DW 1937. Manufactured by Electrical Service Co., Wellington.

'Franklin' 7-valve DW 1937.

Moderne 7-valve DW featuring 'Teledial' tuning. 1938.

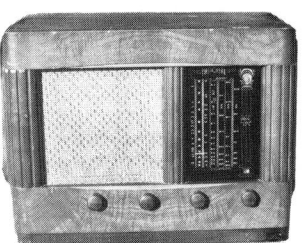

National 7-valve BS 1941. Manufactured by Westonhouse Air Gas Co.

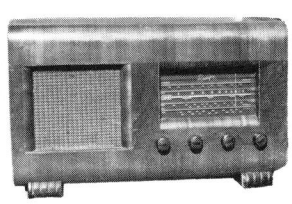

Radiojoy 6-valve DW 1942.

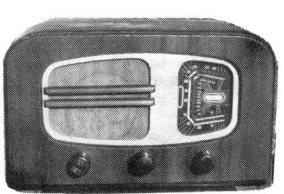

Robertson 5-valve BC 1946. Manufactured by Westco Products Co.

Peerless model 4751, 5-valve 2-band 1947. Made by Megann Ltd.

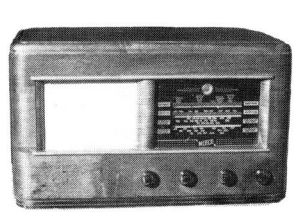

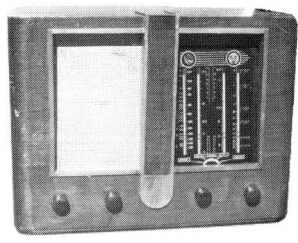

Neeco 7-valve dual-wave 1947. Manufactured by Paramount Radios, Christchurch.

World 5-valve DW 1947.

Bush model 95, 7-valve BS 1948. Designed and built by International Traders Ltd.

Avalon 5-valve BC 1950.

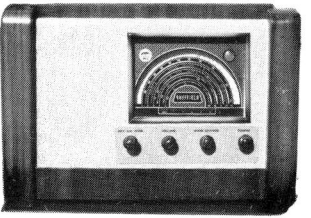

Sheffield 4-valve Superhet 1950.

Murphy TA222, 5-valve 1952. Assembled by Westco Products Co.

Sheffield 856, 8-valve BS with push-pull output. 1956.

Sheffield model 6R3, 5-valve BC 1956.

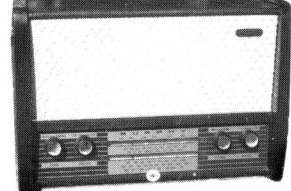

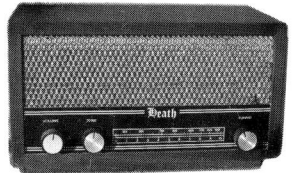

Murphy MD54, 6-valve DW 1957. Made by Allied Industries Ltd.

Avalon 5-valve BC 1958. Manufactured by Swinburne's Radios. Note use of earlier 'Antone' cabinet 1948.

Heath 4-valve 1962. Manufactured by Heath's Electronics, Pukekohe.

Selectra

Radios were made between 1927 and 1930 by a firm called Selectra Radio Ltd. Both battery and AC models were produced.

Sexton

The firm of Sexton Motors Ltd originally made battery sets under the name 'Sexton' in the late 1920s. After about 1931 the name was no longer used as a receiver brand but W. J. Sexton continued to make transformers and power packs and also complete radios for other manufacturers and distributors. In 1939 a firm called Cinevox N.Z. Ltd was formed to manufacture cinema sound systems. Although this enterprise did not survive World War II it is interesting to note that Cinevox commenced to make resin-cored solder and continued to do so until the 1970s.

Silvertone

A brand name originally owned by S. E. Moe

Ltd, an Auckland retailer who had sets made by W. J. Sexton, and later by S. D. Mandeno Ltd and Sheffield Radio Ltd. In 1947 a firm known as Radio Specialities Ltd took over Moe's business but lasted for only a couple of years.

Seven Seas

This brand name was owned by S. D. Mandeno Ltd who made radios between 1935 and 1950. In pre-war days the firm supplied various private-brand owners. The firm's name was later changed to Sonophone Distributors Ltd when they gave up radio manufacture and commenced to make amplifiers and sound systems.

Sheffield

Radios were first made in 1935 by Sheffield Radio Ltd. Early sets carried a picture of a kiwi on the dial. This firm specialised in the production of private-brand chassis and continued to make radios into the 1960s.

Thorn

The last British name to be introduced to the N.Z. market, probably because Thorn Electrical Industries was a newcomer to the British post-war scene. In 1957 Thorn took over the N.Z. firm of Mowat Radio Industries Ltd and formed Thorn Radio Industries N.Z. Ltd. Mowat had previously specialised in the production of tape recorders. For a short time after the take-over radios and tape recorders were sold under the name MRI-Thorn. The last valve radio, the 'Mastiff', was produced in 1967.

World

Manufacture of radios was commenced in 1936 by a firm originally known as Hill Radios, and later, in 1950, as World Radio Industries Ltd. In spite of the somewhat grandiose later name, the firm remained one of the smallest manufacturers, though its products were always of a uniformly high standard. In the early post-war years private-brand sets were made under the names Elco, Neeco and Superdyne.

Yale

House brand of the Westonhouse Air Gas Co., one of the few small pre-war firms to survive World War II, commenced radio manufacture in 1934, specialising in the production of private brand sets. Became Westonhouse Radio Ltd in 1947 and Westco Products Ltd in 1955. Assembled Murphy radios under licence to Murphy Radio, U.K. between 1952 and 1956. Ceased operations in 1957.

The firm of International Traders Ltd imported American Bosch and Bush radios in a partly finished state for final assembly and fitting into locally made cabinets, and was the only firm to handle two different makes of imported sets at the same time. Between 1940 and 1942 the company made sets of its own design using the Bush name when wartime conditions prevented importation. In 1946 manufacture was recommenced using the name 'E.I.L.' (Electric Industries Ltd). Between 1948 and 1950 car radios were manufactured under licence to Motorola Inc., U.S.A. The company ceased operations in 1955.

NEW ZEALAND CAR RADIOS

Because of their specialised nature, coupled with the comparatively limited market in pre-war days, no car radios were made in New Zealand until after World War II. But even then the major manufacturers displayed little interest and most did not enter the field until well into the 1950s. Consequently it was some of the smaller post-war firms who first exploited the field, the most successful being a specialist manufacturer who, for the first 15 years of its existence, made only car radios. Eventually other lines were added to this firm's output, long after it had become well established in the car radio field.

The story begins in 1946 when two young men, George Benson and Perc Wills, formed a partnership known as Benson & Wills and commenced the manufacture of car radios using the name 'Autocrat'. For the first year or so of its existence the 'factory' was only a two-man firm and production was thus on a small scale. In 1947 a move was made to larger premises, when with the addition of a third partner the firm's name became Benson, Wills & Walker. As yet it was still not a limited company. Within two years, however, a third move to much larger premises saw greatly expanded production together with a name change to Autocrat Radio Ltd. A final move to Carr Road, Mt. Roskill was made in 1957.

Up till this time Autocrat had had virtually no competition as the only other company to have produced a car radio was Radio Corp., whose 1947 model MC7 was a dismal failure which deterred that company from further attempts.

From 1949 onwards, however, there was increasing competition from several smaller firms, some of which produced only car radios. During the next few years there were as many as seven different makes on the market which included:

Ariel	made by Webb's Radios Ltd
Avalon	made by Swinburne Radios Ltd
Companion	made by Swinburne for Johns Ltd
Grover	made by Grover Electrical Ltd
Motorola	made under licence by International Traders Ltd
Wayfarer	made by Keith's Radio
Westco	made by Westco Products Ltd

Of these only Motorola had the pre-war style of remote control using flexible metal cables.

Up to about 1952 the major old-established firms had paid singularly little attention to the car radio field but from this time onwards became increasingly interested. It must be recorded, however, that their activities were rather low key and Autocrat continued to be the largest producer for many years. In fact it may be fairly said that most of the larger manufacturers only dabbled in car radio production and in the cases of Collier & Beale and Radio (1936) Ltd only produced two models each. Radio Ltd's first offering, the model RAI of 1949 was actually made by Autocrat and the only other Ultimate valve-operated model was the RBN of 1950-51. Philips entered the field in 1953 with their model 636V/637V and continued to produce valve models for the next five or six years.

Of the remaining large firms Bell Radio-

Autocrat Radio

CAR RADIOS
£34-9-0
Retail Price

SIX-VALVE RECEIVERS BUILT TO WITHSTAND THE ROUGHEST CONDITIONS TO BE EXPERIENCED IN NEW ZEALAND.

Special and exclusive Autocrat features ensure perfect reception under the most adverse conditions. We stand confidently behind any demonstration a prospective buyer may require. Note these features: High gain aerial circuit, latest metal type valves, low current drain. 4½ amps. 6 volt or 2½ amps. 12 volt. Turn to "New Products" page for complete technical description.

★ Approved agents wanted throughout New Zealand. Write for particulars immediately. This car radio has become soundly established and is worth taking over for exclusive representation.

Manufacturers:

BENSON, WILLS and WALKER
118 VICTORIA STREET, AUCKLAND.

The first Autocrat car radios were manufactured early in 1947. This advertisement is dated December 1947.

October 1947.

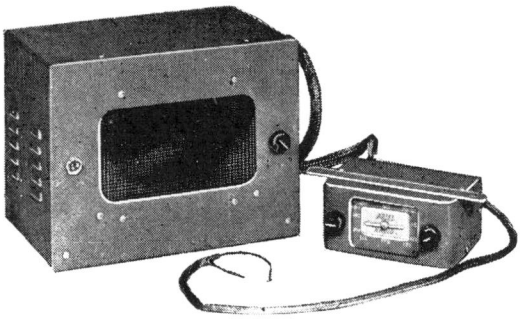

Ariel 5-valve car radio 1947. Manufactured by Webb's Radio Ltd, it was also available in kitset form with pre-wired control head.

This 5-valve Yale car radio made by Westonhouse Radio Ltd was one of the few makes to use the outmoded synchronous vibrator. First advertised January 1948.

SKYSCRAPER "VAGABOND" 6V. Broadcast Auto.

Left: Radio Ltd's first car radio, model RAI 1949. It was actually made by Autocrat but was disguised by having roller controls in place of knobs.

Right: Motorola 6-valve model 1949. Completely made in N.Z. by International Traders Ltd. 1949.

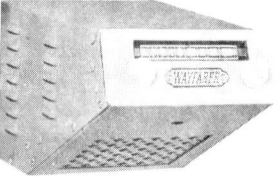

'Wayfarer' manufactured by Keith's Radio Service 1949.

November 1949.

June 1949.

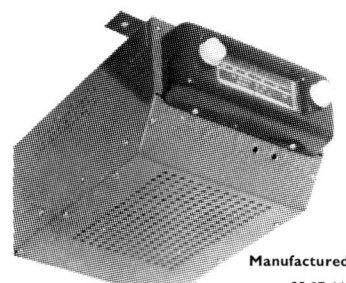

AVALON
SINGLE UNIT
CAR RADIOS

Manufactured By SWINBURNE RADIOS LTD.

85-87 New North Road, Auckland, C.3.

1949

CALL ON US
AT OUR NEW ADDRESS

Visitors entering Auckland from the Great South Road are in a handy position to drop in and inspect the new Autocrat Car Radio factory at The Harp o' Erin. We extend a cordial invitation to all members of the trade who come by car to Auckland on business—or pleasure.

AUTOCRAT RADIO LTD.

285 GREAT SOUTH ROAD (at The Harp o' Erin) - - - - AUCKLAND

Sole New Zealand Distributors: G. A. WOOLLER & CO., LTD., AUCKLAND.

August 1951.

Ultimate
FIRST IN AUSTRALASIA WITH THE SENSATIONAL NEW
"Auto Portable"
TRANSISTOR '8'

3-in-I CAR RADIO

Ultimate-Ekco (N.Z.) Co. Ltd., announce with pride the release of the Ultimate Transistor Eight "AUTO-PORTABLE". This is a new approach to radio enjoyment and is the first of this type of radio receiver to be manufactured in New Zealand. A magnificently versatile piece of equipment, it has the added advantage that it gives outstanding performances in *three separate spheres.*

The one receiver can be used as an AUTO SET, a PORTABLE, and a HOME SET. The "Auto-Portable" is a completely self-contained transistor portable complete with carrying handle and can be fitted to any car or be slipped into a beautifully designed veneered cabinet where it gives a performance comparable with that of a much larger receiver.

ULTIMATE–EKCO (N.Z.) CO. LTD.,
AUCKLAND

March 1960.

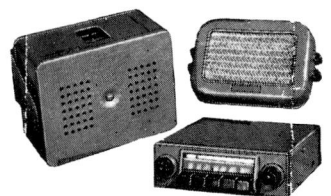

Cromwell

Chassis Model 6154A. 6 Valve Broadcast Auto Radio. Push button three unit. Code word, "Cruiser" (6 volt), "Ranger" (12 volt).

Collier & Beale's model 6154A was the second and last car radio made by this firm. 1954.

7 Tube De Luxe Auto Radio for 6 Volt or 12 Volt Operation.

Collier & Beale's first car radio 1951.

RETAIL PRICE
£35/10/-

SPECIFICATIONS OF MODEL 39 AUTO RADIO

6 Valves. Single Unit. The most powerful auto radio ever made in New Zealand. 5 in. permanent magnet speaker. Two-way tone control switch. Low battery consumption (4.1 amp. on 6 volt, 2.3 amp. on 12 volt). Rigid, simple construction. Special type lock-in tubes. Built-in spark suppression. Supplied with all fittings for installation. Will operate on either polarity of battery. Specially designed to be easily and quickly installed in all types of cars.

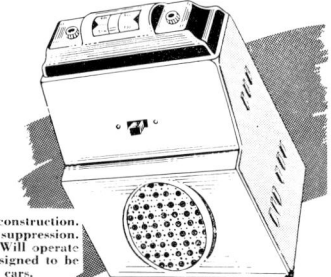

Westco, 6-valve model 39 1951.

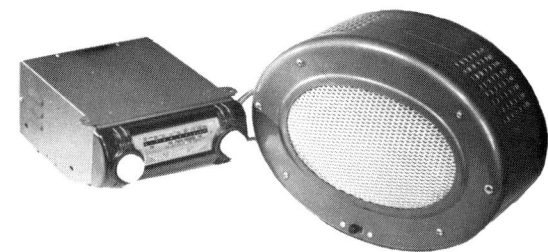

Ultimate 7-valve car radio model RBN 1952.

Philips "Automate" Car Radio

MODEL NZ 656 V

SUPERHETERODYNE RECEIVER

Wave Range: 508 — 1613 kc/s.

Supply: 6 or 12 volts D.C. positive or negative chassis.

I.F. Frequency: 455 kc/s.

Output Impedance: 5 ohms.

Power Consumption: 3.0 amps at 6 volts.
1.6 amps at 12 volts.

The first New Zealand-made Philips car radio. The speaker was detachable for use in a different position. 1957.

SENSATIONAL NEWS
for all Car Owners!

Autocrat proudly present their NEW

TRANSISTORISED

AUTOCRAT AUTO RADIOS

THE NEW AUTOCRAT TRANSISTORISED 'PRESTALOK' MODEL

Custom-built for every modern car, and featuring the outstanding 'PRESTALOK' 5 Button Tuning Unit.

The first transistorised Autocrat, model TP1 was a hybrid using four valves and a single transistor. 1957.

THE HIKER'S ONE

Although the Electric Lamphouse Ltd, in 1937, introduced and heavily promoted the 'Hiker's One' kitset, they did not originate it. Constructional details and the name itself were lifted *in toto* from the American magazine *Popular Mechanics* without acknowledgement.

Its good performance when operating from only six volts 'high tension' was undoubtedly due to the type 49 valve used in space-charge mode. Later versions suffered due to the non-availability of this valve.

Considerably modified versions were still being marketed until well into the early 1950s. In the early post-war years at least two Auckland retailers marketed their own versions in made-up form.

The 'Hiker's' One was undoubtedly the most popular kitset of any type ever sold in N.Z. Many people got their start in radio through building one of these kits. Soon it will be 50 years since the 'Hiker's One' first appeared and it has already become a collector's item in its own right.

The Hiker's One

FIRE WATCHERS AND E.P.S.

The Famous HIKER'S ONE

ASSEMBLED AND IN CABINET.

Just imagine the enthusiasm with which this gift will be received. The newest HIKER'S ONE, famous throughout the Dominion as the most wonderful and economical little receiver ever offered to the public. Used by Hikers, Trampers, Scouts, Motorists, and in hundreds of homes as an extra set for the boys. You just couldn't think of a more useful gift! Cat. No. PK232—Complete with Valve and Batteries **£2/11/-**
(EARPHONES EXTRA)

Wartime uses for the Hiker's One.

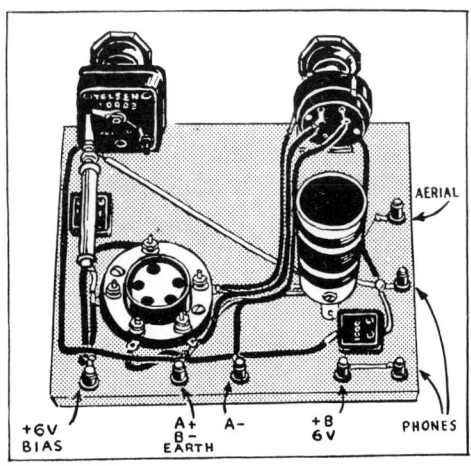

PICTURE SHOWS WIRING.

The Electric Lamphouse's first version as depicted in their 1937 catalogue.

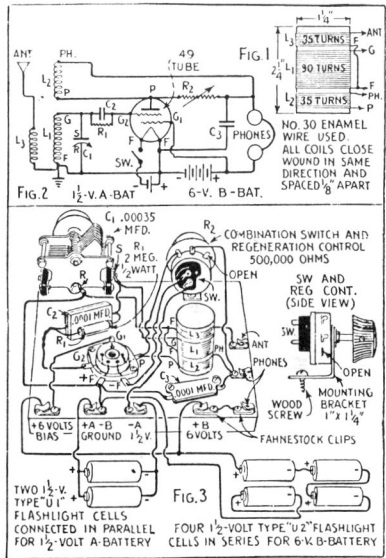

THE CIRCUIT AND PICTURE DIAGRAM.

Experimenters will find the space charge detector of special interest, and, as far as we are aware, this is the first time the principle has been described in New Zealand in a single tube receiver.

In this set the type 49 valve is employed in a regenerative circuit with resistor control of regeneration. A positive basis is applied to the inner grid of the valve, thus permitting the valve to operate efficiently on only 6 volts of plate voltage. The filament supply is 1½ volts, which can be obtained by connecting two single torch cells in parallel as shown or a single No. 6 type dry cell may be used. Four single torch cells connected in series furnish the bias and plate voltage or 9-volt C battery could be used as the B supply.

Coil-winding details are shown in Fig. 1. It is important that all three windings be made in a clockwise direction and connections should be made as shown. The start and finish ends of each coil winding are anchored by passing the wire through two small holes in the former. Be sure and leave the wires long enough to reach the various points as indicated in Diagram 3.

N.Z. CAR RADIOS (cont.)

Television Corp. and the Dominion Radio & Elec. Corp. produced only one model each. No car radios were produced by the Akrad Radio Corp. until 1956, several years after the tie up with Pye Ltd. The first release was the Pye PB8U6 which was followed by a 4-valve model released in 1957 as Pye model PZ305 and Clipper 4CR7.

His Master's Voice (N.Z.) Ltd was the first pre-war firm to become involved with car radios, and this was a result of the British parent company forming an association with Smith's Motor Accessories Ltd in 1948. Smith's and EMI

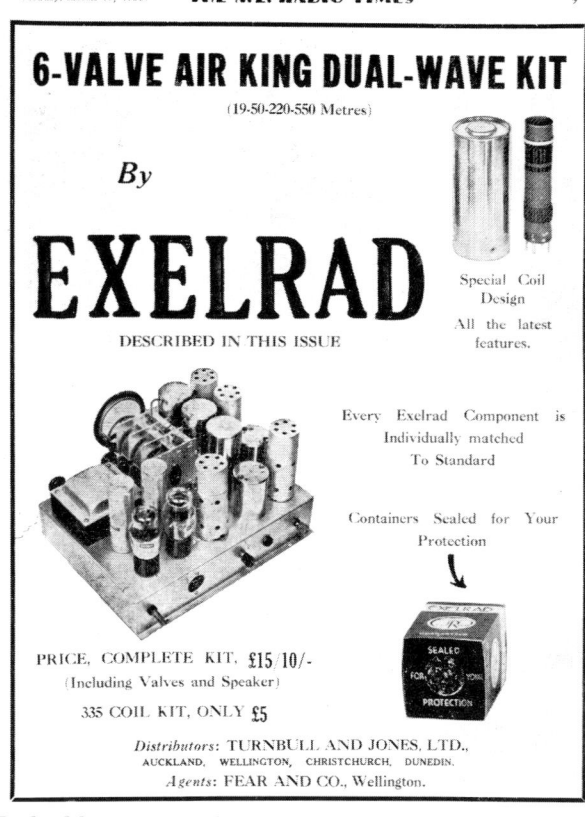
Exelrad kitsets were first marketed in 1935 by Turnbull & Jones Ltd; the parts were made by Radio Corporation of N.Z.

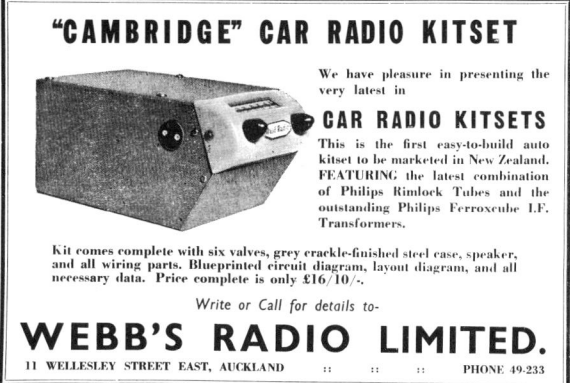
1950

1951

1947

1948

R & E December 1947.   Arnrite kitset portable sold by Arnold Wright Ltd 1949.

Pacemaker 5150, 6-valve AC/Battery 1951. Introduced late in 1950, it remained in production for nearly 5 years and became the largest selling set of its type.

The first Ultimate portable using the then new 1.5 V 'all-dry' valves. 1939.

Collier & Beale's first portable 1940. It had a Rexine covered case.

Pacemaker 5-valve AC/Battery model 517AB 1948.

"Atwater Kent" 5 Valve Portable

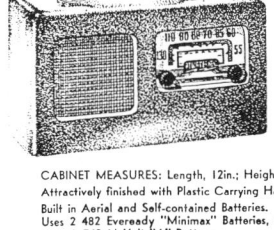

Manufactured by Megann Ltd, Wellington 1948. An example of the pirating of a world-famous brand name by a local firm.

Philips model 545, 6-valve AC/Battery 1948. This was the first Philips set of its type.

Arnrite Battery portable 1948. Available in 4 and 5-valve models and made by R. Chaston Ltd.

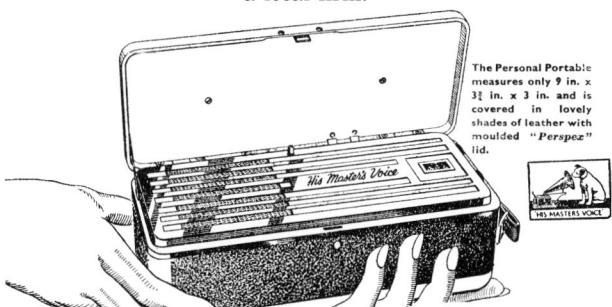

HMV 484P 4-valve portable 1948.

Ariel 5-valve AC/Battery 1948.

Arnrite 5-valve, AC/Battery 1949. Made by R. Chaston Ltd.

Another "Five Star" SMASH HIT!

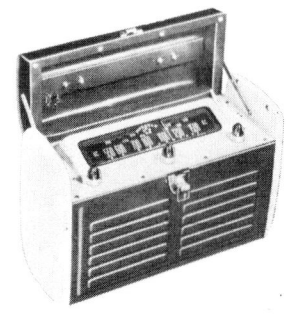

The model 6P9 AC/Battery portable was also sold under the Regent and Pacific brand names. It featured a loop aerial concealed in the lid. 1948.

HMV 6-valve AC/Battery model 476P 1949. It used parallel type 1A5GT valves in the output stage.

Ultimate model RJ 6-valve AC/Battery portable 1948.

Ariel 5-valve AC/Battery 1950.

Ariel 5-valve AC/Battery 1951. Made by Webb's Radio Ltd.

Ultimate model RAW, 5-valve AC/Battery 1952.

Bell model 6P7, 6-valve AC/DC/Battery 1955. An example of the so-called '3-way' portable.

Ltd were responsible for the production of the 'Radiomobile' car radios which were marketed in New Zealand by HMV.

With the advent of transistorised models from 1960 onwards all existing local manufacturers, with the exception of Allied Industries Ltd, became involved in their manufacture.

KITSETS

In addition to making complete radios some manufacturers offered them in kitset form for assembly by home constructors. The boom period for this activity occurred in the years between 1934 and 1940. Amongst N.Z. manufacturers Radio Corp's 'Exelrad' kits were undoubtedly the biggest sellers, runners-up being Johns Ltd and the Electric Lamphouse. However, the N.Z. kits faced fierce competition from the Australian-made products of such firms as Lekmek, Radiokes and

RCS.

After the war there was a brief revival of interest in kitset construction, particularly in the case of portable models. The Electric Lamphouse continued to cater for the kitset market, with other firms such as SOS Radio and Webb's Radio also specialising in this area. By the late 1950s, however, interest in kitset construction had dwindled to almost zero.

NEW ZEALAND PORTABLES

Before 1939 all portable radios seen in this country, apart from a few home-made ones, were of overseas origin as no N.Z. manufacturers were yet making this class of receiver. Although a few imported sets appeared as early as 1927, it was not until the late 1930s that portables made much impression on the local scene. Between 1936 and 1939 such well-known British makes as Ekco, HMV, Lissen, Spencer and Vidor were imported.

The first New Zealand-made portables were of the so-called 'all-dry' variety, one of the earliest being made by Radio Ltd in 1939. During the next two years other firms such as Collier & Beale, Radio Corp. and Wellmade also entered the field. With the production of their model FB in 1941 Radio Ltd became the first N.Z. manufacturer to market a combination AC/Battery set.

Beginning in 1947-48, most existing firms commenced to manufacture 'two-way' portables and in some cases continued production of this type of set until the late 1950s. By 1955 three-way AC/DC/Battery models had arrived, though certain firms, notably Radio Ltd, wisely refrained from producing such troublesome 'hot boxes'. While the elimination of the power transformer made these sets marginally lighter to carry and cheaper to produce, the change brought with it decreased reliability. At least one manufacturer is known to have reverted to the earlier two-way design as a result of the trouble encountered.

As in other countries, the advent of transistorised receivers sounded the death knell of valve-operated portables and by the late 1950s production had entirely ceased.

CHAPTER SEVEN

Some American receivers sold in New Zealand

ATWATER KENT

The story of Atwater Kent Radio is very much the story of one man's life and work—that of Arthur Atwater Kent. He was born in Vermont in December 1873 but the family moved to Worcester, Massachusetts, some eight years later. In 1898 the young Atwater Kent entered the Worcester Polytechnic Institute but proved to be a poor student and left in 1900 without completing his studies.

At the age of 22 he had already established a small electrical manufacturing business in Worcester known as the Kent Electric Mfg Co. Seven years later he moved to Philadelphia and established the Atwater Kent Mfg Works. Here he made, among other products, Atwater Kent automotive electrical parts, including a patented ignition system.

Because of a downturn in business in 1919, following the end of World War I, Atwater Kent turned his attention to making radio parts, even though the market must have been quite small in those pre-broadcasting days. However, the demand proved encouraging and the range of components was steadily increased year by year.

Once broadcasting had started the public demand for receivers encouraged Atwater Kent to enter the market and in 1923 the first complete radios were produced. For the first two years Atwater Kent receivers were constructed in a unique 'bread board' form with all components mounted on a polished mahogany baseboard. Unlike all other contemporary receivers, no front panel was used and all wiring was concealed beneath the baseboard. Extensive use was made of glossy moulded bakelite and polished and lacquered brass, the overall effect of which was most distinctive and extremely eye catching.

The first A K to be enclosed in a cabinet was the model 20, a 5-valve TRF introduced in 1924. Although of plain appearance the cabinet was extremely well finished and the style of cabinet work remained in use for the next few years. Unlike other receivers of the period the model 20

did not use neutralisation, its two RF stages being stabilised by means of 'losser' resistors in the grid circuits. It has been stated that Atwater Kent was unwilling to pay the high cost of the manufacturing licence charged by the owners of the various neutralising systems (such as Neutrodyne) and instead used the losser system even though it resulted in a slightly lower gain. With one exception, the model 50, the basic circuitry of A K receivers remained unchanged for the next five years, even after mains-operated models had appeared. Not until 1929, when screen-grid tubes came into use, was the losser system discarded.

In 1927 the first AC powered set, model 36, was introduced; it used a separate power pack as well as a separate magnetic speaker. The receiver itself was housed in a plain wooden cabinet of the same style as was then in use on battery sets. Later in the same year when the first self-contained AC set, model 37, was introduced a change was made to the use of metal cabinets. Sets continued to be issued in metal cabinets throughout 1928-29 though the first console-style wooden cabinets became available in 1929. Atwater Kent's predilection for metal cabinets even extended to the production of some unique but singularly hideous metal console models during 1929-30.

During the years 1926, 1927 and 1928 A K had been the sales leader of the industry but in 1929 they were overtaken by Majestic who moved into No. 1 position that year. It seems more than likely that the continued use of metal cabinets at a time when other manufacturers were using 'furniture' cabinets was responsible for Atwater Kent's dropping to second place in 1929. In the event they never regained No. 1 position, even though in 1929 the original 11-acre plant had been increased by the addition of a second plant covering 21 acres. With a capacity to produce 12,000 receivers daily it was, with some justification, claimed to be "The World's Largest Radio Factory".

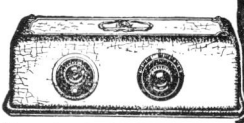
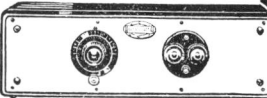

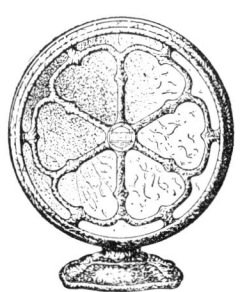

Model 20 Compact 1925. The first bookshelf radio.

Model 32 7-valve TRF 1926.

Model 40, 7-valve TRF 1928.
The first AK to use a dynamic speaker and to have a built-in power supply.

Model 54A Dynamic Speaker.   Model 55, 7-valve SG 1929.

90

ATWATER KENT
presents the new 1935
RADIO

WE have made more progress in the past year than has usually been made in several years of research and engineering work. The new Atwater Kent Radios will enable you, I believe, to get as much out of radio as it is possible to get today, whether you judge it by American or foreign reception. I join with the Atwater Kent dealer in your neighborhood in inviting you to see and to hear the radio for 1935.

A. Atwater Kent.

STANDARD BROADCAST
Model 944 — 4-tube superheterodyne — large speaker with undistorted output of 2 watts — tuning range includes police calls.
$22.50 f. o. b.
Factory

SHORT WAVE and BROADCAST—Model 325E— bringing you the thrill of foreign reception plus all American broadcasting with a high degree of fidelity. 5-tube simplified superheterodyne with six tuned circuits—$3\frac{3}{10}$ watts undistorted output —3 separate tuning bands—2-speed tuning—11-inch speaker. **$49.90 f. o. b.**
Factory

ALL-WAVE—Model 112N—After making scientific tests for fidelity, it is our belief that this is the finest radio receiver we ever built. You can spend much more, but there is no way that you can buy better radio performance than you will get from this beautiful 12-tube, world-wide, all-wave Atwater Kent Radio. **$165.00 f. o. b.**
Factory

SHORT WAVE and BROADCAST—Model 145—5 tubes—foreign short-wave broadcasting, American broadcasting, police, amateur, airplane.
$39.90 f. o. b.
Factory

ATWATER KENT MANUFACTURING CO.   *A. Atwater Kent, President*   PHILADELPHIA, PA.

Other New Models from $22.50 to $190.00 f. o. b. Philadelphia, including the New Self-tuning radio—Atwater Kent TUNE-O-MATIC—also motor-car radio and models for battery, direct current and 32-volt power.

Model 80, 6-valve Superhet
1932.

Model 90, 7-valve Superhet
1932.

Model 70L, 8-valve SG
1931.

Model 84 'Golden Voice'
superheterodyne 1931.

Model 93, Short-wave
converter 1932.

Model 708, 7-valve, 4-band
1933.

Model 567, 7-valve
Superhet 1932.

Model 627, 7-valve
Superhet 1932.

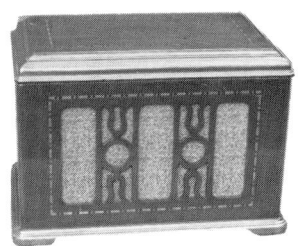   

Model 555, 5-valve BC
1933.

Model 217, 7-valve, 3-band
1933.

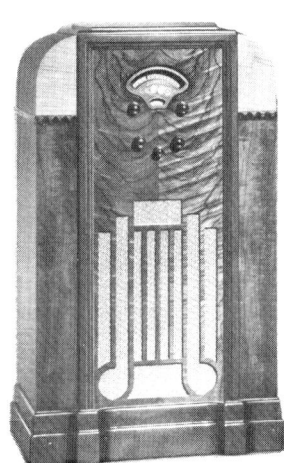 

Model 96, 8-valve TRF
1933. Note 'Tonebeam'
turning indicator.

Model 165, 5-valve, Police
Band 1933.

Model 447D, 6-valve, 4-
band 1934.

Model 318T, 8-valve, 4-
band 1934.

Model 356, 6-valve AW
1935.

Model 717X, 7-valve AW
1936. The last Atwater
Kent.

At this time Mr A. Atwater Kent issued the following statement:

"The Atwater Kent Manufacturing Company has never had any of its shares on the market. It owns outright its business and its manufacturing plant. It has been in business for more than 27 increasingly profitable years, has always done business on its own capital and has never borrowed a dollar.

All its resources and experience are concentrated upon one thing—the making and selling of fine radio instruments. Production in its 32-acre factory is scientifically controlled, so that Atwater Kent dealers have enough radios on hand to meet public demand, and are never overstocked. Its inventory is never excessive.

Single-minded devotion to its one job—the production of the finest radio that can be built—has put Atwater Kent Manufacturing Company to-day in the strongest position it has ever held. Strongest in the excellence of its product— Atwater Kent Screen-grid Radio. Strongest in the confidence of the public. Strongest in stability, which is the keystone of permanence in any business."

By the end of 1929 Atwater Kent had marketed their first screen-grid model, the 7-tube model 55, which was also the first A K to use the then new type 245 output triode. Like its immediate predecessors, it was intended for use with a separate dynamic speaker, both chassis and speaker being housed in metal cabinets.

The first A K superheterodyne, model 72 chassis L, appeared in 1930. Surprisingly, in spite of the fact that it used a total of nine tubes, it did not have an RF stage.

In common with other manufacturers of the day, Atwater Kent turned to the production of 'compact' models in 1931, the model 84 being the first in the series. Although console models continued to be produced, they were not much in evidence during 1931-32. However, during the next two years, 1933-34, many styles of consoles appeared, including some quite ornate six-legged types, the production of which gave the impression that A K had finally realised the importance of the 'furniture' aspect of radio cabinets.

For some reason Atwater Kent produced remarkably few combination radio-phonograph models, the model 75 of 1930 being their first. Only two others are known, the 89P and 99P, of 1931 and 1932 respectively.

The last sets to be produced were the models 637 and 717, both of which used metal tubes and 'aero' dials.

Although sales had been affected by the depressed economic conditions of the early 1930s, the company remained in a strong position and continued to do good business until 1936 when production came to an abrupt halt. What, then, was the reason for the sudden closure of the world's largest radio factory? Actually there were two reasons: By 1936 Mr Kent was 63 years old and had decided that the time had come to retire from business and enjoy something of the good life. After making this decision he had been approached with an offer to take over his business but instead he preferred to close the doors and walk out.

In acting thus it seems he was carrying out a threat made some three years earlier when his company had received the attentions of labour unions. At the time he had granted a 10% increase in pay to all his employees and informed the unions that if they ever returned he would close down the business. True to his word, when the unions returned in 1936 Mr Kent closed the plant.

However, his action did not throw thousands of people out of work, for by this time the factory was virtually at a standstill. From a peak of 12,000 employees in 1929 the staff was down to only a few hundred at the time of the closure in 1936.

Atwater Kent himself moved to Bel Air in California where, for the next ten years, he enjoyed what he once described as "the simple life on a grand scale" in a 32 room mansion attended by 16 servants. He died in 1949 at the age of 76 leaving an estate valued at $8,000,000.

In New Zealand the agency for Atwater Kent radio was taken up by C. & A. Odlin Ltd in the early 1920s, making them one of the first radio importers in the country. Many of the model 20 compacts sold here during 1926-27 are still in existence today as collectors' items.

During the transitional period when AC receivers were evolving from metal boxes to 'furniture' cabinets Atwater Kent was one of the last major manufacturers to make the change. As late as 1929 metal box sets with separate speakers were still in production and certain models, such as the 30, 52 and 57, were even available in metal console cabinets of singularly unattractive styles, though none of these have been sighted in New Zealand.

Even though by 1930 wooden console cabinets had finally arrived, A K clung to the use of metal front panels with an imitation woodgrain finish during this year. Certain models, such as the 60 and 70, were imported in chassis and speaker form and fitted with New Zealand-made console cabinets of various styles.

Odlins continued to import A K's for as long as they were in production and the receivers themselves achieved in N.Z. the same well-deserved reputation for quality as they did in the U.S. Today the firm of Odlins Ltd remains the sole survivor of the many companies who imported radios in the early days of broadcasting.

CROSLEY

Right from its beginning as a wood-working factory making phonograph cabinets in 1920, the firm which became the Crosley Radio Corp. remained under the direct control of its founder, Powel Crosley jun., throughout its existence. Crosley got into radio in 1921 when he commenced to make a line of components, among which was a unique type of variable 'book' condenser made of wood! Later models of this component were made of metal though the 'book' feature was retained.

Crosley model 57 (1931). An example of the use of a one-piece 'Repwood' front panel

Originally the company was known as the Crosley Mfg Co. but after taking over another firm, the Precision Equipment Co., it became the Crosley Radio Corporation. By 1922 a large range of both components and complete receivers was being marketed. For a short while the former company was run as a separate concern but after 1924 this name was discontinued.

Crosley's policy was to mass-produce low cost receivers, and in this he was highly successful. Crosley radios became one of the most popular and best known brands on the market, with Crosley himself becoming known as "the Ford of Radio".

Although Crosley did make headphones for a short time in the early days they did not make horn speakers, but for a short while during 1922 a wooden cabinet containing an enclosed horn was produced. This item was known as a 'Magfone' and was intended for use with a single headphone earpiece which formed the driver unit. In 1925 Crosley became one of the first manufacturers to produce a magnetic cone speaker, this item being sold under the name 'Musicone'. Shortly afterwards another, and quite unique, type of cone speaker known as the 'Dynacone' appeared. In place of the normal permanent magnet this speaker used an energised field magnet which was connected into the receiver's output circuit in

such a way that it did double duty as an output choke, and to this end a blocking condenser was built into the speaker. A third Crosley speaker was the 'Dynacoil', a fairly conventional dynamic (moving coil) type which differed from its contemporaries in having a very 'floppy' cone suspension.

Unlike many other manufacturers of the early period, Crosley made practically all their own parts, a policy which was continued up to, and even after, the advent of the all-electric era. When the manufacture of AC sets was commenced in 1927 a distinctive feature of Crosley and Amrad sets was the use of Amrad 'Mershon' wet electrolytic filter condensers. A much advertised feature of these condensers was their self-healing capability after being subjected to excessive voltage.

Powel Crosley purchased the Amrad Corp. in 1925 and in addition to securing the source of the Mershon electrolytics also acquired a fully equipped radio factory, as Amrad had been making radios for many years previously. Production was maintained under the Amrad name but some of the models were changed to use Crosley designs, which explains why that from 1925 the appearance of some Amrad battery sets was almost identical to Crosley, for example the Amrad S522 and Crosley RFL75.

A feature of some Crosley sets made during the 1930-32 period was the use of one-piece moulded cabinets on even quite large table models, examples being the famous 'Buddy Boy' and 'Super Buddy Boy'. The material used was a dense heavy composition known as 'Repwood', which by a considerable stretch of the imagination could be said to look a bit like wood. Apparently it was cheap to produce and this was its main virtue.

In the case of the model 54 Buddy Boy, issued in July 1930, it is surprising to find that the inbuilt speaker was a moving-iron (magnetic) type because, by American standards, it was very late in the day for any AC receiver to use such a speaker. The reason may have been that the standard Crosley dynamic speaker, the Dynacoil, was too heavy and bulky for use in a table model set. Be that as it may, later models used Magnavox speakers, which may have been made under licence as they differed slightly from standard Magnavox productions.

Another feature, unique to some early Crosley superhets, was the employment of a 'dynatron' oscillator,* a mercifully short lived procedure!

Like many other manufacturers, Crosley

* The dynatron circuit made use of the negative-resistance characteristic of a screen-grid tube to obtain oscillation.

94

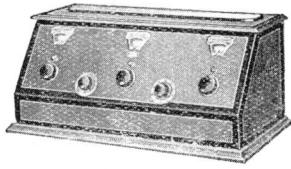
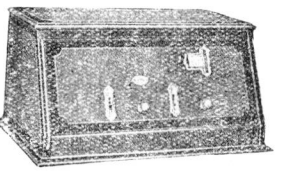
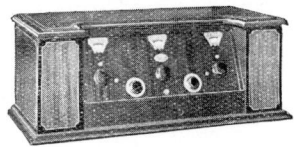
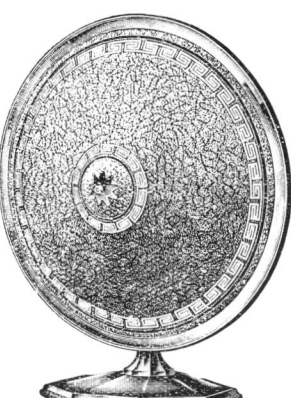
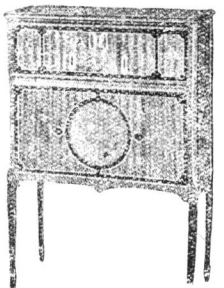

Model 51, 2-valve regenerative 1923.

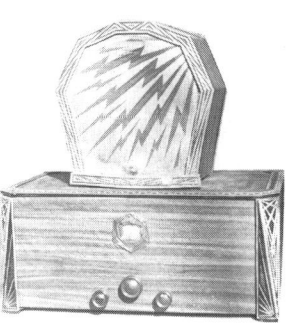

Model 30S, 7-valve S G 'Monotrad' with 'Dynacoil' speaker 1929.

Model 40S, 8-valve SG 'Unitrad' 1930.

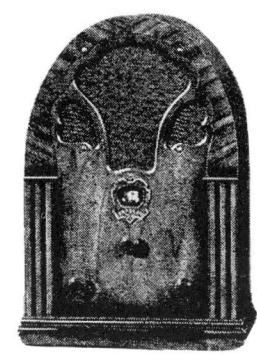

Model 123, 5-valve superhet 1932.

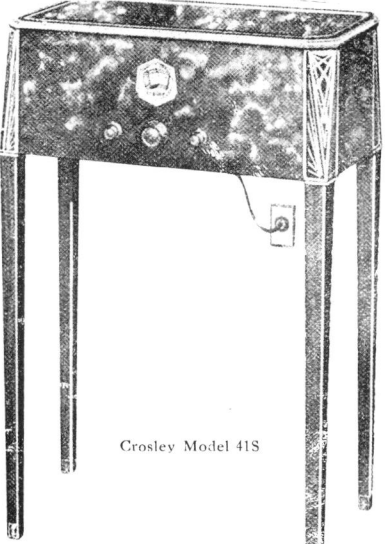

Crosley Model 33S

Crosley Model 41S

The console version of the 'Monotrad' 1930.

The legs were detachable 1931.

Model 154, 4-valve regenerative superhet 1932.

CROSLEY

New Dynamic Speaker DYNACONE $25

The crowning achievement in a history of successes!

6 tube AC Electric GEMBOX $65

Features of the 1928-29 Crosley Radio Receivers

Genuine Neutrodyne radio amplification.

Complete shielding which adds so greatly to the amazing selectivity of Crosley receivers.

Full voltage delivered to the plates of the tubes.

A sensitivity that delights the "old" radio fans and thrills the new ones by the ease with which weak distant stations are brought in.

Positive volume control reduces volume without detuning set.

Adaptability to any type of console.

Modern illuminated dial.

Beautiful gold and brown finish of receivers and matching Musicone and Dynacone delight the eye.

MUSICONE $15

The famous Musicone still leads the world as its greatest magnetic type of speaker.

HERE, in a new line of radios for the season of 1928-29, Crosley presents VALUE such as Radio has never seen . . . . an engineering triumph in *quality* . . . . a production miracle in *price*.

These values are yours today because of the powerful advantage gained through study, work and development acquired in the Herculean task of building and selling nearly 2 million pieces of radio apparatus.

Satisfied by laboratory and actual home installation comparisons that Crosley radio has NO equal Crosley NOW makes it possible for every prospective radio owner to know how well Crosley radio will perform in his or her home before they buy.

5 DAYS FREE TRIAL IN YOUR OWN HOME

This is the NEW way . . . . the CROSLEY way to buy radio. First advertised nationally by Crosley last April.

Study the sets shown at the right. Then go to the nearest Crosley dealer. Ask for a FREE trial. Over 18000 Crosley dealers serve the United States, but if you cannot locate one near you send us this coupon and we will arrange a home demonstration for you at once.

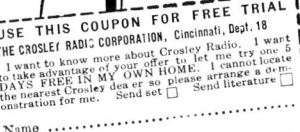

whatever happens in 1928

"You're there with a Crosley"

The Crosley Radio Corporation, Cincinnati, Ohio
Powel Crosley, Jr., President
Montana, Wyoming Colorado, New Mexico and West prices slightly higher.

The 8 tube AC Electric Jewelbox
Genuine Neutrodyne; self-contained; full 180 volts on output tube plates; two 171 output tubes, push-pull. Illuminated dial; Acuminators. $95

The 8 tube AC Electric Showbox
A new completely shielded genuine Neutrodyne, self-contained receiver; illuminated dial; full 180 volts on the plates of two 171 output tubes, push-pull. $80

The 6 tube Improved Battery Type BANDBOX
Neutrodyne; shielded; illuminated dial; Acuminators. Unequalled in its field. $55

The 5 tube Dry Cell Operated BANDBOX Jr.
Modern radio reception for places where electriccurrent is not available or storage battery recharging is inconvenient. $35

Model 59 'Oracle'.

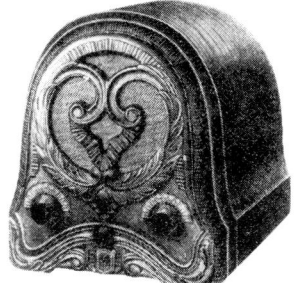

Model 54 'New Buddy'.

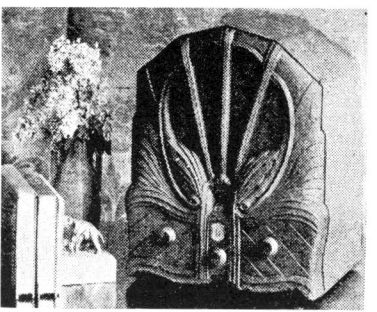

Model 48 'Widgit'.

Model 123 'Super Buddy Boy'.

Model 59 'Show Boy'.

All these 1931 Crosleys made use of cabinets moulded from 'Repwood'.

96

often issued a range of cabinet styles to house a basic chassis model but in doing so sometimes failed to include a cross reference in the relevant service data which made it difficult to identify some of the early AC sets. Also like some other manufacturers, Crosley used named cabinet styles which in Crosley's case were often somewhat fanciful, to say the least. While it is not too difficult to associate a domestic radio as being companionable, hence the names Buddy, Chum, Pal, Partner, Mate etc., or to regard it as being of value, hence Gem Box, Gem Chest, Jewel Box etc., or as a means of entertainment, hence Songster, Musicale, Merry Maker, Minstrel etc., it is more diffficult to account for some of the other names used. Just what was the impression some of the following outlandish names were meant to convey, one wonders—Administrator, Mayor, Congressman or Commissioner?

By 1934 Crosley had grown to be one the largest manufacturers in the industry, ranking third in that year after RCA and Philco. Also in 1934 Crosley entered the refrigerator business with their patented line of 'Shelvador' models, the first to be fitted with the now universally used shelves in the door.

Following the end of World War II, Crosley's company was sold to the Avco Division of the Aviation Company in 1945, though the manufacture of radio and television receivers continued until 1956. Avco finally sold the 'Crosley' and 'Shelvador' names to the Swiss Philco Co. in 1958.

No account of Powel Crosley's activities would be complete without mention of his famous broadcasting station, WLW, Cincinatti, Ohio. This station commenced operation in 1922 but did not come into prominence until 1932 when it went on to the then high power of 50 kW and called itself "The Nation's Station". In 1934 the power was increased to 500 kW making it the most powerful broadcast transmitter in the world. However, this enormous power caused interference with other stations and in 1939 the power was ordered by the Federal Communications Commission to be reduced to 50 kW.

Crosley receivers were early on the New Zealand market, the first sets being imported in 1925 by Abel, Smeeton Ltd in the North Island and L. B. Scott Ltd in the South Island. These distributorships were continued for the next ten years, though Crosley never became such a well-known brand in this country by comparison with other American receivers. In the North Island, at least, this may have been because the partnership of Abel, Smeeton ended in 1935 and was replaced by a new firm, Warwick Smeeton Ltd who gave up handling Crosley when they commenced local manufacture using the name 'Ariel' for their sets.

The last Crosleys seen in New Zealand were car radios, which were imported in 1937 by a different company. Of these sets the 'Fiver Roamio' was the first single-unit car radio seen in this country.

In spite of Crosley's undoubted success as a radio, television and refrigerator manufacturer it is said that his first love was really automobiles and in the early post-war years a Crosley car was actually produced and marketed. Its engine was notable for the use of a cylinder block made up from laminated copper stampings.

GILFILLAN BROS

The history of Gilfillan Bros Inc. is of more than passing interest to New Zealanders as nearly all of the many brands of radios imported from the West Coast of the U.S. in pre-war days carried the name Gilfillan on their chassis. Because the company at one time had factories in both Los Angeles and San Francisco, it was consequently the closest American manufacturer and, with a regular and frequent shipping service available, was well placed to serve this country's radio needs.

It was in 1912 that two brothers, Senet and Jay Gilfillan, set up in business as refiners and smelters of precious metals for supply to dentists and jewellers. Two years later they established the firm of Gilfillan Brothers Smelting & Refining Co. However, shortly afterwards this work was relinquished in favour of manufacturing automotive accessories, including moulded bakelite ignition parts. Here, it is of interest to recall that at almost the same time another manufacturer on the opposite side of the country, Atwater Kent in Philadelphia, was similarly engaged and he also later turned to radio manufacture.

By 1921 the Gilfillan brothers, then known as Gilfillan Bros Inc., became interested in radio and in that year commenced to manufacture a line of bakelite moulded radio parts. From the manufacture of parts the supplying of kitsets and complete radios was but a step and in 1924 Gilfillan Bros became a member of the Independent Radio Manufacturers Inc., the exclusive licensees of the Hazeltine Corp., an organisation formed to exploit the Neutrodyne patents. Thus Gilfillan, along with such other well-known companies as Amrad, Fada, and Freed-Eisemann, became one of the first names to be associated with the word Neutrodyne; in fact the letters GN used as a prefix to the first model numbers stood for Gilfillan Neutrodyne.

First issued in 1924, the GN series of receivers ran from the GN1 of 1924 to the GN6 of 1926. Of these models the GN1, 2, 4 and 5 are

S. W. Gilfillan

J. G. Gilfillan

Radiette model F12 1930.

Kemper 'Kompact', 5-valve
SG 1930.

A Gilfillan RA-1 2-valve reflex kitset as assembled and sold by Radio Ltd 1923.

The Gilfillan patent licence notice as used on the backs of dozens of different 'West Coast' chassis during the 1930s.

Patterson 8-valve All-wave 1934.

GILFILLAN NEUTRODYNE

A new powerful set of greater Clarity Distance, Simplicity and Beauty

In a handsome two-tone American Walnut Cabinet, 33 ins. long, 12 ins. wide and 10 inches high

Complete, without Loud Speaker, phones, tubes batteries **$175.00**

The introduction of the GILFILLAN NEUTRODYNE set is the longest forward step in Advanced Radio Engineering

The engineers who designed and built this Set are leaders in Radio Invention and Construction. They reviewed and analyzed every American receiver and have given their best in producing this highly sensitive, accurate, selective NEUTRODYNE set. Extremely simple to operate, convenient to install and of an artistic design that will be a handsome addition to any room.

In the GILFILLAN NEUTRODYNE every detail has been reviewed and corrected to assure highest amplification, finest selective reception and positive neutralization. Its well-balanced, neutralized circuit gives distortionless reproduction of speech and music of ample volume and great clarity.

It is truly a marvel in the radio world and the first "straight line" set with a properly proportioned and beautifully designed and finished cabinet which can be completely closed whether in use or not.

Manufactured at 3 convenient shipping points, addresses below, assures prompt delivery and national distribution.

JOBBERS and DEALERS—looking for a high grade set of assured merit, ample power and real beauty, will write at once for our sales proposition and place their orders early to prepare for sales of unheard-of volume!

Send for Descriptive Literature showing Special Features and Details

GILFILLAN BROS. Inc.

Kansas City, Mo.
2525 West Penn Way

Los Angeles, Calif., 1816 West 16th St.

New York City
225 West 57th St.

 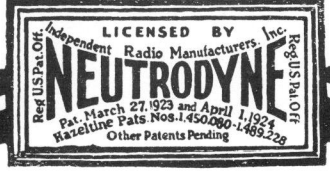 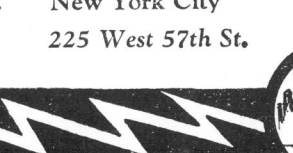

LICENSED MANUFACTURER — UNDER NEUTRODYNE PATS.

This 1930 model 7-tube SG was being sold in N.Z. in 1931.

Radiette model 60, 6-valve
SG 1931. (Keller Faller
Mgf Co.)

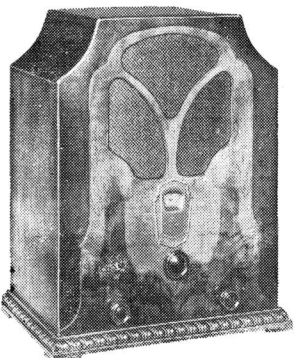

Radiette model 80, 9-valve
Superhet 1932.

Gilfillan model 63B, All-
Wave, 1937.

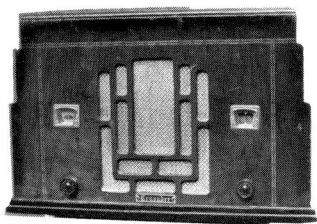

Gilfillan Crusader model
5T 1934.

Mission Bell 5-valve 1934.

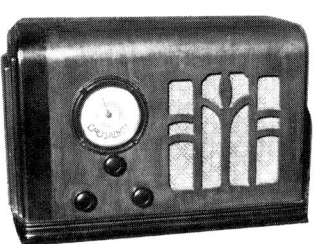

Gilfillan Crusader model
57X 1935.

100

known to have been sold in New Zealand. Later battery sets seen here were the models 10 and 25.

By 1927 Gilfillan Bros had been successful in obtaining a manufacturing licence from RCA (by no means an easy task) and thus equipped were ready for the all-electric revolution then just getting under way. Twelve years later, in 1939, the company could claim to be one of the four oldest licensed still in existence.

In this case the terms of the licence were quite remarkable for the company was granted an exclusive manufacturing licence for an area comprising no less than eleven western states, a sizeable chunk of real estate, even if much of it was sparsely populated. Included in the terms of the licence was a clause which allowed Gilfillan to sub-license all other manufacturers in the area, whether in existence or in the future, a state of affairs which seems to have been unique. Also unique was the manner in which Gilfillan chose to carry out the sub-licensing arrangements.

The first all-electric Gilfillan, the 7-tube model 60, which appeared in 1927, used four type 226s, a 227 detector and a 171 output tube. In 1929 came the first screen-grid model, a 6-tube console using four 224A's and a single 245 output tube.

However, it was a development occurring in 1930, the introduction of the so-called 'midget' receiver, which really put the name Gilfillan on the map, or at least on the licence decals of dozens and dozens of different brands of sets. Midget radios were small, self-contained AC models which could conveniently be placed on a mantelpiece, hence the alternative description— 'mantel' models.

Strictly speaking, at least one receiver qualifying for the description midget had been in existence before 1930 because the Echophone Radio Corp., a Gilfillan licensee, claimed to have marketed their model 'C' in November 1928. This was a 6-tube regenerative TRF using three type 201A battery tubes, a 227 detector and a 171A output tube feeding an inbuilt magnetic speaker. An almost identical receiver was produced by the Keller Fuller Mfg Co. as their model 'M'.

It has been stated that the reason for the introduction of midget radios was to provide a low-priced second set for people already owning large console models, but as things turned out, the midget came to play a more important role than this. With worsening economic conditions during the depression years midget radios became the only sort of set many people could afford. By 1933 other manufacturers in the eastern part of the country were busily engaged in producing smaller radios which by then were usually of the AC/DC variety. So although midget radios had really originated on the West Coast their later

development took place in other areas and Gilfillan did not make AC/DC models until after 1940.

From about 1930 Gilfillan adopted what seems to have been a unique and flexible method of handling the business of sub-licensing. Apart from making complete receivers on a contract basis for private brand owners, Gilfillan also offered several alternatives: they would supply chassis only, or even partly wired chassis, for finishing by the customer; they would make sets to a customer's own design; they would even hire out factory space where customers could make their own sets, using either their own or Gilfillan's designs. But regardless of exactly how they made them the chassis all had to carry a patent licence decal bearing the words—"Licensed by the Radio Corporation of America".

The foregoing explains how it was that so many different makes of radios bore the Gilfillan decal on their chassis yet the name Gilfillan itself seldom appeared on the front of many sets. At the height of the sub-licensing boom there were at least 24 different companies working under the Gilfillan licence, some of the brand names being: Angeles, Baldwin, Breting,* Cardinal,* Chanticleer,* Echophone,* El Rey,* Falck, Flint, Jackson Bell,* Kemper,* Lyratone,* Mission Bell,* Packard Bell, Patterson,* Peter Pan,* Plymouth,* Royale, Radiette,* Sky Raider,* Troy. In addition there were Remler* and Rola* which were made at Gilfillan's San Francisco plant. Those names indicated by an asterisk are known to have been sold in New Zealand. Furthermore there were at least two N.Z. brand names, Crusader and Skyscraper, which at one time were used on sets having chassis made by Gilfillan.

Apart from radio production the company was, at various times, engaged in other areas of manufacturing ranging from power tools to refrigerators.

After World War II Gilfillan Bros continued to make radio and TV receivers but the previous sub-licensing arrangements were discontinued. The company retired from the consumer electronics field in 1948 to concentrate on the production of radar equipment and later came under the control of the International Telegraph & Telephone Corp., when it became known as ITT-Gilfillan.

GULBRANSEN

Gulbransen radios took their name from the Gulbransen Company of Chicago, a firm which had been established in 1907 and which claimed

* The author is indebted to Mr Floyd A. Paul of Glendale, California for permission to use material on the history of Gilfillan Bros which appeared in the California Antique Radio Gazette, Vol. 9, No. 3.

Gulbransen 7-tube AVC Superheterodyne 1932.

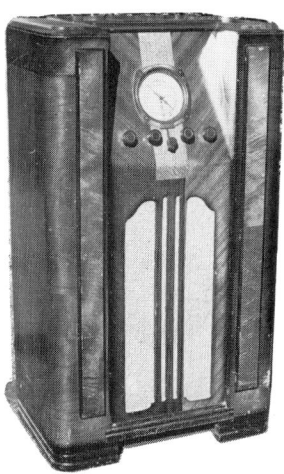

Chassis 7G, 7-valve DW 1935.

Chassis 7D, 7-valve DW 1934.

Chassis 7L, 7-valve, 3-band 1936. The addition of a magic eye increased the valve complement to eight.

Chassis 7L, 8-valve AW 1936. This model was more commonly seen in an upright cabinet.

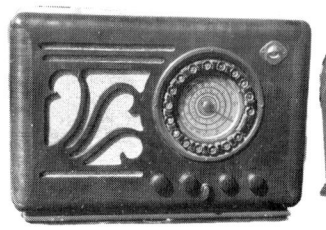

Chassis A-1 'Telephone Dial' sold under Airline name 1937.

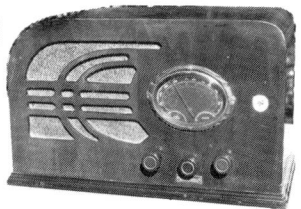

Chassis 5K, 5-valve, 3-band 1937.

to be the world's largest manufacturer of pianos. This company's entry into the radio market was obviously in response to the way in which radio broadcasting was affecting the sale of pianos, but, in the event, the Gulbransen Company's involvement with radio did not last for long.

Chassis for Gulbransen radios were provided by Wells-Gardner & Co., a Chicago manufacturer specialising in the production of 'private brand' radios. This company claimed to have been established in 1924 and the chassis nameplates of early AC sets carried the marking 'WG24'. However, it has not been possible to obtain details of the firm's activities prior to 1929. It is possible that a firm known as the Wells Mfg Co. which made battery sets in the early 1920s was the predecessor to Wells-Gardner, though this is only speculation. Although Wells-Gardner remained in business until well into the 1960s, the name Gulbransen disappeared in the U.S. after about 1936.

In New Zealand the firm of H. W. Clarke Ltd acquired and held the agency for Gulbransen, and it is interesting to note that chassis imported after 1936 carried a metal nameplate inscribed with the words "Chassis by Wells-Gardner, successors to Gulbransen".

The first Gulbransen seen in this country was a 9-valve TRF using triodes in all stages except the detector. Known as the 'Nine-in-Line', it was advertised in 1930 as a screen-grid model on the strength of a solitary screen-grid valve used as the detector. The first models to have screen-grid valves in the RF stages were the series 63 and 160 which appeared in the following year.

Also in 1931 came the first superhet, known as the series 60 and notable for the use of automatic volume control (AVC) obtained by the use of a separate AVC tube. An unusual model produced in the same year, the 12-tube O2A, used push-pull 45 triodes running with 400 volts on their plates with fixed bias provided by another 45 used as a half-wave rectifier.

The 10-tube series 20 of 1932 featured diode detection using a type 27 triode wired as a diode, whereas the series 50 and 53 used a separate 24A tube to obtain AVC without diode detection. When, in 1933, 6.3-volt tubes came into use that year's model O7A made use of a type 76 triode wired as a diode in the manner of the previous year's model.

In 1934 the dual-wave model 7D was the first Gulbransen to use an 'aero' dial, and it also continued an earlier tradition of using a separate oscillator tube, a feature which became a hallmark of all but the lowest priced Wells-Gardner sets. From this time onwards Gulbransen steadily became one of the best-known American radios on the New Zealand market, taking the place of Majestic which had gone out of production in 1934.

Model 7GM was the first Wells-Gardener chassis to use metal valves and the first to incorporate variable selectivity in the IF stage, a feature thereafter used in all but the cheapest models. Selectivity was controlled by a two-position switch marked "Broad-Sharp" which was connected to tertiary windings on each of the two IF transformers.

Instead of using a separate selectivity control on the model 7L of 1936 the switch was combined with the tone control in such a manner that when it was turned to maximum treble the selectivity was switched to 'broad'. In this position the tone indicator then indicated the words "Hi-Fi". The 7L was also the first model to use a glass dial scale and a separate illuminated pointer for each waveband.

In 1937 the model A1, in keeping with industry trends towards larger and larger dials, featured one of 4 inches in diameter surrounded by a ring of 17 push buttons which resulted in an overall diameter of 7 inches. This somewhat clumsy and heavy mechanism was actuated by keeping one of the buttons depressed while rotating the entire ring in a similar manner to using a telephone; in fact this model was advertised as having "Telephone Dial Tuning".

The last American Gulbransen seen in New Zealand was the console-only model A14 of 1938 which featured a conventional 'slide-rule' dial and six separate push buttons. From then on all Gulbransens appearing on the local market were made by Collier & Beale Ltd and bore no resemblance to those of American origin.

MAJESTIC

During its brief but spectacular existence the company which produced Majestic radios rose with remarkable speed to become within 18 months of its inception the largest manufacturer in the industry, and that meant the largest in the world at that time. In the words of a contemporary writer it was—"expansion in production so rapid as to take one's breath away". During its second year of operation, in 1929, the company produced over two million receivers, putting it ahead of such giants as Atwater Kent and RCA. The story of the amazing effort that made possible this unparalleled achievement is now part of the history of radio's 'Golden Age' but it remains a fascinating story to this day.

The Chicago based company that started it all was originally known as the Grigsby-Grunow-Hinds Co. and in 1926 was engaged in the manufacture of battery eliminators. Business was brisk during the next two years enabling the

company to build up a nation-wide distribution network which, as events turned out, was to be an important factor in its later success.

Grigsby-Grunow-Hinds got into the radio business as a direct result of the falling sales of battery eliminators consequent upon the advent of the all-electric receiver in 1928, which brought with it a sharp decline in the popularity of battery sets. In order to survive G-G-H had to switch to the production of the new receivers, and do it quickly. However, before any production could commence, or at least before any sets could be sold, it was necessary to secure a manufacturing licence from RCA and other patent holders, but RCA's policy at that time did not make it easy for newcomers to get started. Ostensibly in order to discourage fly-by-night operators, an applicant was required to be selling at least $100,000 worth of receivers annually, but just how a non-licensed manufacturer could admit to doing this without prejudicing his chances of obtaining a licence was not explained! There was a way round it though, a way which others in the same position had used, and that was to buy out an existing licence holder. So it was that early in 1928 Grigsby-Grunow-Hinds acquired the Pfanstiel Co., an RCA licensee who had been making radios since 1924.

Now, secure in the possession of the necessary licence, it was a case of full steam ahead. The company was reorganised as the Grigsby-Grunow Co. and by late 1928 production was in full swing. And what production! The figures were almost unbelievable. Early in 1929 the factory output had risen to 4,000 sets a day, with over one million being produced in that year alone. During the first 18 months of operation over two million sets were produced, the daily average being 6,000.

Although these figures were exceeded numerically by at least one other manufacturer it must be realised that whereas other firms, such as Atwater Kent, were making smaller table models Grigsby-Grunow were making only massive and elaborate consoles. And not only were the cabinets massive but so were the innards; in the case of the model 70 the weight of the main chassis, power pack and speaker amounted to no less than 70 lbs.

By 1929 production of Majestic receivers accounted for 25% of the entire industry's output, sales for the year being $120,000,000. Without a doubt the "Mighty Monarch of the Air" had well and truly arrived!

First off the production line was the model 70, released late in 1928. It was an 8-valve TRF using push-pull 171As feeding an inbuilt dynamic (moving-coil) speaker. As it happened, Grigsby-Grunow's decision to use a speaker of this type in 1928 gave them a decided edge on their competitors and was probably a key factor in their early success. For years the listening public had had to put up with 'tinny' reproduction, first from horn speakers and then from cone speakers, but now they could "listen to the bass". And listen they did, Majestic's sales figures proved it.

In 1930 Grigsby-Grunow commenced to make tubes to equip their receivers, being at the time the only independent radio manufacturer to do this.* Production of tubes continued for as long as the company remained in business. Reference to tube manufacture would not be complete without mention of Majestic 'spray shielded' tubes which were introduced in 1931, the company being the only one in the U.S. to make such tubes.

On the technical side Grigsby-Grunow was not a particularly innovative company although, with the help of Radio Frequency Laboratories Inc., they were able to chalk up a few 'firsts'. For example, with the release of their model 15 in April 1931 they became the first manufacturer to market a receiver using the new 'variable-mu' tubes. In November of the same year they were the first to combine the use of these new tubes with full-wave diode detection in their model 25.

Quite early in the history of the company Grigsby-Grunow became associated with the Canadian firm Standard Radio Mfg Corp., makers of 'Rogers' radios and this led to the formation of a new company, the Rogers-Majestic Corp. It is interesting to note that this company became one of Canada's leading manufacturers and remained in business long after the demise of the American company.

In common with others in the industry, Grigsby-Grunow did not do as well in 1930 as in the previous year, their sales figures being beaten by Philco who moved into No. 1 position. It would be difficult to decide exactly when the turning point in the company's fortunes occurred, although it is known that B. J. Grigsby left the company in 1930. During the next three years production continued at a somewhat reduced level, due to the depressed economic conditions prevailing, and never again was the company to reach former heights. By 1933 Grigsby-Grunow were in receivership and in 1934 the last Majestic radio was produced. So ended the brief history of one of America's largest radio manufacturers, a company whose rise and fall may fittingly be described as meteoric.

However, this was not the end of the Majestic name for in 1935 a new company, Majestic Radio & Television Corp., was formed. Using the same Majestic 'eagle' trade-mark and logo the new company engaged in radio manufacture for the

---

* Apart from Sparton, who ceased tube manufacture in 1929.

MAJESTIC
ALL-ELECTRIC
Radio Receivers

Have created a sensation in the Radio World. The most wonderful value ever offered in Radio Receivers. Compare the model illustrated with anything on the market—

7 Valves
and Rectifier
with Genuine
MOVING COIL
LOUDSPEAKER

Beautiful Walnut Consoles with front panels of Matched Burl Walnut. Single dial control, amazing sensitivity, simple to operate. Majestic has "out-distanced" and "out-picked" anything on the market. Coupled to an electric pickup makes a perfect Electric Gramophone, equal to machines selling at £100.

A beautiful piece of furniture that will adorn the most elaborate drawing-room at the price of the "Tin Box" Receivers offered for sale! Those who buy an Electric Radio Receiver before seeing the Majestic will regret it later. Shipments arriving shortly.

Only £48

Complete. Ready to plug into the Lighting Socket.

"WAIT FOR THE MAJESTIC"

Distributors' names will be published later.   Dealers interested should communicate with—

THE MAJESTIC FACTORY REPRESENTATIVES   ::   C.P.O. BOX 462, AUCKLAND.

First N.Z. advertisement for the first Majestic radio, model 70 February 1929.

Model 50, 8-valve superhet 1931.

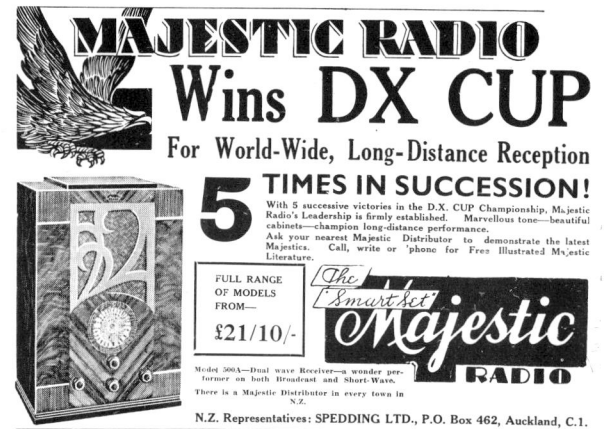

Model 500A, 6-valve, dual wave 1935. A pale shadow of the former glory. Made by Majestic Radio & Television Corp.

Model 151 'Ravenswood' using model 15 chassis 1932.

106

Model 50, 8-valve superhet 1931.

Gothic table model of American Walnut finish. Entire front panel is of imported Australian Lacewood. The receiver is a 7-tube superheterodyne.

Dimensions: 17⅝" high, 15" wide, 10" deep

M O D E L   3 3 1

A Conventional Console of grace and dignity expressed in perfect lines and proportions. Center panel is of V-matched African Zebrawood, top panel of Australian Lacewood and side panels have Lacewood Medallions. Receiver is a 7-tube superheterodyne.

Dimensions: 40½" high, 24½" wide, 11½" deep

Two examples from Majestic's 1933 range. The big feature that year was Syncho silent tuning.

Model 463 1934.

Model 461 1934.

These two sets used the 460 chassis. Note the square knobs on one and spiked knobs on the other, the idea of some idiot furniture designer!

Model 310A, 7-valve superhet 1933.

Model 465 'Lido' 1934.

next 10 years or so, but at least some of the models marketed in later years appeared to have been made by other producers.

Meanwhile, William Grunow after leaving Grisgby-Grunow in 1934 formed his own company, known as General Household Utilities, and commenced making radios using the brand name 'Grunow'. The new company rose rapidly to become one of the foremost producers during the next few years but by 1941 had ceased operations.

Majestic in New Zealand

In New Zealand the agency for Majestic radios was acquired by the Auckland firm of Spedding Ltd, a company which had had an interest in radio since 1923. Speddings imported the first Majestic sets right from the start of production late in 1928 and retained the agency throughout the time Grigsby-Grunow remained in existence. In 1929 Speddings claimed to have sold 3,000 sets, an extremely respectable figure for New Zealand, even if it was only half a day's production for Grigsby-Grunow! An interesting point is that in spite of their immense production the firm was prepared to make special export models which unlike the products of other manufacturers of the 1928-30 period, did not require the use of a separate step-down transformer.

Following the demise of Grigsby-Grunow in 1934 Speddings were left without any radios to sell and so took up the agency for Patterson, a small Los Angeles manufacturer.

Early in 1935 Spedding Ltd were successful in obtaining their first shipment of receivers from the newly formed Majestic Radio & Television Corp. but these proved to be but a pale shadow of the Grigsby-Grunow product. Apparently word got round quite quickly that there was a difference between the 'old' and 'new' Majestics with the result that Speddings felt constrained to publish a warning notice, a copy of which is reproduced here. In the event, the name Majestic soon disappeared from the N.Z. scene and was not seen again for nearly a quarter of a century when it was used by a local manufacturer.

PHILCO

The history of the manufacturers of Philco radio goes back a long way further than that of most independent producers as it can be traced to 1892 when the Helios Electric Co. was founded. In 1906 this company became the Philadelphia Storage Battery Company which for the next 20 years or so specialised in the manufacture of Philco 'Diamond Grid' automobile batteries.

Following the advent of radio broadcasting, which opened up an entirely new market for batteries, Philco commenced to make radio 'A' and 'B' (LT and HT) wet batteries. Although wet A batteries were used extensively during the early 1920s wet B batteries were far less common and presumably to encourage use of the latter Philco commenced to make A and B chargers.

From the manufacture of chargers to the manufacture of battery eliminators was but a step and in 1925 Philco marketed their first 'socket power unit'. For a battery manufacturer to start making eliminators might seem a self-defeating step, but in the event the company did good business during the next two years. By the end of 1927, however, something had gone wrong for sales had dropped alarmingly following the arrival of the first 'all-electric' radios. This left Philco no choice but to become a receiver manufacturer too if they were to remain in the radio business.

So it was that in 1928 the first steps were taken which were to lead to Philco's eventually becoming one of the giants in the industry.

One of the first requirements was to obtain a manufacturing licence from RCA and other patent holders but at the time RCA was maintaining a closed-door policy and was not issuing further licences. To enter the field Philco was forced to buy out an existing licence holder, in this case the William J. Murdock Co., a company already licensed by RCA and Neutrodyne. After this Philco were able to proceed with their plans to become a large-scale manufacturer.

By the winter of 1928 Philco were ready to launch their first receiver, known as 'Neutrodyne Plus'. It was a 7-valve TRF using three neutralised type 26 triodes in the RF section with a single type 71A providing the output to a separate magnetic speaker. The receiver chassis, which featured an integral power pack, was housed in either a metal box or in a highboy console, though in both cases the speaker was a separate unit. It seems strange that the company which pioneered the concept of an integral power pack did not include a speaker in the console model but this may have been because the metal box cabinet carried with it the inherent need for the speaker to be a separate unit and perhaps this requirement was carried over without question when producing a console version of the receiver.

At this point it is interesting to make a comparison between the first radio produced by Philco and the first by its main rival, Majestic. Both companies commenced production in the same year and both had previously been making battery eliminators. The first receivers made by each company were very similar in all respects except when it came to the output section. Whereas Majestic used push-pull 71A valves

Stop! Look! Think!
—and you'll get your Philco now

Safety demands the strongest, toughest, most powerful battery you can get—a battery that will stand by you in emergencies—that won't expose you to the embarrassments, humiliations, and DANGERS of battery failure.

Thousands upon thousands of car owners today—in record-breaking numbers—are replacing their ordinary batteries with dependable, long-life, *super*-powered Philco Batteries.

They know the Philco Battery—with its tremendous power and staunch, rugged, shock-resisting strength—will whirl the stiffest engine—give them quick, sure-fire ignition—*get them off at a touch of the starter.*

The Philco Battery is guaranteed for two years—the longest and strongest guarantee ever placed on a battery of national reputation. But with its famous Diamond-Grid Plates, Slotted-Rubber Retainers, Quarter-Sawed Hardwood Separators and other time-tested features, the Philco Battery *long outlasts its two-year guarantee.*

Why continue taking chances on ordinary batteries? Why wait for an emergency to show you the absolute need for a dependable, power-packed Philco? Install a Philco NOW and be safe. It will cost you no more than just an ordinary battery.

Philadelphia Storage Battery Co., Philadelphia

The famous Philco Slotted-Retainer Battery is the standard for electric passenger cars and trucks, mine locomotives and other high-powered, heavy-duty battery services.

with the famous shock-resisting Diamond-Grid Plates

3-Point Superiority

1. The Famous Diamond-Grid—the diagonally braced frame of a Philco plate. Built like a bridge. Can't buckle—can't warp—can't short-circuit. Double latticed to lock active material (power-producing chemical) on the plates. Longer life. Higher efficiency.

2. The Philco Slotted Rubber Retainer—a slotted sheet of hard rubber. Retains the solids on the plates but gives free passage to the current and electrolyte. Prevents plate disintegration. Prolongs battery life 41 per cent.

3. The Quarter-Sawed Hard-Wood Separator—made only from giant trees 1,000 years old; quarter-sawed to produce alternating hard and soft grains. Hard grains for perfect insulation of plates. Soft grains for perfect circulation of acid and current—quick delivery of power. Another big reason why Philco is *the* battery for your car.

LOOK FOR THIS SIGN

of Philco Service. Over 5,000 stations—all over the United States. There is one near you. Write for address, if necessary.

A 1926 advertisement for Philco 'Diamond Grid' batteries.

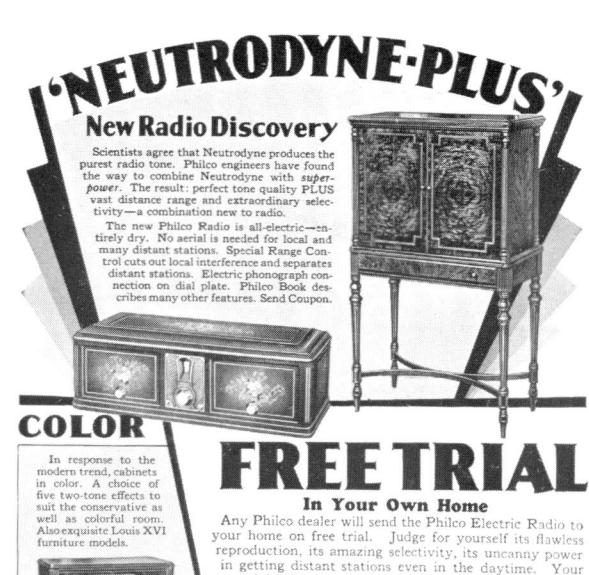

The first Philco. This advertisement is dated October 1928.

Model 77, 7-tube SG 1930.

Right: Model 91E in console cabinet by Lofley Cabinet Co., Balmoral 1932.

The famous 'Baby Grand', Philco's first cathedral model 1930.

Model 70E, Philco's first Superhet cathedral 1931.

Model 81E, 4-valve 1933.

Model 89E 1933.

Model 43E, 8-valve, 3-band 1934.

Model 84E, 4-valve Superhet 1934.

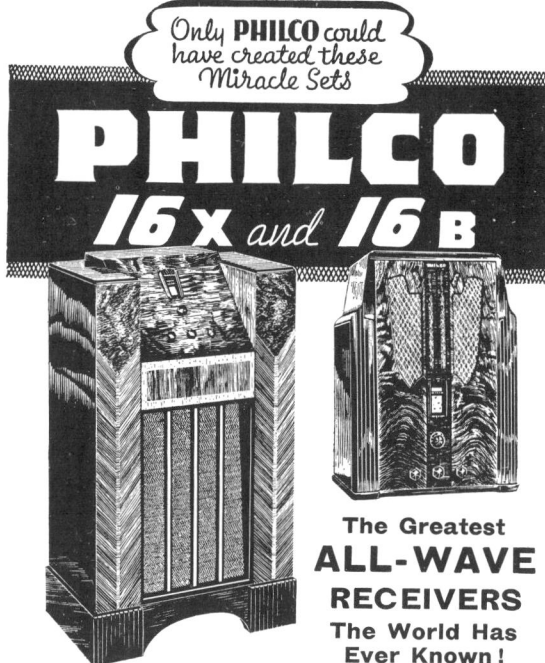 
110

feeding a dynamic (moving coil) speaker, Philco used a single 71A feeding a magnetic (moving iron) speaker. By comparison the Philco product was inferior in the matter of bass response and furthermore it cost a lot more than the Majestic; $275 for a 7-tube set against Majestic's $135 for an 8-tube model. In the first six months of operation, i.e. the last six months of 1928, Philco sold 96,000 sets compared with Majestic's total of over 300,000.

Although 1929 was Majestic's big year, with production reaching nearly one million sets, Philco were coming up fast and sold 408,000 in that year. To achieve such an increase Philco had to reduce its prices considerably; for example the cheapest model now sold for $149, which represented a large reduction from 1928 prices. Furthermore, all sets now had push-pull output and were fitted with inbuilt dynamic speakers which made them fully competitive in this respect. Price reduction was achieved largely by the adoption of mass production techniques.

Late in 1929 the model 95 'Screen Grid Plus' was released for the 1930 season. As the use of screen-grid valves was not uncommon in 1930 one may wonder about the "Plus". Here it can be said that with the production of the model 95 Philco introduced innovative trends (continued in the years ahead) which must have had a considerable bearing on the company's success in the marketplace. In 1930 diode detection and automatic volume control (AVC) were, generally speaking, some two years away, yet the model 95 featured both. It seems the particular circuit used had been developed by the Hazeltine Corp. and was available to all Hazeltine licensees. But in 1930 Philco and Edison were the only two manufacturers progressive enough to produce receivers incorporating it. It is interesting to note that variable-mu tubes were not then in existence and that the sets were of the TRF variety.

It was in 1930 that Philco attained No. 1 position, having produced 616,000 receivers out of an industry total of 3,827,000. Part of their success in that year was due to the introduction and energetic promotion of their first 'Baby Grand' cathedral type radio. Philco was the first major manufacturer to produce this style of receiver and their model 20, a 7-valve TRF, selling at $49.50 accounted for about half the company's production that year.

In the following year, 1931, the first Philco superheterodyne was marketed and also the first cathedral superhet, the model 70B, which sold at the same price as the previous year's TRF. The company retained No. 1 position that year by a comfortable margin and came close to achieving a production goal of one million sets, the actual figure being 977,000.

With economic conditions at their worst in 1932 it might be thought hardly the best time to launch an expensive multi-tube set but Philco offered two, the 112X and 15DX, both 11-tube models. These "Balanced Superheterodynes" as they were called, were claimed to be the first high-fidelity receivers on the market and featured a sloping baffle-board which tilted the axis of the speaker upwards at an angle which improved the distribution of the higher musical frequencies. Another innovation in 1932 was the first use of 6.3-volt tubes in AC operated home receivers, for example in the model 80B.

The prevailing tough economic conditions caused many manufacturers to produce extremely cheap 'midget' or 'pee wee' models at this time, some of which sold for as little as $9.95. Although Philco entered this market their cheapest set, the model 80B, sold for $18.75. At the opposite end of the scale the model 15DX sold for $250.

Although sales were down in 1932 Philco were still on top, accounting for the sale of 609,000 sets out of an industry total of 3,000,000. Because at this time low selling prices were vital to achieving a satisfactory level of sales Philco consequently sought every means of lowering production costs. The manufacturing licences issued by RCA called for 5% (it was 7½% prior to 1932) of the ex-factory selling price to be paid as royalties. In the case of large console models the cost of the cabinets amounted to quite a large proportion of the total and Philco didn't see why they should have to pay royalties on cabinets. After all, there weren't any of RCA's patents involved in cabinet manufacture! Accordingly Philco devised a scheme whereby they sold the complete chassis and speakers to another company who supplied the necessary cabinets before selling the completed radios to the distributors. The other company was the Philco Radio & Television Corp., really just a 'paper' company formed expressly to circumvent RCA's licence requirement.

Naturally RCA was not too happy over this turn of events and in 1934 attempted to cancel Philco's licence. Philco countered with legal action against RCA but the case dragged on for five years before being settled in Philco's favour.

During 1933 Philco introduced 39 new models ranging in price from $20 to $175 and retained its place as the largest producer in the industry. The following year, 1934, was one of Philco's best; for the first time the company sold over one million sets, about 30% of the total industry production.

An even larger range of models was introduced for the 1935 season, a total of 49 as compared with 39 for the previous year. At the top of the line was the model 200X, claimed to be the first true high-fidelity receiver ever produced.

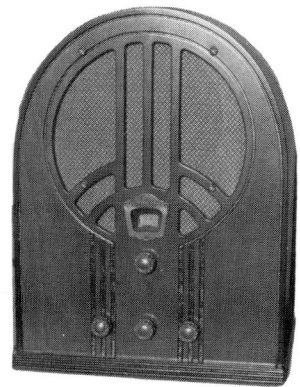

Model 60E, 5-valve 1934.

Model 91E, 9-valve, 3 band
1934.

Model 37-620EZ 1936.

Model 37-89 1936.

Model 37-610 1937.

Model 37-620E 1937.

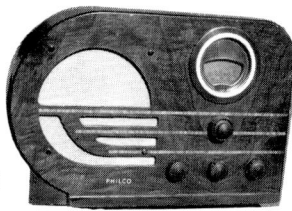

Model 38-10 EZ 5-valve, 2-
band May 1937.

It featured variable selectivity enabling a flat audio response to be obtained up to 7,500 cycles. A pair of 42s connected as triodes in Class AB push-pull provided 15 watts output to a speaker operating in an enclosure. With the production of this model Philco stole a march on the rest of the industry, putting them at least a year ahead of other manufacturers who, with the exception of one or two specialist firms such as Scott, did not

market any high-fidelity models until 1936-37.

The year 1935 was a good one for the industry with over six million sets being sold. It was the first time that sales figures exceeded those of the boom year of 1929. A much talked of event of 1935 was RCA's introduction of metal tubes, but Philco, as RCA's arch rival, not only completely eschewed the new tubes but actively campaigned against their use, even to the extent of taking out full page advertisements in the *New York Times* claiming the superiority of glass tubes.

As an initial counter measure Philco pioneered the use of octal-based glass tubes until they could come up with something better—an 'all-glass' tube. By early 1939 Philco had something better, or so it was claimed, the so-called 'Loktal' tube developed by Sylvania.

Although 1936 was another bumper year for Philco, with two million receivers being sold out of an industry total of eight million, the company profits were actually down slightly for the year. Sales figures for 1937 dropped even further and for the first time Philco actually lost money. Two reasons were given for the loss: trouble with labour unions and a minor trade recession in the U.S. However, in spite of everything Philco still retained its position as sales leader in 1937.

During 1938 Philco were facing increasing challenges from other giants in the industry, in particular RCA whose sales figures were climbing at a faster rate than Philco's, and Zenith who rose to No. 3 position in that year. Incredibly, after a six months' strike at their plant Philco still came out in No. 1 position at the end of the year, though the company again lost money.

The total industry production reached a staggering figure of over 10 million receivers in 1939 and although Philco's share continued to decline the company still retained their position as No. 1. In this year the company's finances were richer by $750,000 as a result of a Supreme Court ruling in the case against RCA when Philco were awarded this amount as being excess royalties paid over the last five years. This enabled Philco to do away with the need to maintain two separate companies and in 1940 the former two were combined as the Philco Corporation.

By this time Philco had been the No. 1 sales leader for ten years in a row, having produced over 15,000,000 sets since 1930. In 1940 alone they sold over two million, the industry total being 11.8 million for that year.

The outbreak of World War II in Europe provided a considerable impetus to radio sales and in 1941 the industry produced over 13 million sets. Philco were still at the top at the end of the year but with America's entry into the war production of receivers for civilian use was halted in 1942. For the duration of the war the company were engaged in the production of military equipment for the government.

By the end of 1945 the first post-war models were in production on a small scale but supplies were limited due to shortages of materials. Extensive plant expansion was carried out in 1946, one of the first moves being the purchase of one of the old Atwater Kent factories. By the end of 1946 Philco had 16 different plants in operation, though some were making non-radio products such as refrigerators. By 1947, in fact, the production of refrigerators and other "white" goods accounted for nearly half of the company's income.

Philco were marginally slower in getting television production under way and this initial lag was just enough to prevent the company from becoming the leader in the new field, the company remaining in No. 3 position after RCA and Zenith.

From 1951 there was a small but steady downward trend in the company's profitability which continued until 1956. In spite of all that was done to remedy the matter Philco remained in a somewhat shaky position and in 1961 sold out to the Ford Motor Company. Ford held on to Philco until 1974 when they sold the Philco Consumer Products Division to General Telephone-Sylvania. GTE-Sylvania in turn sold the division to North American Philips in 1981 and that was the end of Philco.

Philco in New Zealand

The New Zealand agency for Philco was held by Chas Begg & Co. Ltd whose head office was located in Dunedin. In 1930 two of the first Philcos imported were the model 76 metal box series and the model 20 TRF cathedral. Philco were one of the very few American manufacturers to supply export models in those early days, and even made 230-volt DC models, an example being the 46E which used special Philco tubes, types 14 and 17.

As early as 1932 cabinets for console models were being made in New Zealand, an example being the model 91, which when sold by Begg's Auckland branch was fitted with a cabinet made by the Lofley Cabinet Co. of Balmoral.

Following the introduction of import restrictions in 1938 all cabinets, both mantel and console, were then made locally. After 1939 no further chassis were imported, complete receivers

then being made by the Dominion Radio & Electrical Corp. Ltd.

PILOT

During the late 1920s and early 1930s Pilot occupied a unique position in the industry as a company which made every single part that went into the kitsets they produced. The only exceptions were headphones, speakers and tubes, but as these items were classed as accessories and not as part of a kitset they did not count, though even tubes were later made by Pilot.

The beginnings of the Pilot Electrical Manufacturing Co. go back much earlier than the 1920s, however, for it was in 1908 that a one-man business known as the Beacon Electrical Co. was established by a certain Isidor Goldberg and for the rest of its history Pilot remained under the sole ownership and control of this man. By 1925 the firm had become the Beacon Radio Mfg Co., located at 323 Berry Street, Brooklyn, New York, and was by then engaged in the manufacture of complete radios which were sold under the name of 'Trinity'. These sets were supplied complete with Beacon-Trinity "Duo-Phonic" horn speakers which were fitted with Stromberg Carlson driver units.

In 1926 there was a company named the Pilot Electrical Mfg Co. located at 100 South Third Street, Brooklyn, and it was this firm which in the same year combined with Beacon and moved to the Berry Street address where it remained until late in 1930. Under the new set-up the production of complete receivers was discontinued and only parts were produced. By August 1928 Pilot claimed to be "The World's Largest Radio Parts Plant", and there is no reason to dispute the claim. Right from the start a policy of making every single component was adhered to. Because they were such a large parts manufacturer it was only logical that Pilot should enter the kitset field, which was booming at the time, and this they did at the end of 1926 when the 'Pilotone Universal' kit was marketed. This kit differed from those of competing manufacturers in that it could be assembled in various ways to use four different circuit hookups.

Next came the 'Pilotone Electric', a 6-tube AC set with a built-in filament transformer and a separate 'B' eliminator, and in the same year, 1928, the first short-wave kit the 'Pilot Wasp', a 3-tube regenerative set.

It was the wasp's successor, the 4-tube 'Super Wasp' which really put the name Pilot on the map. Developed during the winter of 1928-29, it was announced in June 1929 and became an instant success. The use of a tuned RF stage ahead of the detector was a notable feature at the

The AC Super Wasp and Pilot's first midget both appeared in 1929.

time and such was the excellence of the Super Wasp's design that production was continued in the original form for the next three years. An AC version was not long in making its appearance and in December 1929 the 'AC Super Wasp' was announced. It differed from the previous battery version only in the use of indirectly heated tubes.

Just prior to this, in September of the same year, Pilot announced the commencement of tube manufacture under the name 'Pilotron', the necessary manufacturing licence having been obtained from RCA. One reason given for the new venture was that it had been found impossible to obtain 227 tubes which did not give rise to hum problems when used as detectors in the AC Super Wasp. Pilotron 227s were specially developed to overcome this problem. It was at this time that the name of the company was changed to the Pilot Radio & Tube Corp.

In July 1930 Pilot announced the availability of a car radio kitset which was marketed under the name 'Auto Pilot'. Like all car radios of the day, its HT supply was provided by three 45-volt 'B' batteries. Apparently Pilot was the only firm ever to market a car radio in kitset form.

September 1930 was an important month for Pilot for it was then that a move was made to a completely new location in Lawrence, Massachusetts. This move, which was brought about by the need for greatly increased factory space, marked a turning point in the history of the company, but, unfortunately, not one for the better. After little more than two years at the new location the company collapsed, but not, as might be thought, as a result of the then current depression conditions.

Meanwhile it was a matter of business as usual and production of both versions of the 'Wasp' continued. The first self-contained AC broadcast model, the 'AC Midget' was introduced in November 1930 and a console model (Pilot's first) followed in March 1931. By this time the kitset market had largely evaporated although production of the 'Wasps' was still carried on as a result of a continuing demand. The last kitset, also available in a factory-built form, was the 'Universal Super Wasp', a 6-tube all-wave model featuring band-switching and a built-in speaker; it was announced in April 1931.

From then on there was a move towards the production of plain broadcast receivers, although in December 1931 Pilot's first all-wave superhet, the 'New Super Wasp', was announced. This particular model was actually two separate receivers combined on a single chassis which functioned as a double superhet on short-wave. Pilot's first broadcast superhet was the S-148, a 7-tube model released in 1932. During the years 1931-32 there were 28 different chassis produced which, when assembled into various styles of cabinets, amounted to 48 different models ranging from the 4-tube 'Rainbow' to the 10-tube model C-153.

Production at Lawrence finally ground to a halt and the company ceased operations at the end of 1933. Isidor Goldberg left to return to New York where he founded a new company—the Pilot Radio Corporation in Long Island City.

Initially the new company carried on with some of the earlier designs and name styles, producing such models as the '8-Tube Dragon' and 'Dragon All Wave'. However, by 1935 all traces of the earlier ancestry had disappeared and the receivers produced from then on had a new look about them.

From this time Pilot became very active in the export market, producing many special export models, including 230-volt DC models, all of which were equipped with long-wave coverage to suit European conditions. In fact, in the immediate pre-war years, it might be said that Pilot receivers were better known outside the U.S. than in it!

Following the end of World War II radio production was continued and Pilot also entered the TV field as well as making a brief foray into the hi-fi market in the late 1950s. The company went out of business following the death of the founder, Isidor Goldberg, in 1960.

In 1936 a British branch, Pilot Radio Ltd, was established in London and British-made versions of the American designs were initially produced. But, over the years, the British receivers became less Americanised and more British, until by 1940 they had lost much of their American look. After the war the British company became quite active in the field of television manufacture which was continued up to about 1960. As in the U.S., British Pilot also made hi-fi amplifiers for a period during the late 1950s.

The name Pilot became known quite early in this part of the world; first in Australia when the agency was taken by United Distributors Ltd and later by Harringtons Ltd. The latter firm had a New Zealand branch which thus became the distributors for this country. The agency was retained by Harringtons until they were taken over by Kodak (N.Z.) Ltd in 1934. This firm continued to sell Pilot receivers and parts until existing stocks were exhausted. A few Pilot sets somehow arrived in New Zealand after this time but they were thin on the ground until well into 1935. It was in this year that the firm of Fisher & Paykel Ltd took up the agency and in 1936 they commenced to assemble partly completed chassis which were then fitted into . locally produced cabinets made by G. C. Goode Ltd. This

The famous Pilot 'Super Wasp' 1929. 4-valve battery set with plug-in coils.

The second Pilot midget 1931 used the same valve line-up as the 1930 model but had a tone control.

Pilot's first superhet midget 1931.

Model 43, 5-valve TRF 1932.

Model 12, 6-valve superhet 1933. First use of a bakelite cabinet by Pilot.

Pilot 'Dragon' 7-valve, 4-band 1933.

Model 63B, 6-valve, 3-band 1935.

Model G752B, 4-valve, 2-band 1935.

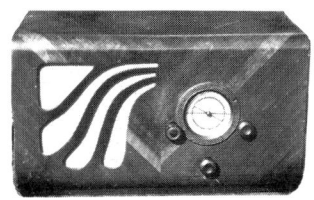

Model Y43B, 4-valve, 2-band 1935.

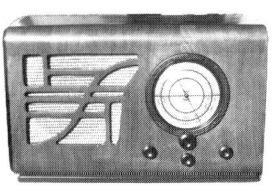

Model 403B in horizontal style cabinet 1937.

Model X664, 6-valve, 3-band 1938.

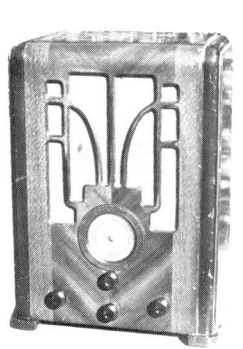

Model 103B, 5-valve DW 1936.

Model 403B, 7-valve, 3-band 1937.

Model H554, 6-valve, 3-band 1938.

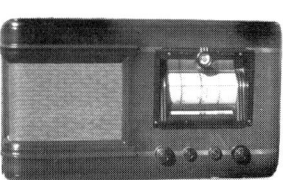

Model H664 7-valve, 3-band 1938.

116

They are different!

AND THEY ARE BETTER ON BOTH SHORTWAVE AND BROADCAST RECEPTION

The NEW ALL-WAVE PILOT RADIOS

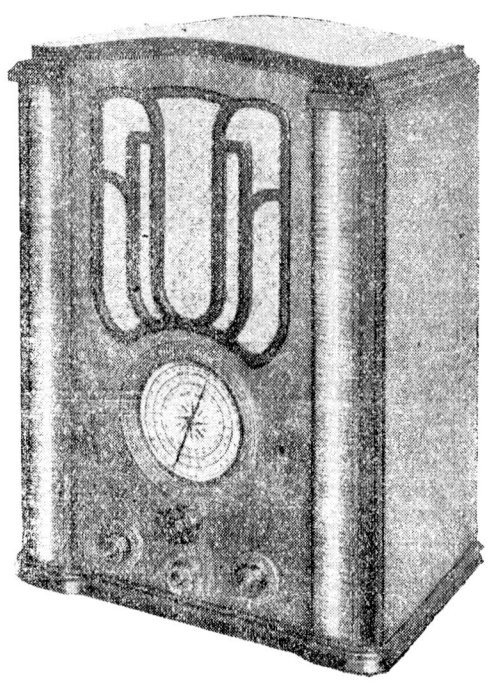

In design, construction and materials the new All Wave Pilot Receivers are basically different to all other All Wave machines. They differ as follows: Whereas other All Wave Sets are fundamentally of Broadcast design with Short Wave added, the new Pilots are basically SHORT WAVE receivers with Broadcast incorporated! The result is, that the finer materials and the superior, more accurate construction necessary for efficient Short Wave reception combine to make an All Wave receiver that will out-perform all other All Wave Sets on both Short Wave AND Broadcast reception! This is no idle claim as even the most non-technical listener can prove by testing a new Pilot against any other All Wave set!

Be fair to yourself! Make the Test before you choose that new Radio.

Illustrated

is PILOT MODEL 63, just one of the complete PILOT line including table models, consoles and phonograph combination receivers. It is an ultra modern All Wave Superheterodyne, 16-550 metres (18,800 to 545 k.c.), with R.F. pre-amplification increasing sensitivity and selectivity. It features the famous two-speed PILOT Compass Dial, 10:1 ratio for fast tuning; 80:1 ratio for micrometer Short Wave tuning; illuminated scale showing metres and kilocycles simultaneously on all wave bands; Diode detection; Class "A" power pentode output stage; phonograph jack; Tone Control for reducing treble tones; Automatic Volume Control; and an eight inch full range Electro-Dynamic Speaker. D.C. models also available.

FISHER & PAYKEL LTD.
CUSTOM ST. E., AUCKLAND.
Sole New Zealand Agents for

PILOT
ALL WAVE RADIOS

TRADE MARK REGD.

Fisher & Paykel's first advertisement for Pilot radios, February 1935.

arrangement continued until wartime conditions prevented further importation. After the war Fisher & Paykel did not return to handling radios for many years, by which time conditions had changed completely.

RCA

The Radio Corporation of America (RCA) did not originally make radio apparatus, in fact for the first ten years of its existence—between 1919 and 1929—it functioned (among other things) as a selling agent for other companies, mainly General Electric and Westinghouse. From 1922 receivers were sold under the name 'Radiola', apart from some very early types made by Westinghouse which were sold under the name 'Aeriola'. The name Radiola had been suggested for use as a trade-name some two years earlier, in 1920, and it is interesting to speculate on its origin as this name was also in use in France at the same time, but it is not known which was actually the first country to use it.

The fact that RCA did not possess its own manufacturing facilities soon became a source of dissatisfaction to the firm's general manager, David Sarnoff, and it was he who was largely responsible for RCA's establishing a separate manufacturing unit.

The first step in this direction was taken in December 1929 when RCA purchased the Victor Talking Machine Co. of Camden. N. J. Victor, like other phonograph companies, had by this time been hard hit by the burgeoning new medium of home entertainment, radio broadcasting, and was then in the hands of bankers. Even so, Victor's assets were valued at $69,000,000.

With the purchase of Victor, RCA acquired a vast manufacturing facility which, within a short space of time, was to be turned into an equally large radio factory. A small but valuable acquisition which came as part of the deal was the rights to the world famous Listening Dog trademark, 'Little Nipper', and the accompanying slogan 'His Master's Voice'. Incidentally, these were not of American origin, having come to Victor when that company had acquired a 50% interest in the British firm, the Gramophone Co. Ltd, in 1920.

The initial plan was that GE and Westinghouse, who were partners in the new enterprise, should be responsible for designing the radio products and running the new factory but shortly after the plan had been put into effect the U.S. government brought an anti-trust action against the combine claiming that it constituted a monopoly. At this time RCA also controlled the National Broadcasting Co. as well as owning other subsidiary companies such as the RCA Photophone Corp. and RCA Communications Inc.

As far as we in New Zealand are concerned, the first American Radiolas sold here were the models 20 and 26, both of 1925. As with other later models, they were imported by Amalgamated Wireless (A/sia) Ltd, an Australian firm having a depot in New Zealand.

The first true all-electric Radiola, the model 17 of 1927, was seen here in 1928. It was a 7-tube model using type UX226 triodes in all stages except the detector and output. In keeping with industry trends of the day it was housed in a metal cabinet and supplied with a separate magnetic speaker.

Although RCA had marketed an AC superhet as early as 1925 it was really only a battery set with an added AC power supply and output stage. The first true all-electric super was the Radiola 60 of 1928, a 9-tube set using type UY227 indirectly-heated triodes in all stages except the output.

In 1929 came the first screen-grid models, Radiola 44 and 46. By comparison, the model 33, which was released in the same year, used triodes in all stages.

Because the receivers marketed by RCA at this time came from two different sources, a word of explanation may be in order. When RCA took over the Victor Talking Machine Co. they used the factory to produce radios which were sold in the U.S. under the name 'Victor'. Because of copyright restrictions this name could not be used in certain countries, including New Zealand, and in such cases the name 'His Master's Voice' was used instead. At the same time RCA's original suppliers, GE and Westinghouse, were still producing radios which, as before, were being sold under the name Radiola. This duality of production sources sometimes led to confusion when it came to assigning model numbers to the respective products. For example, the Victor R32 and the Radiola 32 were quite different receivers. However, with the temporary cessation of receiver manufacture by GE and Westinghouse the name Radiola disappeared from the American scene. From then on the newly formed RCA-Victor Co. commenced production on its own account under the name style 'RCA Victor'.

In this part of the world a change in distribution occurred in 1930 when AWA ceased handling American sets, though continuing to distribute RCA Radiotron valves in both Australia and New Zealand. The N.Z. agency was then taken up by His Master's Voice (N.Z.) Ltd, a company which had been established here in 1926 by the Gramophone Co. of England.

Since about 1925 AWA had been producing a line of Australian-made receivers under the Radiola name, but in general these had no resemblance to any American models. Prior to

Radiola 20

The Supreme 5 Valve Set

Amalgamated Wireless (A'sia) Ltd.

Box 830   **Wellington**

This 1925 model Radiola 20 was still being advertised in 1927.

The two newest features in fine radio set design are both found in the new

RCA

SCREEN-GRID

Radiola

46

with the incomparable RCA Electro-Dynamic Reproducer $179 *less Radiotrons*

All-electric screen-grid—the latest thing in 1929.

RCA Radiola 17

MUSIC *from your* LIGHTING SOCKET

RCA Radiola 17, one of the first all-electric receivers. A separate repeater was still necessary. It was sold in N.Z. during 1928.

Hear the New RCA RADIOLAS

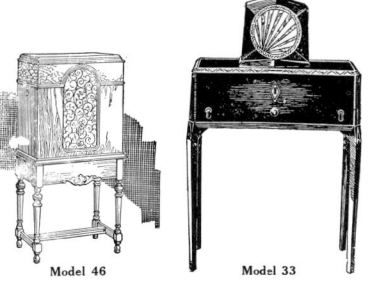

Model 46   Model 33   Model 44

Most Complete Line on the Market
GREATEST VALUES TODAY

First get acquainted with this wonderful new line of RCA Radiolas. Use them as standards of comparison. No lesser instrument can then satisfy you.

There's a RCA Radiola to fit your purse and your home. Small models or large. Various styles. Screengrid, with all the advantages of this new circuit and many other features besides. The finest reproduction you ever heard—mirror-like reproduction of the living voice of the artist in the broadcasting studio.

Many new refinements give RCA Radiolas their superiority over anything on the market.

Come in for a Demonstration.   **Be Prepared for a Surprise**

FARMERS TRADING CO.
LTD.   AUCKLAND.

Advt. of

Amalgamated Wireless
(Australasia) Ltd.

119

RCA RADIOLA 60
SUPER-HETERODYNE

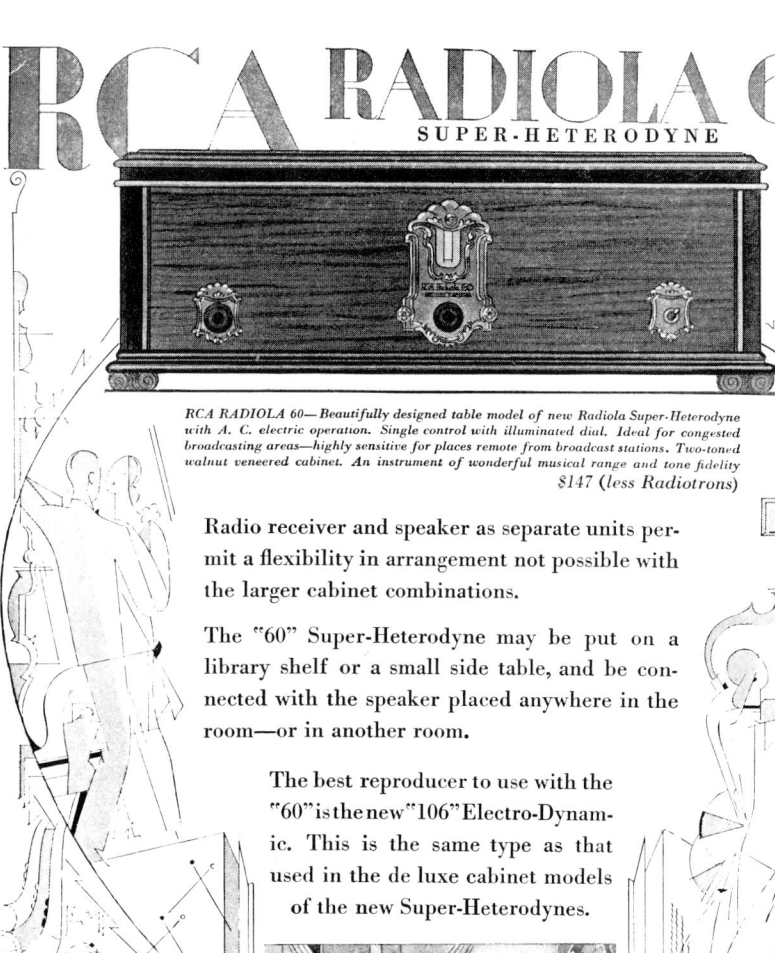

RCA RADIOLA 60—Beautifully designed table model of new Radiola Super-Heterodyne with A. C. electric operation. Single control with illuminated dial. Ideal for congested broadcasting areas—highly sensitive for places remote from broadcast stations. Two-toned walnut veneered cabinet. An instrument of wonderful musical range and tone fidelity **$147** *(less Radiotrons)*

Radio receiver and speaker as separate units permit a flexibility in arrangement not possible with the larger cabinet combinations.

The "60" Super-Heterodyne may be put on a library shelf or a small side table, and be connected with the speaker placed anywhere in the room—or in another room.

The best reproducer to use with the "60" is the new "106" Electro-Dynamic. This is the same type as that used in the de luxe cabinet models of the new Super-Heterodynes.

Buy with confidence where you see this sign

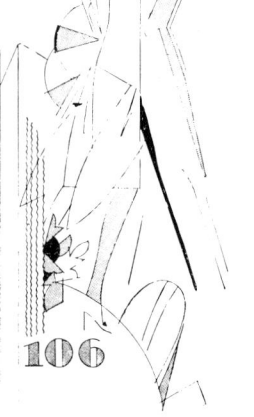

RCA ELECTRO-DYNAMIC SPEAKER 106—The incomparable reproducing instrument of the type used in the new cabinet Radiolas now available as a separate unit. Operates from A. C. house current. A beautiful little piece of furniture as well as a reproducer of amazing range and tone. **$88**

RADIO CORPORATION OF AMERICA

New York   Chicago   Atlanta   Dallas   San Francisco

Model R-4, 7-valve superhet 1931. One of the 'Superette' models.

Model R-5, 4-valve SG 1932. The first 'Radiolette'.

RCA Radiola 62 1929.

RCA-HMV model R7 'Superette' 1932.

Model R28P, 6-valve superhet 1933.

Model R-37, 6-valve, 2-band 1933.

Model R22S, 5-valve AC/DC 1933.

Science develops a "Magic Brain"

that makes All-Wave Radio actually think!

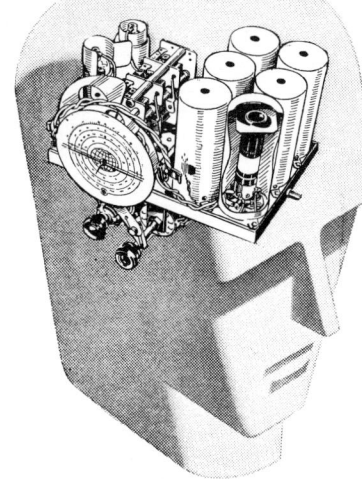

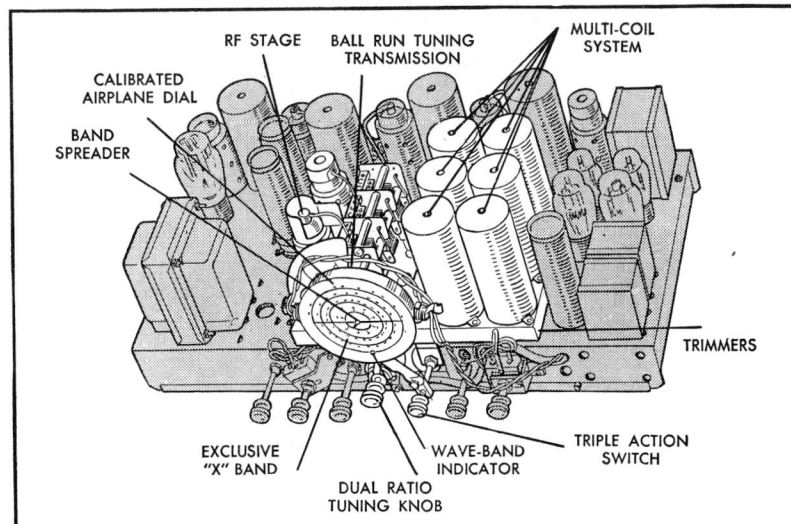

CALIBRATED
AIRPLANE DIAL

BAND
SPREADER

RF STAGE   BALL RUN TUNING
              TRANSMISSION

MULTI-COIL
SYSTEM

TRIMMERS

EXCLUSIVE
"X" BAND

DUAL RATIO
TUNING KNOB

WAVE-BAND
INDICATOR

TRIPLE ACTION
SWITCH

Here you see the relation of the "Magic Brain" to the rest of a typical 12-tube RCA Victor all-wave chassis. Indicated by the pointers are those parts of this unit which, acting in unison, produce the finest all-wave reception you've ever heard!

RCA Victor engineers produce uncanny governing unit in all-wave chassis that is directing force for superior long- and short-wave performance

Deep in the center of RCA Victor's new all-wave radios is placed the "Magic Brain".

It is a new and exclusive RCA Victor development that permits far greater latitude in all-wave performance. Human in its power of selection and direction of discovering signals, it can be compared to the human brain.

There are two principal engineering features which give the "Magic Brain" its outstanding performance characteristics. First, the radio frequency stage *ahead of the first detector*. RCA Victor engineers have succeeded in designing this stage so that it functions with equal efficiency on all bands. It amplifies the signal you tune, *four times*, without acting on noise, cross-talk, image frequencies or other interfering factors. Thus, the wanted signal is *supercharged*, resulting in a four-to-one signal-to-noise ratio and a practical elimination of background noise and cross-talk from the speaker output. Reproduction is clear, with a higher-fidelity tone, and freer from interference than ever before.

The second great "Magic Brain" advantage is the RCA Victor multi-coil system. A separate and distinct set of three coils act for each band —so no coil performs more than one function. Furthermore, each coil is trimmed or adjusted individually for maximum performance. In effect, then, these RCA Victor "Magic Brain" all-wave sets are really three, four or five sets in one, depending on the number of wave bands covered.

You get an enormously increased range in these new receivers—as much as 140 kc to 36,000 kc! Everything, practically, in the world of radio is yours, including the new ultra short-wave police signals. Also, in "Magic Brain" chassis of 8 tubes or better, an exclusive "X" band is provided—for hourly U. S. Government weather aviation reports.

An interesting pamphlet is offered you, free. It tells, in detail, the fascinating story of the "Magic Brain". Write today for it. Use the convenient coupon.

GET THE INTERESTING ANSWERS to these "Magic Brain" Questions!

What is the "Magic Brain"?
Why you get higher fidelity tone?
What are the 3 reasons for the RF stage?
How does the multi-coil system work?
Why is it so necessary?
Why is high "Signal-to-noise" ratio good?
What extra mechanical features has it?
How wide is the KC range?

—the answers to these and many other questions are given for you in a free pamphlet. You are invited to get your copy. Use this coupon now.

TABLE MODEL 128. "Magic Brain" Superheterodyne, domestic, foreign, police, amateur wave bands $69.95

"X" Band is in all sets of 8 tubes or more

•

A RADIO AND A PRICE FOR EVERYONE!
RCA Victor Instruments priced from **$18.75** to $375, including Standard Receivers, Auto Radios, Air-Cell Battery Radios and Radio-Phonographs. All RCA Victor Instruments equipped with RCA Micro-Sensitive Radio Tubes. All prices subject to change without notice. Any short-wave radio performs better with an RCA World-Wide Antenna.

RCA Victor Co., Inc., Camden, N. J.
Dept. N
I'm interested in getting more details on the "Magic Brain". Kindly send me the pamphlet you mention.

*Name*_____

*Address*_____

*City*_____ *State*_____

RCA VICTOR

RCA VICTOR CO., INC., ONE UNIT OF RADIO CORPORATION OF AMERICA...THE WORLD'S LARGEST RADIO ORGANIZATION. OTHER UNITS: NATIONAL BROADCASTING CO., INC. .... R. C. A. COMMUNICATIONS, INC. ... RCA RADIOTRON CO., INC. ... RADIOMARINE CORPORATION OF AMERICA

The model 128 was the first in the series of 'Magic Brain' receivers developed by RCA.

"His Master's Voice"

RADIO for every PURSE and PURPOSE!

There's an "HIS MASTER'S VOICE" radio to suit your every need. At prices you can afford to pay! Here are four splendid models—go to your nearest "HIS MASTER'S VOICE" dealer, and ask him to demonstrate any one that interests you. Tell him to explain his EASY TERMS system.

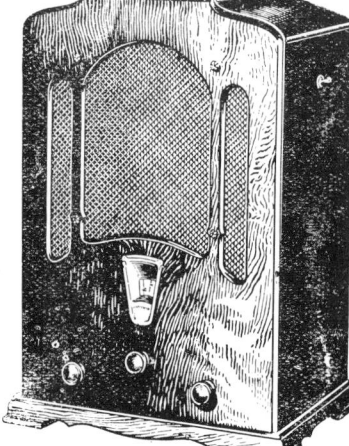

R7 - £32/10

An 8 valve screen grid super-heterodyne priced at a figure that sets a new standard of radio value! Small enough to be conveniently moved around the home or to take up little space in your week-end bach . . . but gives performance bigger than you've ever experienced! Brings in local and the most distant stations with extraordinary ease . . . and with fine, full, undistorted tone!

R-5 £18/10

The greatest local receiver to-day! Complete with four valves, including the marvellous Pentode tube. Sets a new standard of value at the sensationally low price, £18/10/-. Housed in a handsome cabinet only 15in. high. Weighs but 16 lbs. Can be conveniently carried anywhere.

And The
R-9 Console £45

A super-heterodyne with sensitivity that gives you even the low-powered distant stations, and selectivity that enables you to bring in ANY programme—precise, clear-cut, free from interference! Single knob tuning—volume control and tone control! And priced at only £45!

And
RE-16 Radio-Gramo.

Giving you the advantages of all the music of the air plus all recorded music. Entertainment at any hour of the day or night! All for £65.

His Master's Voice (N.Z.) Ltd.
Wellington

1932

Model 118, 5-valve DW 1935.

Model 125, 6-valve AW 1935.

RCA model 211, 5-valve, DW 1934.

RCA model 121, 6-valve, 1934.

Model 66BX, 6-valve AC/DC/Battery 1947.

Left: Model 9SX, a 5-valve AC/DC, 2-band 1937. This 110-volt model needed an extra line-cord resistor for 230 V.

1931, few, if any, Australian Radiolas were seen in New Zealand but when after 1931 RCA gave up using the Radiola name, in the same year Australian Radiolas were imported extensively. The first 'Victor' receiver imported was an unusual TRF model, the 'Micro Synchronous' R-32 (sold here as 'His Master's Voice'). It used an ingenious system of multiple trimmer adjustments mounted on a special 'turret' type ganged tuning condenser.

A landmark receiver released in 1930 was the model 80, the first AC screen-grid superhet, the design of which set the pace for much of the later development of this type of receiver. Prior to 1930 the industry in general had been prevented from exploiting the superheterodyne circuit because RCA, as the patent holder, had not previously granted licences to independent manufacturers. However, the introduction of the model 80 seemed to mark a turning point for the industry as henceforth RCA commenced to license the independents who were quick to take advantage of the new situation. Within a couple of years the superhet had almost completely ousted the TRF.

From 1931 on, a very noticeable shrinkage in the size of most American radios became apparent, and RCA's products were no exception. The often enormous and sometimes lumbering consoles of the previous two years were being superseded by smaller and cheaper table models. The model R-5 'Radiolette' and R-7 'Superette' were examples of RCA's contribution to the genre. Incidentally, the use of the word Radiolette as a trade-name had been suggested as far back as 1922, by none other than David Sarnoff, as being a suitable name for a portable receiver, but this was the first time that a Radiolette had been produced, and it was not a portable. For some reason the use of the name was not continued in the U.S. but it was later taken up enthusiastically by AWA in Australia who produced a series of Radiolettes between 1933 and 1938.

Small radios were the order of the day during the next few years of the Great Depression, two of the smallest made by RCA being the R28 and R22. Both were 1933 models, the latter being an AC/DC type which was first seen in the U.S. in that year. As mentioned earlier, RCA receivers were now being sold in this country by His Master's Voice (N.Z.) Ltd, and this arrangement continued until the outbreak of World War II.

Announced in December 1934 was the first of the so-called "Magic Brain" models which ushered in the era of simplified all-wave tuning for the ordinary listener. In essence the Magic Brain was no more than an all-wave coil assembly mounted together with band switch, tuning gang and RF and mixer tubes on a separate sub-chassis. The coils were provided with holes in the tops of their shield cans through which a "tuning wand" could be inserted to check whether a particular circuit needed trimming adjustments during the servicing of a receiver. It is interesting to note that exactly the same type of construction, minus the separate sub-chassis, was used in England by EMI in their 1936 models, e.g. 441.

Not content with just a Magic Brain RCA added in 1936 a 'Magic Eye' and a 'Magic Voice'. The first of these features was the now well-known electron-ray tuning indicator, at the time a fascinating novelty which soon became a feature of all better class receivers. The Magic Voice was a form of speaker enclosure used only on console models. Imagine there being three sorts of magic in one radio!

Comparatively few RCA receivers were seen in this country after 1937, as, for one thing, imports of English HMV sets had by that time largely replaced those from the U.S. Finally, in 1938, Government import restrictions effectively prevented importation from either source.

STEWART WARNER

The company which made Stewart Warner radios was soundly and widely based in other areas of manufacturing long before entering the radio field, and this may well have had some bearing on its subsequent success in this area. Companies in the group were some of the largest in the business and included: the Alemite Mfg Corp., the Bassick Caster Corp., and the Stewart Speedometer Corp. The radio division, known as the Stewart Warner Corp., commenced operations in 1925 at the height of the battery set boom.

The first Stewart Warner receivers produced were known as the '300' series, the earlier issues of which were notable for the absence of grid biassing in the output stages! This omission was surprising because by 1925 the use of biassing had become almost standard practice in receivers of the day. Not until the sixth model in the series had been issued was provision made for the use of a 'C' battery.

In appearance the 300 series were typical 'three diallers' of the period, but their circuitry differed from most others in that the two RF stages were stabilised by means of a grid circuit potentiometer instead of the more common neutralising as generally used. Right from the start Stewart Warner made their own speakers and the 300 series were sold complete with a model 405 horn speaker. The model 345 issued in 1926 was the first single-dial model; it was equipped with a model 415 cone speaker.

Mains-operated models were introduced in 1927, and following current practice, they used separate power supply units and separate

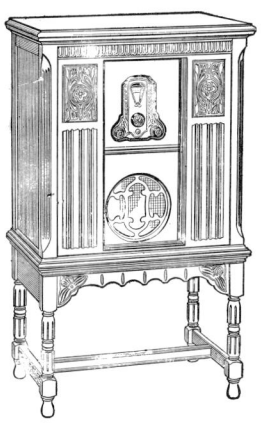

Model 300, 5-valve TRF battery set fitted into a N.Z. cabinet 1925.

Model 950, 8-valve SG 1930.

"SILENCE" IS GOLDEN!

WHAT would you give for a really quiet "silent" superheterodyne, powerful to a degree, with amazing sensitivity for distant station programmes?

Here you have it in Stewart-Warner's latest radio. Modern to a degree in technical design, and, from a musical standpoint —tone perfect.

But, gone are the awkward noises that any powerful radio is prone to receive. Instead, a smooth, silent background out of which comes the perfect reproduction of your favourite station.

STEWART-WARNER HAS THE BIGGEST FEATURE THIS YEAR IN THE QUIET SUPERHETERO-DYNE.

Make your test. Our splendid radio will win its way into your home eventually—why not now?

Broadcast, low-wave, or combined radios—and at the Lowest Prices in Radio History.

TUDOR NO. 2
Combined Short and Long-Wave Console

INSTAL NOW FOR MAXIMUM WINTER PROGRAMME TIME

STEWART-WARNER
Round-the-World RADIO

1932

1926

Model R-105, 11-valve AW 'Magic Dial' 1932. It used a separate power pack.

Left: Model R-104A 6-valve BC in an unusual style of cabinet 1932.

STEWART-WARNER RADIO
"The Voice of Authority"

NEW ZEALAND DISTRIBUTORS

HOPE GIBBONS LTD.

Wellington

The R-102, 6-valve Superhet 'Apartment' model 1932. Note the words "New Zealand", but only the cabinet was N.Z. made.

Model R-104A 6-valve BC Superhet 1932. It used a 'Wunderlich' detector valve.

Model R-111, 6-valve AC/DC 1933. Cabinet in the form of three volumes of books.

Model R-116, 5-valve with large cabinet 1933.

Model R-116, 5-valve with Police Band 1933.

Model R126, 7-valve, 4-band 1933.

Model R-136X, 6-valve, 3-band 1936.

Model R-119 6-valve 1933.

Model R-166 Air Chief 1938. Made for the Firestone Tire & Rubber Co.

speakers. The company continued to make their own speakers throughout the entire period during which radios were in production, being one of the very few receiver manufacturers to do so. Incidentally, the power packs of the first AC sets were made by Grigsby-Grunow and not until the production of the 900 series in 1929 did Stewart Warner make a complete AC radio.

When, towards the end of 1929, the first screen-grid model, known as the 900 series, appeared it incorporated all that was good in American design and constructional methods of the day.

In 1931 Stewart Warner became one of the first non-specialist manufacturers to market an all-wave model, and in the same year also marketed a 2-tube short-wave converter.

A feature of the 1932 all-wave models was the use of their so-called 'Magic Dial' wherein individual scales for each tuning band were brought into view one at a time as the band switch was manipulated. This feature was retained for the next two years, after which circular (areo) dials came into use. The name 'Magic Dial' continued to be used in advertising, even though the new dials bore no resemblance to the earlier type.

With the advent of metal tubes in 1935 Stewart Warner claimed to be the first manufacturer to design a chassis especially suited to the new tubes. This was the R136 'Ferrodyne', so called because in addition to using metal tubes it also used iron-cored IF transformers.

Up to about 1936 Stewart Warner had sold radios under their own brand name only, but after this time both home sets and car radios were also made for the Firestone Tire & Rubber Co. who sold them under the name 'Air Chief'. In the post-war years several more private brands were added.

Following the end of World War II, Stewart Warner continued to manufacture both radio and television receivers until 1954.

Stewart Warner in New Zealand

The agency for Stewart Warner radios was held by Hope Gibbons Ltd, a Wellington based firm of motor accessories importers whose association with radio went back to 1923 when they held a one-sixth share in the International Radio Co. In this regard it is interesting to note that in a 1932 advertisement Hope Gibbons claimed to have been established even earlier than Stewart Warner, although the exact date was not given.

It was in 1926 that the first Stewart Warner radios were imported, the 5-valve '300' series, and from then on the name Stewart Warner grew to be one of the best known of the many American manufacturers whose products were marketed in this country in pre-war days.

When in 1930 Hope Gibbons fitted a series 950 chassis and speaker into a New Zealand-made console cabinet they became one of the first importers to adopt the practice of using locally made cabinets. Similarly, in 1931, locally made mantel cabinets were used, and in addition locally made step-down transformers were fitted because the American chassis came equipped with 110-volt power transformers. Some sets were also fitted with locally made line filters. The effect of all this N.Z. content was enough for Hope Gibbons to advertise one 1932 model as "New Zealand Built", a slight exaggeration, to say the least.

Another innovation was the combining of a 2-valve short-wave converter and a standard 6-valve chassis into a console cabinet in 1932, thus producing an early all-wave model.

For some reason the use of New Zealand-made cabinets ceased after about 1936 at just about the time when most other importers were starting to use them in order to take advantage of the lower rate of duty applicable.

After the war Hope Gibbons did not re-enter the radio business, presumably because of the changed post-war conditions.

ZENITH

The firm which became the Zenith Radio Corporation evolved from a two-man business established in 1918 by R. H. G. Matthews and Karl E. Kassel which originally traded under the name Chicago Radio Laboratory, using the brand name 'C.R.L.' In the pre-broadcasting years components for 'ham' radio use were made but in 1922 the first complete radio was marketed. In the same year the name of the firm was changed to the Zenith Radio Corporation, said to have been chosen because Matthews' ham call-sign was 9ZN.

In 1923 a third person, Eugene F. McDonald, joined the fledgling company and quickly acquired control of the business. It was under his leadership that Zenith grew to be one of the largest manufacturers in the industry which, by 1936, had displaced Crosley as No. 3 after RCA and Philco.

Quite early on Zenith adopted a policy of producing high quality receivers and emphasised this point in contemporary advertising using the slogan "They Do More—But They Cost More". Some two months later, in March 1925 this rather apologetic slogan was changed to "They Cost More—But They Do More".

Released in December 1924 was the 'Super Zenith VII', a 6-tube set in a table model cabinet

which sold for $230, without tubes, batteries or speaker; the same set in a console cabinet equipped with *two* inbuilt horn speakers sold for $550. However, these prices pale into insignificance when compared with those applying to models marketed a couple of years later. In 1926 the same Super Zenith chassis in a "Spanish De Luxe" cabinet was priced at $2,500 making it probably the most expensive set ever produced.

Throughout 1924-25 advertising was confined almost entirely to publicising the fact that a Commander Donald B. McMillan had used a Zenith receiver on his two polar expeditions. In fact, one might imagine from a perusal of contemporary ads that the ad men could think of nothing else.

Zenith's first AC set, the model 17 of 1927, used 201A battery type tubes with series-connected filaments, though prior to that earlier models could be electrified by the use of Zenith 'A' and 'B' eliminators. The first models to use the then new 227 indirectly heated AC tubes became available in 1928.

An extremely short-lived feature originated by Zenith was the use of push-button station selection in some of their 1930 models.

In mid-1931 the first superhets appeared, the 'Zenette' an 8-tube mantel model, and the models 91 and 92, both being 10-tube sets fitted with tuning meters.

The first Zenith car radio, model 460 of 1933, was unusual in that instead of having remotely-controlled tuning and volume controls operated by flexible steel cables it had the front end housed in the control head. It was the only model so constructed, all subsequent car radios using the conventional method of control.

A point of interest, perhaps not commonly known, is that for a short period during 1933-34 Zenith marketed receivers which were not their own manufacture and as this seems uncharacteristic a word of explanation is called for. Not many different models were involved, the first example being the model 730, a 5-tube battery set using 2-volt tubes which was made by Wells Gardner, being that firm's standard model 06A. Another example is the model 702, a 5-tube AC/DC set having a European long-wave band; it was made by Belmont, being that firm's standard model 530. In both cases these were types of sets not previously made by Zenith and it seems likely that in order to satisfy a demand Zenith found it expedient to buy in ready-made sets from other manufacturers to avoid losing substantial orders. Another explanation could be that the factory facilities were fully committed at the time, but whatever the reason this procedure was not repeated in later years.

Presumably because it conflicted with

It Tunes Through *Everything*
The New SUPER-ZENITH

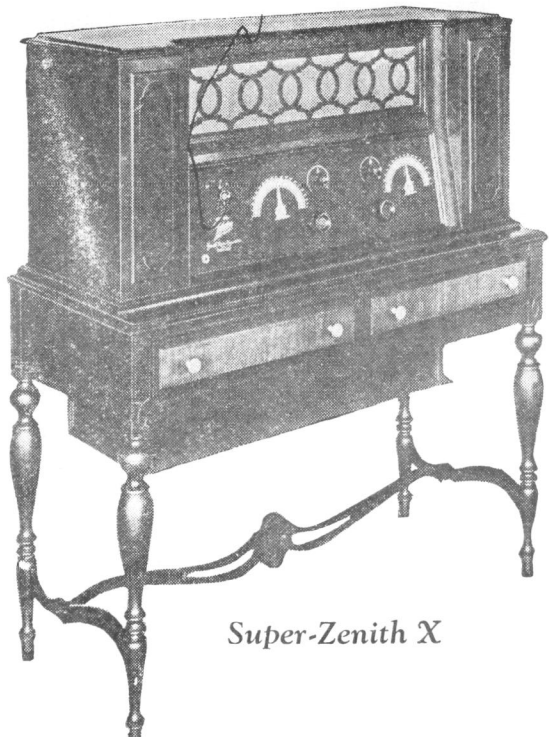

Super-Zenith X

Super-Zenith VII
—Table Model
(Not regenerative)—6 tubes—2 stages tuned frequency amplification—detector and 3 stages audio frequency amplification. Installed in a beautifully finished cabinet of solid mahogany—44⅞ inches long, 16¾ inches wide, 10⅝ inches high. Door panels inlaid. Slanting panel of sheet bronze, mahogany finish, with scales and indicators in metallic relief. Gold plated pointers, to prevent tarnish. Compartments at either end for dry batteries. Can be operated on either wet or dry batteries. Either inside or outside antenna. Price (*exclusive of tubes and batteries*) **$230**

Super-Zenith VIII
Same as VII except—built with mahogany legs of well-proportioned appropriate design, converting model into console type. Price (*exclusive of tubes and batteries*) **$250**

Super-Zenith IX
Same as VII except—built with legs and additional compartments containing built-in Zenith loud speaker on the one side and generous storage battery space on the other. Price (*exclusive of tubes and batteries*) **$300**

Super-Zenith X
Contains two **new** features superseding all receivers. 1st—Built-in, patented, Super-Zenith Duo-Loud Speakers, perfectly reproducing both high and low pitch tones otherwise impossible with single-unit speakers. 2nd—Zenith Battery Eliminator. Requires no A or B batteries or charger. Price (*exclusive of tubes*) **$550**

The new Super-Zenith is NOT regenerative. It is a six-tube set in four different models ranging from $230 to $550, with a new, unique and really different patented circuit controlled exclusively by the Zenith Radio Corporation. Amplification is always at a maximum in each stage for any wave-length. *The Super-Zenith line is not affected by moisture.* For the first time, you have here a set that—

1—tunes through *everything* and selects the station you really want.
2—requires only *two* hands—*not three*—to operate.
3—brings in each station *at only one point on the dial.*
4—affords such mathematical precision and simplicity that you can run over the entire dial in 1½ minutes and pick up *more* stations with greater clarity and volume than any other set on the market. Direct comparisons invited. The new Super-Zenith was perfected in Zenith's laboratories in the center of the eleven powerful Chicago broadcasting stations. Even under these extremely adverse conditions the new Super-Zenith tunes through everything and "gets the outside" on loop, inside, or outside antenna.
5—produces not only the seemingly impossible in perfect selectivity, but also possesses such artistry of design, such finished craftsmanship, that it lends distinction and exclusiveness to any living-room or library.

Write for the name of the nearest dealer from whom you can obtain a demonstration of this outstanding marvel of the radio world.

Dealers and Jobbers: Write or wire for our exclusive territorial franchise.

ZENITH RADIO CORPORATION
Branch Office: *General Offices:*
1269 Broadway, NEW YORK   332 So. Michigan Avenue, CHICAGO

The exclusive choice of MacMillan for his North Pole Expedition. Holder of the Berengaria record.

Zenith Radio Corporation
Dept. 11E
332 S. Michigan Ave., Chicago, Ill.

Gentlemen: Please send me illustrated literature giving full details of the Super-Zenith.

Name...

Address..

....

Built to Sell —
In *Your* Market *
NEW 1934 MODELS
Presented By

Featuring the

ZENITH
CHALLENGER LINE

All products of experience, skilled workmanship and advanced engineering and designing extending for a period of over eighteen years in the construction of notable radio values in above the average tone qualities, selectivity, sensitivity, dependability of performance and superlatively beautiful modern design.

FOR ALL WAVE BANDS
STANDARD
STANDARD AND SHORT
STANDARD AND LONG

MODEL 288. 8-valve superheterodyne—Short-standard wave lengths, 12 to 560 meters. Automatic volume control, noise reducer—sensitivity control, phono jacks.

MODEL 790. 7-valve Superheterodyne, wave band 180 to 2100 meters (Standard-Long). Automatic volume control, Shadowgraph tuning, sensitivity and tone controls.

* Each ZENITH chassis is especially engineered for export trade and designed to withstand climatic conditions of various International markets.

Note These Sales Inducing ZENITH Features:

Advanced superheterodyne circuits. All purpose transformers for operation on all voltages and all cycles. Advanced engineering developments. Clear, undistorted tone and dependable reception. Compactness, Beauty, New features . . . and a sales franchise backed by complete financial and merchandising stability.

MODEL 702
LONG AND
STANDARD WAVE

A new 5-valve AC-DC Superheterodyne, automatic volume control, wave band 200-2000 meters or 175-560 meters. Calibrated in meters. Phono jacks weigh about 8 lbs.

Now Note Below Our Very Newest ZENITH

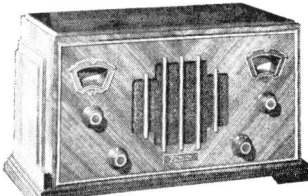

MODEL 827

A 7 tube Superheterodyne, 8½" high, 15½" wide, 7½" deep. 6 inch extra heavy dynamic speaker. 3 gang condenser — functioning on bands. Wave band 560 meters to 25 meters. Tuning, tone and volume controls. Hair line, shadow dial indicator.

Write or cable your particular market requirements.

EXPORT DIVISION
ZENITH RADIO CORPORATION
3616 Iron Street, Chicago, Illinois, U. S. A.
Established 1913, Cable Address: ZENCO—ALL Codes

JUNE, 1934

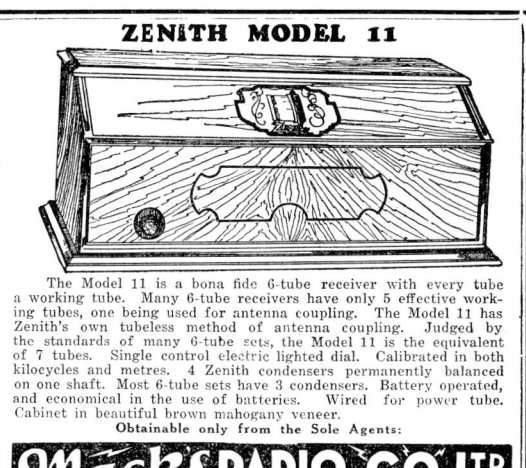
This advertisement appeared in May 1928. The set was a 1927 model.

Zenette, 7-valve, Superhet 1931.

Model 288, 8-valve AW 1934.

Model 6S-129, 6-valve, 3-band 1937.

Model 7D-127, 7-valve, 3-band 1937.

Model 6S-229A, 6-valve AW 1938.

Model 7S-238, 7-valve, 3-band 1938.

Zenith's quality image only two AC/DC models were made in the years before World War II. In post-war years it was another matter, however, for in keeping with the rest of the industry practically all table model radios were of the AC/DC variety.

An unusual and most elaborate receiver produced in 1934 deserves mention because in its day it used more tubes than any other set on the market. The set in question, the model 1000Z 'Stratosphere', used no less than 25 tubes, including eight type 45 triodes in the output stage. It is difficult to believe that this large number of output tubes was used for any other reason than to build up the total tube complement as four type 2A3 tubes would have done the same job.

No comments on specific models would be complete without mention of the famous 'Trans-Oceanic' portables, originally one of the earliest all-wave models of this class of receiver. The first Trans-Oceanic, model 7-G-605, was produced in 1941 being a 7-tube, 5-band set for operation on batteries or AC and DC mains. Production of the Trans-Oceanic series was continued for many years with tube-equipped models being made until the 1950s.

During the 1930s Zenith continued to grow steadily but it was not until 1936 when the now famous Big Black Dial models were introduced that Zenith edged its way into No. 3 position on the sales ladder. From this time on the company remained one of the industry's sales leaders.

Amongst American radio manufacturers Zenith must be counted as one of the most successful and it is interesting to reflect that, unlike some of its competitors, such as Admiral, Philco and Sparton, the company never diversified into the so-called "white goods" field. Its success was achieved entirely in the area of radio and television, or "Radionics", as Zenith liked to call it, with an incursion into hearing-aid manufacture included.

Amongst manufacturers of combination radio-phonographs Zenith was a leader in introducing an entirely new type of light-weight pickup in 1948. The mechanism is of technical interest in that its action depended on a hitherto unused principle, different from anything seen before or since. This new pickup arm was named 'Cobra' because of its snake-like profile. Apart from Zenith's own use the Cobra arm was used by at least one juke-box manufacturer who reported getting three times the length of life of the 78 rpm records then in use.

Zenith became extremely active in television manufacture from 1948 onwards, eventually rising to No. 2 position, after RCA.

Zenith radios were seen on the New Zealand market as early as 1927, being imported by the N.Z. Express Co. of Dunedin. However, Zeniths were not widely distributed until the late 1930s, possibly because the N.Z. Express Co. had other radio agencies. Also it must be remembered that the early Zenith sets were quite expensive by comparison with other makes and that in itself would have limited the market in this country. When N.Z.E. gave up handling radio in 1934 the agency lapsed until it was taken up by C. & A. Odlin Ltd, Wellington. Odlin's had previously held the agency for Atwater Kent but when this firm went out of business in 1936 it left Odlin's without an agency. This, then, was how Zenith came back on the local market and how it replaced Atwater Kent as a top selling American set. Because Zenith would not supply radios in chassis and speaker form, that is they would not supply without cabinets, it made their sets dearer by comparison with those of other American manufacturers such as Belmont, Patterson and Wells Gardner. This was because local import duties were higher on radios which came into the country complete with cabinets.

With the coming of World War II the name Zenith disappeared from the local scene, never to reappear.

ROGERS-MAJESTIC

Because the Canadian radio industry has long been dominated by the offshoots of American and British companies it is interesting to know that one of the world's first, if not actually *the* first, manufacturer of all-electric receivers was originally a purely Canadian concern.

The story begins in 1924 when a young Canadian, Edward S. Rogers, returned home from a visit to the United States where he had been successful in acquiring manufacturing rights to a new type of AC radio tube as yet only in the laboratory stage. In order to appreciate Rogers' far sightedness it must be realised that in those days the idea of an 'all-electric' radio was barely dreamed of, yet he was quick to realise that the future of the domestic radio receiver lay in the area of 'batteryless' operation. To this end he devoted all his energies to the development of such a radio, together with the necessary special tubes.

In May 1925 Rogers, then aged only 25, formed the Standard Radio Manufacturing Corp. Ltd of Toronto and in the same year marketed the first 'Rogers' radio. Although described as 'batteryless' this first model nevertheless used a concealed dry-cell bias battery, but this fact cannot really be held against him as even several years later some American manufacturers of mains-operated receivers are known to have done

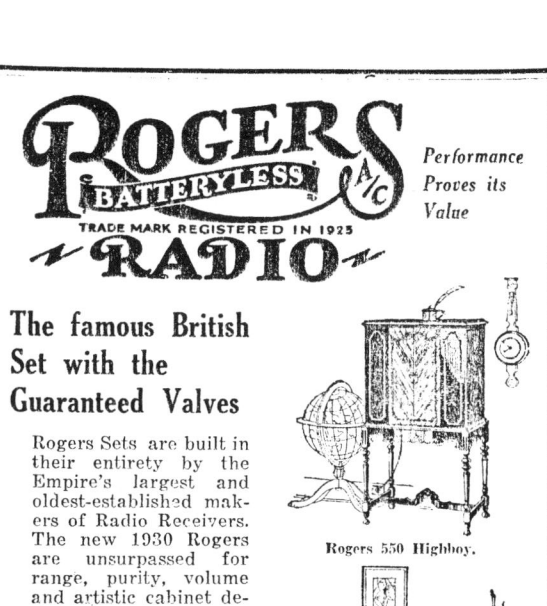
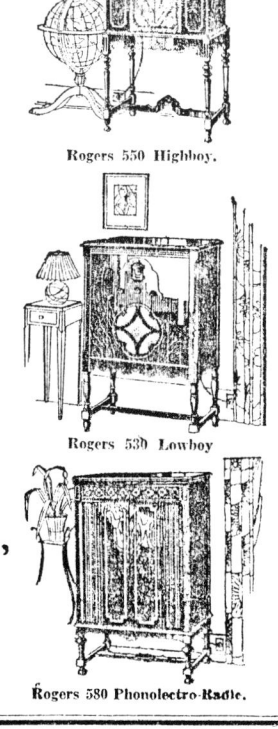

Model 610, 6-valve S G 1931.

Model 861, 7-valve superhet 1933.

Model 646, 6-valve S G 1931.

Model 371, a 3-valve superhet using special Rogers tubes 1933.

likewise.

After little more than four years of independent operation the Standard Radio Mfg Corp. formed a connection with the Grigsby-Grunow Co. of Chicago who acquired a substantial holding in the Canadian firm, resulting in the formation of the Rogers-Majestic Corporation Ltd in 1929. This event marked a turning point in the company's history as henceforth the American company's designs and constructional methods exerted a considerable influence on Rogers receivers and on the tubes used in them.

However, the failure of the Grigsby-Grunow Co. in 1934 seemingly had little effect on the Canadian company which continued to operate as before, though from then on had to rely on its own initiative in developing new receivers and tubes. Even so, the American influence could be detected lingering on into the late 1930s.

Another event occurring at much the same time was a merger with an existing Canadian

Freshman 'Masterpiece', 5-valve TRF 1925.

Grebe Synchrophase MU-1, 5-valve 1925.

Crystaldyne, Made in U.S.A. c. 1925.

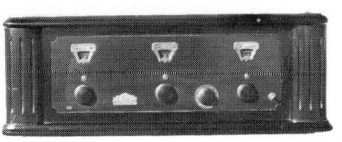

Amrad Neutrodyne S522 5-valve battery set 1926.

Standardyne Multivalve 1927. It used a special 3-in-1 valve.

Splitdorf 6-valve All-electric 1928.

Baldwin internal-horn speaker 1928.

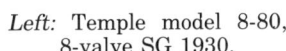

General Motors 'Little General' 6-valve SG 1931.

Left: Temple model 8-80, 8-valve SG 1930.

Master 6-valve SG, TRF 1930.

Jesse French 'Junior' model 'G' 5-valve TRF, Loftin-White audio 1930.

Crown 5-valve SG TRF 1931. Manufactured by Custom Built Radio Co.

Colonial 36, 6-valve TRF 1931.

Zaney Gill 7-valve SG 1932.

Colonial 60E, 6-valve BC 1931.

Brunswick AC10, 5-valve TRF 1932. Manufactured by Transformer Corp. of America.

Erla 5-valve SG TRF 1932.

Colonial 345E, 6-valve superhet 1932.

Wurlitzer 8-valve DW 1934.

Wurlitzer 7-valve AW 1934.

Colonial model 650EU 5-valve dual wave 1934.

Fairbanks Morse 70, 7-valve AW 1935.

Left: Belmont 878, 7-valve AW 1936.

Left: Emerson U6, 5-valve AC/DC DW 1934.

Right: American Bosch 653AA 5-valve 3-band 1937.

Right: Fairbanks Morse 66, 5-valve DW 1936.

McMurdo Silver 'Masterpiece VI'. The 21-valve 1937 version.

Scott 'Philharmonic' 30-valve, deluxe all-wave 1937.

company, De Forest-Crosley Ltd (itself an offshoot of two American firms, which, incidentally, were not connected in the U.S.). Under the new setup a company known as Canadian Radio Corporation Ltd was formed as a manufacturing division of Rogers-Majestic Corp. to produce a unified line of receivers under the previous Rogers and De Forest-Crosley brand names.

With the death of Edwin S. Rogers in 1939 at the early age of 39, the Rogers family interest in the company was disposed of, though the firm remained under Canadian control until 1957 when it was taken over by Philips of Holland and renamed Rogers-Majestic Electronics Ltd. Fittingly the Rogers name was preserved for at least a while longer, as befitted a pioneer Canadian manufacturer.

It is not known exactly when Rogers receivers were first sold in New Zealand but the earliest advertisements of the N.Z. agents, the A. R. Harris Co., can be traced back to 1929. From about 1935 both De Forest-Crosley and Rogers radios were marketed here until, as in the case of other imported sets, they were effectively removed from the local scene by the introduction of import restrictions in 1938.

THE RICH MAN'S RADIO

No story of American radios would be complete without mention of two of the most well-known luxury receivers—McMurdo Silver and Scott. Both these makes were seen in New Zealand, the agency for the former being held briefly during 1934-35 by Megann's Radio Service, Wellington, and the agency for Scott by Chas Begg & Co. and later by Warwick Smeeton Ltd. The first Scotts were imported in 1932 and the last in 1939. Today there are surviving examples of most models made during this period now in the hands of collectors. Scotts are of particular interest to New Zealanders as E. H. Scott himself was born and educated in New Zealand, although he never made radios in this country.

This class of receivers—expensive, multi-valve, all-wave, high-fidelity models with chromium-plated chassis—were a peculiarly American development the high prices of which put them well out of reach of the average radio owner. To cater for those buyers who could not afford a McMurdo Silver or Scott, the Midwest Radio Corp. produced what might be called "a poor man's Scott", a multi-valve, all-wave set at less than half the price. Midwest radios were seen briefly in New Zealand, being imported by Midwest Import Distributors Ltd during 1936-37.

In 1934 this 15-tube model was described as "The World's Finest Radio Receiver". By 1937 the company slogan had become "The Stradivarius of Radio".

133

CHAPTER EIGHT

Some British imports

By comparison with those of American origin very few British receivers were seen in New Zealand, and of those that were, only a comparatively few makes were represented. This is true of both early battery sets as well as later AC models, for throughout the period that radios were imported—from about 1923 to 1940—probably no more than 10% were British-made.

Two of the first British battery sets seen in this country were the 2-valve Marconiphone V2A and the 2-valve Gecophone set, both of 1924 vintage. During the next few years other sets such as the Burndept 'Empire Four', the Cossor 'Melody Maker' and the Radio Communication Co's 'Polar Twin' also appeared.

However, when it came to crystal sets it was another matter for here there were far more British than American to be found. This was probably because comparatively few American manufacturers went in for crystal sets and their products were also more expensive. British makes seen in New Zealand included Brownie, B.T-H., Edison-Bell, Ediswan, Fortevox, Gecophone and Transant, all of which were marketed between 1925 and 1930.

In the early days of mains operation British sets were conspicuous by their absence, none being seen in this country before 1930. Two of the first makes to appear were HMV and Philips, details of which will be found under their respective listings. Blue Spot, a receiver of German origin though also made in England for a short time, was sold in New Zealand during 1930-31 but distribution seems to have been very limited. Another make, seen briefly here during 1933, was Ferranti, but only one model was imported. Small quantities of Lissen receivers, mainly 'transportable' table model battery sets, were first imported by the Electric Lamphouse Ltd in 1934. The same firm subsequently continued importation up to 1938.

Not until the late 1930s did any British radios make much impression on the N.Z. market and even then less than half a dozen makes were represented. Apart from Philips and HMV the best-known of these were Bush and Ecko. Bush sets were partly assembled in New Zealand and fitted into locally made cabinets. During the early

war years when imported sets were no longer available, New Zealand designed models were made in small quantities until the total prohibition of domestic set manufacture came into effect. Bush had the distinction of being the only British set to be copied by a N.Z. manufacturer. In 1940 the firm of Radio (1936) Ltd produced a model the outward appearance of which bore a striking similarity to the Bush model PB63.

Ecko receivers made their mark in this country mainly with the SW86, a 6-valve, 3-band bakelite cased model which was introduced in 1937.

Another British set, though one seen in small numbers only, was Kolster Brandes, a product of British S.T.C. This was probably because most models were imported from Australian S.T.C.

From about 1937 several different brands of British portable battery operated sets were seen in this country; makes included Ekco, HMV, Lissen, Spencer and Vidor/Burndept. By 1939, however, importation had largely ceased due to the commencement of local manufacture of this class of receiver.

Overall it may be said that in spite of the then extant "Be British" sentiments, patriotism was not enough to prevent many, or even most, people from buying American receivers, mainly because they represented better value for money. Furthermore, British sets were generally difficult and expensive to service, a state of affairs caused in part by the plethora of different types of valves used in them.

Yet another factor contributing to the dearth of British sets on the local scene was the British manufacturers' attitude towards overseas markets which they just did not seem to think worth troubling about. Not until 1936 did any British manufacturer produce an export model in which the long-wave band was omitted in favour of an extra short-wave band. Similarly, British manufacturers earned a reputation among local importers of being difficult to do business with, their "take it or leave it" attitude causing the *N.Z. Radio Times* to run an article in 1932 entitled "Are English Manufacturers High Hatting the N.Z. Market?". From a perusal of the text it was quite apparent that this journal thought they were.

The famous Marconiphone
V2 1923.

The famous Marconiphone
V2 1923. Not many were
sold in New Zealand.

Radiola crystal set 1924.
Made by British Thomson-
Houston Co.

Gecophone Junior crystal set
1924.

Cosmos Radiophone type V.R.2 1923. This is the tuner unit
only, part of a complete receiver.

Left: Gecophone 2-valve
1924.

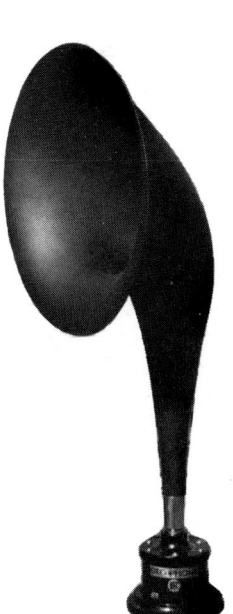

Gecophone speaker
1924.

Left: This advertisement
was dated 23 December
1927, by which time the
Gecophone set was
somewhat out of date.

135

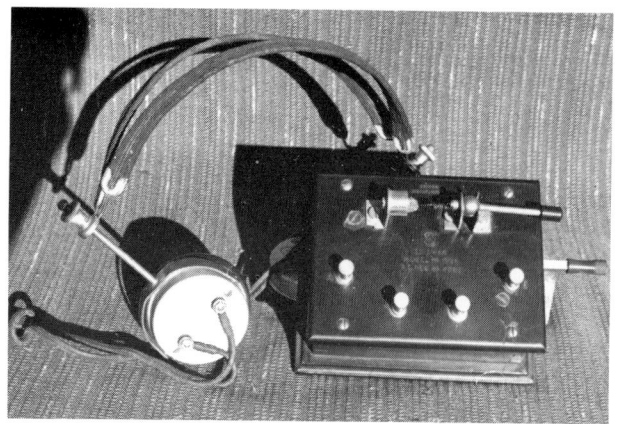

Ediswan model No. 1 1924 crystal set 1924.

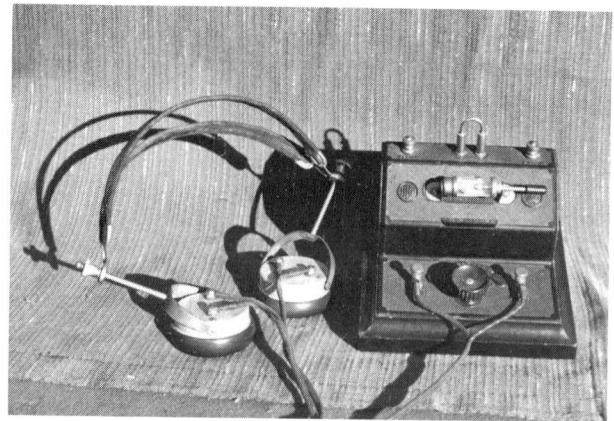

Brownie No. 2 crystal set 1925.

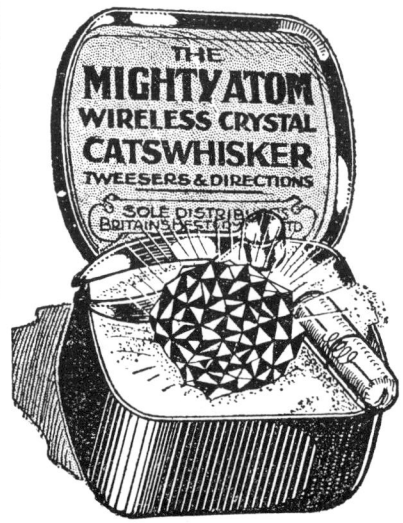

THE MIGHTY ATOM WIRELESS CRYSTAL CATSWHISKER TWEESERS & DIRECTIONS

SOLE DISTRIBUTORS BRITAIN'S BEST

The Mighty Atom Crystal

Complete with tweezers and **1/-**
Catswhisker in Sealed Box
Write for FORMO Price List.

A. E. STRANGE

404 Worcester Street, CHRISTCHURCH.
Wholesale and Retail.

Tweesers or tweezers? 1927.

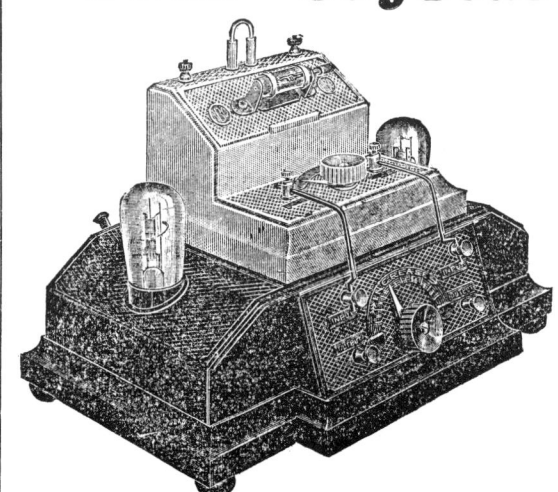
Advertisement from the *N.Z. Radio Record* 1927.

The Polar Twin, 2-valve battery set 1927.

N.Z. Radio Guide and Call Book 1931.

The SENSATION of the RADIO WORLD

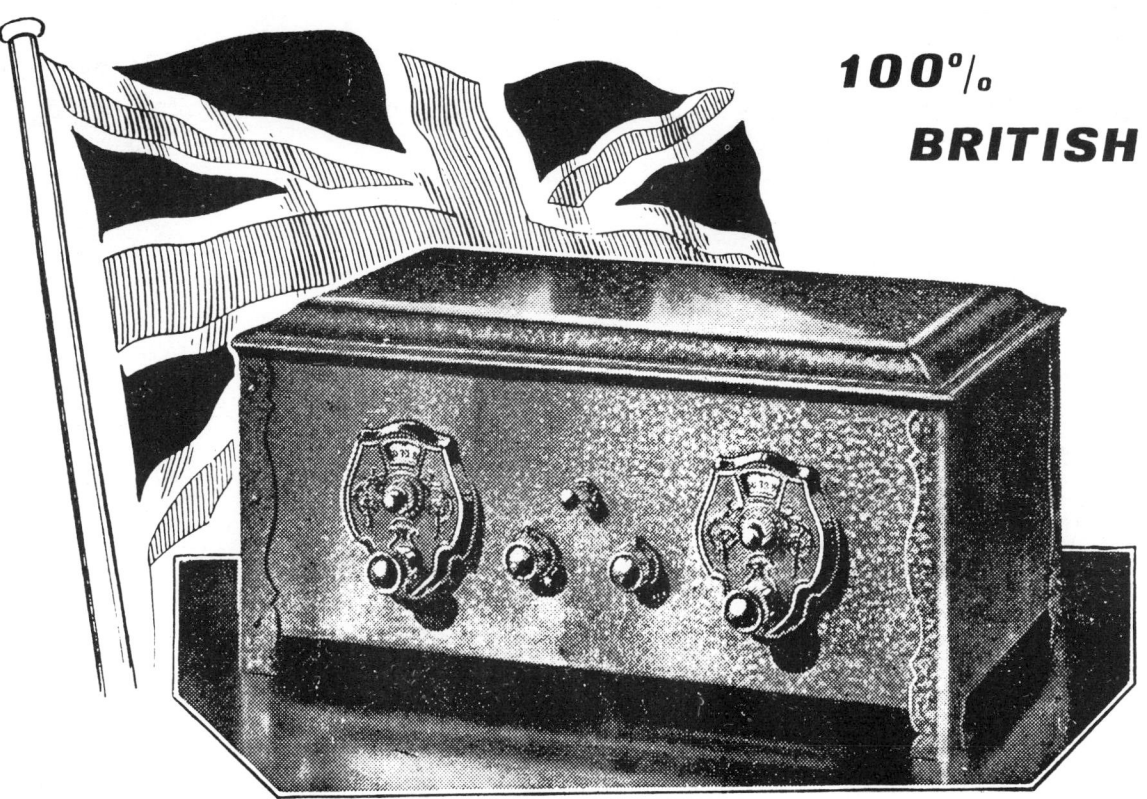

100°/₀ BRITISH

For only £10 you can buy

THE WONDERFUL

Cossor
"Melody Maker"

BRITAIN'S GREATEST RADIO SUCCESS

Never before has *any* Radio Set created such an enormous sensation. Thousands of delighted Cossor Owners throughout N.Z. testify to the wonderful performance and value of the Cossor Receiver - the set that has 2000 miles range - that cuts out unwanted stations like magic - that brings in all the usual programmes - the most powerful and efficient Receiver ever produced at such a modest price. Send for a Free Constructor Envelope which tells you how you can assemble the Cossor Melody Maker even if you know nothing of radio. No soldering - no sawing - no drilling - it's as simple as Meccano - success is certain even if you know less than nothing about Wireless - act now!

Before deciding on a battery model or electric receiver, secure latest particulars of Cossor Products.

The 1930 releases are of a revolutionary nature and are a wonderful advancement in Radio Science.

Enquire for details of Cossor's latest 2 and 3 valve A.C. Receivers and the wonderful—

NEW PROCESS VALVES

South Island and Wellington:

GEO. HOWES & CO.
259 CUMBERLAND ST., DUNEDIN.

Auckland and Hawkes Bay:

RADIO LTD.
ANZAC AVENUE :: AUCKLAND

This advertisement was dated March 1930 but the set was not 100% British. The two dials were by Pilot, U.S.A.!

Celestion cone speaker 1927.

Columbia model 303, 'Transportable' 1928.

Telsen cone speaker 1933.

Ferranti 7-valve superhet 1933.

LISSEN SIX-VALVE ELECTRIC SUPERHETERODYNE RECEIVER.

This fine new Six-Valve All-Mains Superheterodyne Receiver is in a class by itself. It is the receiver for the connoisseur. No receiver, whatever its

price, could surpass it in performance.
Cat. No. BZR154 .... £19/10/-

Lamphouse catalogue 1934.

Ekco SW86 in deluxe console cabinet 1937. Note addition of magic eye tuning indicator.

Ekco SW86, 6-valve, 3-band 1937. Note use of metal ring grille.

At Right! Another Radio Sensation by BUSH — now available at John Burns' Radio Dept.! Note the magnificent cabinet and spectacular tuning scale. This is the famous 7-stage BUSH All-Wave Model with

Bush PB63, 6-valve, 3-band 1940.

Kolster Brandes 750, 7-valve AW 1938.

Bush Model PB61, 5-valve, 3-band 1940. It had a N.Z. made cabinet.

Ekco Model AW88 5-valve, 3-band (LW) 1938.

138

LISSEN

TRANSPORTABLE
BATTERY RECEIVER (K)

You can take this set just where you like —you have no aerial or earth to think of— they are inside the set. It is an inexpensive receiver, yet it has 4 valves and "Class B" output to give ample undistorted volume, and iron-cored coils for increased selectivity and sensitivity.

(Complete with Batteries.)

Cat. No. FR711 .... £19/10/-

BATTERY SUPERHET (K)

Has power, range, and can be easily tuned so that there is no interference. Outstanding features: An ingenious A.V.C. arrangement to facilitate tuning by ear and to avoid side band screech. Positive quiescent control. Three position tone control. Highly sensitive moving coil speaker employing nickel aluminium iron alloy type of magnet.

(Complete with Batteries.)

Cat. No. FR712 .... £21

Lamphouse catalogue 1937.

HIS MASTER'S VOICE

The story of the Gramophone Company began in 1897 when a small group of English businessmen acquired the necessary patent rights from the Victor Talking Machine Co. in the U.S. to enable production of disc gramophones and records to commence in England. Initially the name 'His Master's Voice' was not used on the company's products for the following reason, and although an oft-told tale it is worth repeating.

In 1899 a minor artist by the name of Francis Barraud came to the office of the Gramophone Company in Maiden Lane, London, with an unusual request: He wanted to borrow a brass gramophone horn. When questioned as to his reason for such an odd request he explained that he had recently painted a picture of a dog listening to a phonograph and now wanted to alter the picture.

It appeared that Mr Barraud's painting depicted a fox terrier named 'Nipper' listening attentively to the black horn of an Edison cylinder phonograph. However, Mr Barraud had had no success in selling his picture and a friend suggested that if a brass horn could be substituted for the black one it would add a bit of colour and make the picture more attractive. The picture was entitled "His Master's Voice".

Barraud's request aroused the interest of the firm's manager, W. B. Owen, who requested that the picture be brought in for him to see. When that was done Owen was immediately impressed by its possibility for use as a means of advertising his company's gramophones and requested that the artist paint out entirely the rival Edison machine and substitute a Gramophone, complete with brass horn, of course. When this was done the company purchased the picture and retained the name which in the course of time came to be known as the world's most famous trade-mark.

Some years later, in 1920, the Victor Talking Machine Co. purchased a 50% interest in the Gramophone Company for $9,000,000 and thus acquired the right to use the British company's trade-mark. So it was that Little Nipper crossed the Atlantic and became as well-known in that part of the world as he was in Europe.

The Gramophone Company's interest in radio did not become apparent until the end of 1929 when in December of that year they purchased the Marconiphone Co., the domestic products division of the Marconi Co. With this move the Marconi Co. retired from the entertainment field and as part of the deal agreed to refrain from trading in this area for a period of twenty years, i.e. until 1949.

With this move the Gramophone Company was obviously responding to a move on the part

139

At a Touch of a Switch!

Gramophone or— Radio Entertainment

Something new in radio, and something different in gramophone reproduction! Tune in with the new Super-Automatic Station Selector. All stations are plainly and permanently visible. Just slide the knob to right or left—you have—exactly—the one you want. It is to-day's most modern musical instrument. It reproduces electrically both recorded and broadcast music, with the actual realism of the personal performance. Your nearest accredited "His Master's Voice" dealer will gladly give you a demonstration and particulars of easy terms.

The NEW
"His Master's Voice"
GRAMOPHONE AND RADIO IN COMBINATION

The Victor 'Micro-Synchronous' model R35 was one of the first radios sold by HMV (N.Z.) Ltd.

The HMV 491 was similar to the previous year's model but had an extra short-wave band extending down to 7 metres making possible the reception of television sound signals in the London area. New Zealand buyers were led to believe that they would be ready for television when it arrived! When sold in N.Z. this model was fitted with a different dial scale. 1937.

This ad from the *N.Z. Radio Record* of 29 Sept. 1933 reads: "His Master's Voice English Made Radio". Well, this RCA Model R37 certainly wasn't English made!

The model 442 featured "Fluid Light" tuning, a fancy name for a visual tuning meter. Separate scales were used for MW and LW. The N.Z. price was nearly double that shown. 1934.

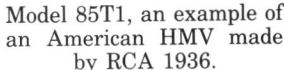

Model 85T1, an example of an American HMV made by RCA 1936.

HMV model 656, 7-valve, 3-band 1938.

RCA model 5T5, 5-valve, 2-band 1936. Another American model sold in N.Z. as HMV.

The famous 6-valve, 4-band model 471 1936. It did much to popularise British sets in N.Z. It was fitted with 6.3-volt American (RCA) valves and was EMI's first export model, though the LW band was still included. The 441 was a home market model using 4-volt valves. The circuitry of these sets owed much to RCA's "Magic Brain" of 1935.

141

Tour The World
in your armchair ! !

All the world's a stage when you have an "His Master's Voice" All-Wave Receiver in your home! American, Continental, Asiatic, Australian and English programmes —all are at your command with the greatest of ease and with that thrilling realism, undistorted volume and perfect tonal fidelity one expects from "His Master's Voice"—the greatest name in the science of sound. Explore the waveways of the world yourself witht the latest triumph of "His Master's Voice." Thrill to the perfect **All-Wave** reception and world-wide range.

Model 141 8-Valve All-Wave Superhet. Gives brilliant, realistic tone, undistorted power, high sensitivity, efficient, economical performance.

Model 122 6-Valve All-Wave Superhet. No other radio provides such tone excellence, ease of operation, noiseless background interference.

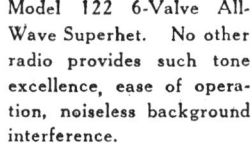

OUTSTANDING FEATURES
Include:

All-wave 6 and 8-Valve Superhet. Circuit—New Airplane Type Full-Vision Tuning Dial—Automatic Volume Control—Tone Control—Full-size dynamic Speakers—Beautiful Modernistic Cabinets. No other radios include so many refinements and new features of engineering design.

"His Master's Voice"
All Wave Receivers

Any "His Master's Voice" Dealer will gladly arrange a demonstration.   Or write to "His Master's Voice" (N.Z.), Ltd., Wakefield Street, Wellington, for full particulars.

Two RCA models sold in N.Z. as HMV 1934.

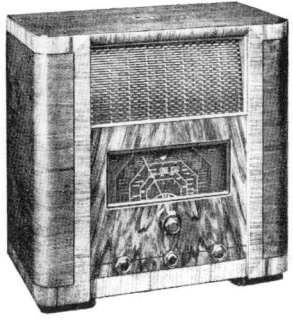

Model 653, 5-valve, 3-band 1938.

Model 482, 6-valve, 3-band 1938.

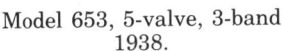

Left: The 472 was another export model using American metal valves. It still had the L.W. band fitted. 1938.

of the rival Columbia Graphophone Co. who had already been marketing radios in 1929, but in the event, no His Master's Voice radios appeared on the scene until 1931.

As mentioned earlier, the Victor Talking Machine Co. had acquired an interest in the Gramophone Company back in 1920 and when in turn Victor was purchased by the Radio Corporation of America (RCA) in 1929 this interest thus passed to RCA. It was RCA's David Sarnoff who was largely responsible for persuading the somewhat reluctant Gramophone Company to become involved in radio in the first place.

So it was that the year 1931 became an important one in the history of the British home entertainment industry. It was marked by the amalgamation of the two rivals, HMV and Columbia, and the formation of a new company known as Electric & Musical Industries Ltd (EMI). Initially the two 'gramophone' firms continued trading as separate entities but eventually the name Columbia was withdrawn. Over the years EMI grew to become one of the largest firms of its kind in Europe and it is interesting to note that in 1935 was in a position to buy out RCA's interest for the trifling sum of $215,000,000!

Under the new set-up radio manufacturing was concentrated in the Hayes, Middlesex factories of the Gramophone Company, receivers

being produced under the brand names—His Master's Voice, Columbia and Marconiphone.

Of these brands only the first two were marketed in N.Z.; there already existed established agencies for the respective brands, extending back to the early years of the century. Originally HMV gramophones and records had been imported by the firm of E. J. Hyams Ltd, but in 1926 His Master's Voice (N.Z.) Ltd was established as a New Zealand branch of the Gramophone Company. Incidentally, the Australian branch, the Gramophone Co. Ltd (Incorporated in England), was established a year earlier, in 1925, and for some reason many of the American sourced HMV radios later sold in New Zealand bore the Australian company's imprint.

Although EMI had commenced making radios under the HMV brand in 1931 none were marketed in New Zealand until 1933. From then on both British and American HMV sets were sold side by side in this country. However, the British sets did not achieve the same degree of popularity as did the American ones, at least in the early days. Not until the Gramophone Company made definite efforts, in 1936, to cater for the overseas market did British models make appreciable headway in New Zealand.

The first special export model seen in New Zealand was the 471, a 6-valve all-wave set marketed in 1936. It was identical to the 441 'Home' model except for the use of 6.3-volt American valves. Its design was based firmly on RCA's 'Magic Brain' model 128 of the previous year.

Undoubtedly the most interesting feature of the 471 was the use of an unusually small diameter speaker, taking into consideration the comparatively large size of the cabinet. This speaker was specially developed by EMI and although measuring only 6½ inches across, the use of an extremely narrow rim on the cone housing enabled the effective cone area to very nearly equal that of most other 8 inch speakers. A lot of work had obviously gone into the design of this speaker and its performance was much superior to the average run-of-the-mill type, including RCA's very ordinary one as used in their model 128.

Advertisements of the day claimed the HMV 471 to be "All British", but it must be recorded that in addition to using American (RCA) valves there were other American components to be found, such as CTS volume controls and Yaxley wave-change switches. The same also applied to other pre-war models.

A feature of many later pre-war HMV receivers was the use of oval or elliptical speakers, an EMI first. The particular shape had a definite advantage in providing a larger

A 5-valve broadcast model made in N.Z. 1939.

This N.Z.-made used two multi-function valves, types 12B8 and 25A7G. 1940.

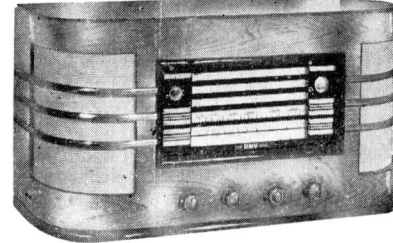

Made by HMV (N.Z.) Ltd, this 1947 model 467SB was the company's first bandspread set.

The 5-valve, dual-wave model 465D was also issued in broadcast-only form 1945.

Model 476D, 5-valve D.W. 1947.

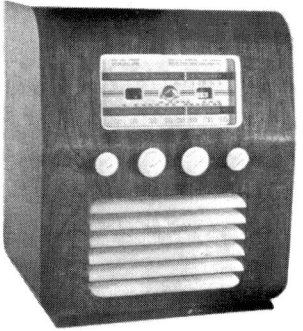

HMV 'Westminister', 7-valve D.W. 1948.

The model 495, a 5-valve set, 1949 was known as the 'Little Nipper'. Made by Collier & Beale, it was the equivalent of their Pacemaker model 519P.

7-valve bandspread, model 467 1947. In spite of the double-ended cabinet there was only one speaker.

4-valve 'Minor' made in N.Z. by Collier & Beale Ltd 1954.

effective cone area than could be obtained when using a conventional round speaker in certain shapes of cabinets.

British HMV receivers always maintained a well-deserved, high quality image and at no time was any attempt made to compete in the marketplace with the "cheap and nasty" products of some manufacturers. The Gramophone Company long held the coveted right to use the Royal Warrant "By Appointment" as suppliers to more than one Royal Household, an honour indicative of the standing of the firm and its products.

HMV in New Zealand

As mentioned earlier, HMV (N.Z.) Ltd first marketed British-made radios in 1933. Before this, however, they had sold American RCA-Victor receivers under the HMV name since 1930. After 1933 they continued to sell American sets alongside British ones, but were at pains to conceal the fact that not all the sets marketed in

this country were of British origin. From the middle to late 1930s unbranded RCA sets carried a transfer (decal) on the top of their cabinets worded: "Made for the Gramophone Company Ltd, Homebush, N.S.W.".

Although nearly all the British-made receivers marketed by HMV in this country were sold under the HMV label, there were a few also sold under the Columbia name for a short period in 1933. On the other hand, the name Marconiphone, well-known in Great Britain, was not used by HMV in New Zealand.

After 1938, as a result of the newly introduced import restrictions, HMV in common with other N.Z. importers, were faced with the need to either establish their own factory or else arrange for a local manufacturer to make sets for them. They did both. In 1939 the first locally made receivers to carry the HMV label were produced at the company's newly established Wellington factory. At the same time some models were made by Collier & Beale Ltd. These arrangements were continued until the closure of HMV's factory in 1957. After this time receivers were obtained from such companies as Philips and Pye.

For a short period after World War II Radiomobile car radios, which had been introduced in the U.K. in 1946, were assembled here by HMV. One or two models, such as the 516AR, were completely made here.

CHAPTER NINE

Made in Australia

In spite of the fact that Australia is New Zealand's closest neighbour (and British too!) remarkably few Australian receivers were imported into this country. The reason for this state of affairs is a little hard to fathom because some makes did become well-known on the N.Z. market.

Apart from AWA's Fisk Radiolas and Radiolettes there were little more than half a dozen makes of Australian sets seen in this country. Some of the better known are listed below.

Airzone

One of Australia's largest manufacturers. Sets were first imported in 1932. After a gap of a few years importing was resumed by Airzone (N.Z.) Ltd during 1936.

Kreisler

Although better known in this country as a supplier of kitsets, complete receivers were also marketed, mainly during 1933.

Lekmek

Another firm specialising in kitset production but whose complete receivers were also marketed here by the N.Z. agents Electric Lamphouse, Wellington.

Raycophone

Marketed in this country during 1932-33 by the N.Z. branch of Harringtons Ltd.

STC

Imported between 1932 and 1937 by Standard Telephones & Cables Pty Ltd of Wellington. Although the manufacturers were part of a world-wide organisation, IT & T, the receivers bore no resemblance in either design or appearance to sets made in England by Kolster-Brandes Ltd. Incidentally, small quantities of the latter sets were imported during the later 1930s.

Stromberg Carlson

A wholly Australian owned firm having connections with the American company of the same name. The Australian receivers had no similarity to the American models. Imported by Gough, Gough & Hamer Ltd of Christchurch during 1934-36.

Tasma

Manufactured by Thom & Smith Ltd and sold in New Zealand by N.Z. Electrical Equipment Ltd, Wellington, during 1936-37.

In addition to the above there were also certain models of Mullard (made by Airzone) and Philips (made by Tasma) imported from time to time by the respective N.Z. companies to fill gaps in their ranges.

A name seen only on this side of the Tasman was 'Stannage', the brand name being that of the importer, John Stannage, who was in business briefly during 1936-37. The radios themselves were made by Thom & Smith Ltd (Tasma).

AMALGAMATED WIRELESS

Prior to 1913 the commercial side of wireless in Australia, consisted of two local agencies for the rival overseas firms of Marconi's Wireless Telegraph Co. and the German firm of Telefunken GmbH. The latter was represented by a company known as Australasian Wireless Ltd which had been formed in 1910. On the other hand, Marconi's did not have a representative until the following year when a Marconi shipboard wireless operator, Ernest Fisk, was appointed resident engineer to the company.

Not long after this a patent dispute between the overseas rivals made it prudent for the two Australian firms to combine their interests, and in 1913 a new company, Amalgamated Wireless (Australasia) Ltd, was formed. Henceforth this company became and remained a major influence in the development of all areas of radio in Australia.

As well as maintaining close links with the Marconi Co., AWA also became closely associated with the Radio Corporation of America (RCA), a move which was to have a lasting effect in the fields of both receiver and valve manufacture in the years to come. Initially AWA were concerned with the sale and installation of imported spark

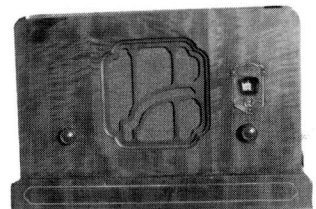

Audiola model 492, 4-valve
Superhet 1932.

MODEL 535
The Standard Console
with lift-up lid.

*Radio Dealers are invited to
send for full particulars of
the S.T.C. range. You in-
cur no obligation at all.*

STC, 5-valve SG 1932.

The New
STC
RADIO

will build
bigger business for you!

Standard Telephones and Cables, pioneers
in radio research, with the largest laboratories in the British Empire, announce the
new S.T.C. silent tuning radio—a new combination of worthy British manufacture and
world-wide research, specifically built for
New Zealand listeners.

The S.T.C. is constructed by the builders of
broadcasting apparatus for all the important
stations throughout New Zealand and

Australia and is destined to capture public
preference and build big business for active
Radio dealers. A model will be available
for every class of buyer on liberal easy pay-
ment terms. Prices will be competitive and
margins generous.

A limited amount of territory is still available. If you are genuinely interested write
immediately for full particulars.

Airzone model 602, 6-valve
1935.

Standard
Telephones and Cables (A/sia) Limited.

Head Office: Box 638, Wellington.   Auckland: Box 1897

Stannage model 437, 6-valve
DW 1937.

Airzone model 458, 5-valve
BC 1946.

Stromberg Carlson model
564 1935.

STC model 58A, 5-valve
1936.

STC 5-valve DW 1936.

147

Raycophone, 5-valve TRFs 1931.

Airzone model 404, 5-valve BC 1932.

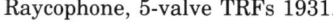

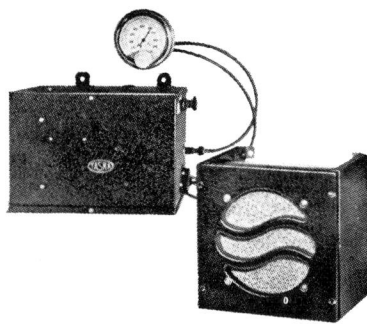

Left: Airzone, 5-valve model 550 1937.

Right: Mullard model 50, 5-valve 1937. Made by Airzone.

July 1936.

equipment but before long a factory was established to commence local manufacture of certain components and even valves. From there it was but a step to the assembly of complete transmitters and receivers.

A few years after the end of World War I AWA commenced production of a line of components suited to the needs of the growing number of experimenters and amateurs who had become interested in 'wireless'. These components were sold under the name 'Expanse'* as were certain built up items such as wavemeters and loose couplers. Expanse equipment was also being sold in New Zealand through AWA's Wellington office and by 1922 the volume of business seems to have become sufficiently large to justify the printing of catalogues in this country. The author has in his possession two different issues dating back to 1921-22, printed by Andrew, Baty of Christchurch.

With the advent of broadcasting, in which AWA naturally became deeply involved, the company, in 1925, commenced to manufacture a line of broadcast receivers under the name 'Radiola'. Although the use of this American name can be taken as indicative of the closeness of AWA's association with RCA, the sets themselves were, with one exception, of Australian design.

Listed in AWA's catalogue No. 25 dated August 1925 were the following receivers: Radiola crystal sets, 2-valve Radiophone, Radiola III, Radiola IV and Radiola Super. The last named was an Australian version of RCA's massive 'catacomb' superheterodyne which was available in two 'portable' styles and as well in a 'Sheraton' console. Production of all three models was continued through 1926 and 1927. Superhets, including the newly introduced Radiola Super 8, predominated in 1927 when four were issued compared with one TRF. However, with the advent of the first Radiola AC sets in 1928 superhets disappeared completely and were not seen again until 1933. Battery sets produced during the same period were likewise of the TRF variety.

Since 1930 in Australia heavy import duties had been levied against all imported receivers in order to protect local manufacturers, with the result that American Radiolas were not seen there. The situation in New Zealand was different in that similar restrictions were not introduced until much later and thus AWA in N.Z. were able to import sets from either Australia or U.S.A. In spite of a preferential tariff in favour of British goods AWA's N.Z. branch seemed to prefer to import American RCA receivers, probably because as franchise holders for RCA products they would have been likely to have lost the

agency if they had not sold any American receivers in this part of the world, and the N.Z. market was their only opening for this trade. Even so it was not long before the receiver agency changed hands and in 1930 the firm of His Master's Voice (N.Z.) Ltd became the New Zealand distributors. After this time AWA receivers were then sold here in direct competition with sets of American origin, but by that time RCA was no longer using the name Radiola so there was no confusion in the marketplace.

One of the first Australian Radiola AC sets sold in New Zealand was the model 46E, a 6-valve TRF console of 1931. It was also the first of the so-called 'Fisk Series', the name Fisk being that of the previously mentioned E. T. Fisk who in 1916 had become managing director of AWA. From 1931 his name appeared in conjunction with the word Radiola when AWA's receivers became known as 'Fisk Radiolas'.

The year 1933 marked the reintroduction of the superheterodyne circuit in Australia, this time in all-electric form. The Fisk Radiola 120 was the first of the 5-valve 'supers', a class of radio which became very popular in Australia and New Zealand during 1933-34.

A feature introduced in 1934 was the use of reflex circuitry whereby the IF stage did double duty by acting as the first AF stage as well. It has been claimed that the gain of a receiver so constructed can come within 6db of a similar model using separate IF and AF stages, but in practice it is extremely doubtful if this figure was ever reached. Apart from the matter of gain there were other more important practical disadvantages which eventually led AWA to abandon the use of reflexing, but not before many thousands of reflexed models had been produced. Its demise was unlamented by anyone who had anything to do with receivers using it.

Probably the most well-known AWA receivers sold in New Zealand were the 'Radiolette' series. This word, like Radiola, was also of American origin and came directly from RCA who had produced their first Radiolette (model R5) in 1932. The first Australian Radiolette, model C87, was a 4-valve TRF announced in December 1932 as a 1933 model. It was notable for the use of a bakelite cabinet, a 'first' for this part of the world. Following this a 5-valve model housed in an almost identical cabinet was released in August 1933.

For some reason the use of bakelite cabinets was discontinued in 1934, the model 24 of that year being housed in a diminutive wooden cabinet

* As well as being a registered trademark the word EXPANSE was also the registered telegraphic address of both AWA and the Marconi Co.

"RADIO"

An "Expanse" Panel Unit Receiver assembled with various types of panels that may be used.

The Expanse 'PX' receivers were based on the American De Forest 'Interpanel' sets. Up to six separate units could be assembled in various combinations. 1921.

Miss Gladys Moncrieff, the well-known musical comedy actress, recently invested in a Radiola Super and Amplion Loud-speaker. It is hardly necessary to say that she is delighted with her purchase, forming, as it does, an enjoyable distraction after the arduous hours at the theatre.

The Radiola Super in action. Note turntable under the base to allow positioning when using the inbuilt loop aerial. 1925.

THE RADIOPHONE

The necessary controls and adjustments have been reduced to a minimum. Many of these sets are giving excellent results up to 150 miles from Sydney.

Cat. No.	Description.	List Price. £ s. d.	Section.
RR.3	Radiophone 2-Valve Receiver. Instrument only, with Aerial Plug and Cord; Earth Plug and Cord; L.T. and H.T. Plug and Cords; 1 Instruction Booklet; 1 Table Type Condenser. (Only sold complete)		

AWA's 2-valve Radiophone model RR3 sold for £10 minus valves in 1924.

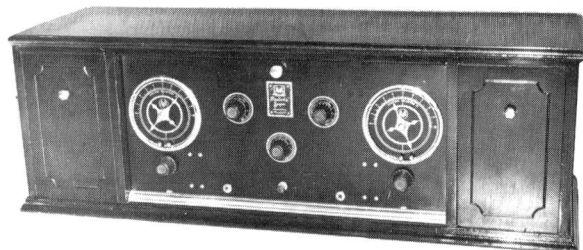

This massive 'transportable' Radiola Super of 1925 was the first commercial superheterodyne marketed in Australia and New Zealand. It used six UV-199 valves and had a built-in loop aerial. Batteries were contained in the end compartments but a separate speaker was needed.

The Radiola Super Sports Model with Amplion loud speaker.

The portable model of the Radiola Super required a separate box to have the batteries. 1925.

150

RADIOLA IV.

The RADIOLA IV is noted for its great sensitivity, selectivity and simplicity of operation. Designed and manufactured in the Company's Radio Electric Works. Constructed to ensure perfect reception at all times.

Cat. No.	Description.	List Price. £ s. d.	Section.
* RR.8	Radiola IV. Instrument only, with 9 Tuning Coils, as follows: 2 only No. 65, 1 only No. 75, 2 only No. 110, 2 only No. 210, 2 only No. 275 ; 1 A. Cord and Plug ; 1 E. Cord and Plug ; 1 L.T. Cord and Plug ; 1 Instruction Booklet	37 0 0	B
* RR.9	Radiola IV. With Accessories (Dry Cell equipment), complete. Same as RR.8, but includes 1 Weston Telephone Plug ; 1 6ft. L.S. Cord ; 4 A.W.A.33 Valves ; 2 H.T. 60-v. E.R. or Hellesen Batteries ; 2 E.R. 4½-v. Bias Batteries ; 3 Diamond Commonwealth or E.R. X type 1½-v. Cells ; 1 Radiola Aerial Equipment Box, senior ; 1 pair Brandes Telephones	44 0 0	B
* RR.10	Radiola IV. With Accessories (Accumulator equipment), complete. Same as RR.9, but 1 4-v. 22 A.H. Accumulator in place of 3 Dry Cells	45 10 0	B

RADIOLA III.
An excellent Four-Valve Receiver.

* RR.6

Radiola III. Instrument only, with A. Cord and Plug ; E. Cord and Plug ; H.T. Plug and Cord ; L.T. Plug and Cord ; 4 Tuning Coils, i.e., A1, A3, RT1, and RT3 ; 1 Instruction Booklet   29 0 0   B

Australian-made Radiolas listed in AWA's 1925 catalogue.

WIRELESS WEEKLY   Friday, May 1, 1931

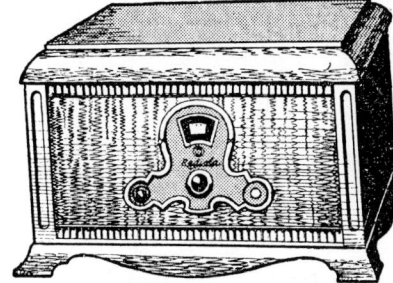
The model C49 was AWA's first AC operated set. It was a 6-valve (plus rectifier) TRF which used a separate magnetic speaker. 1928.

The "Radiola Thirty-Four" Receiver

Radiola 34/C 76, a 4-valve TRF using a magnetic speaker. 1930.

The first Australian Radiolette model C87, a 4-valve regenerative TRF. It was the first Australian set to use a bakelite cabinet.

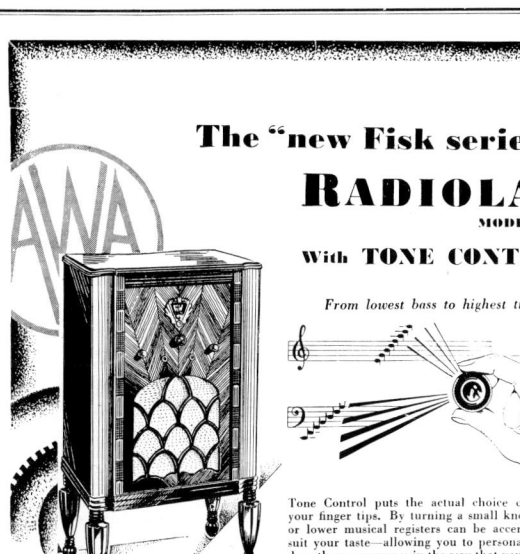

One of the first Australian AC Radiolas sold in N.Z. was the model 45E. It was a 5-valve TRF and featured a tone control.

Radiola 45/C 79, 5-valve TRF 1931.

C87 Radiola Junior 4-valve TRF 1932.

151

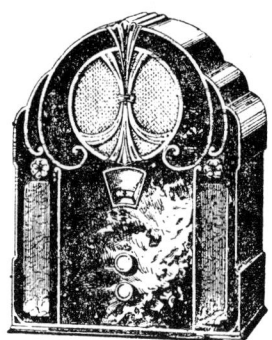

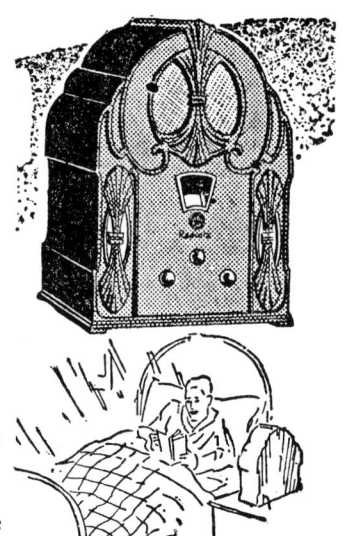

RADIOLETTE
The Little Receiver with the Big Performance

A.W.A.'s New Portable All-Electric Radio. Four Valves including rectifier. New Type Dynamic Speaker. Efficiency and beauty in small compass.
CASH PRICE, **£17/17/-**

A.W.A. "FISK" RADIOLETTE
All-Electric 5-Valve Table Model
Cash Price, £22/10/-

The first Australian Radiolette, model C87, 4-valve TRF, 1932.

The first 'Fisk' Radiolette. Model 110/C104, 5-valve Superheterodyne 1933.

Model 120/C105   Model 110/C104

These were AWA's first AC superhets, both were 5-valve models using the same chassis. 1933.

5-valve Radiolette model 24 1934. It had no dial light.

The Radiolette 29 was the first of a line of reflexed models housed in bakelite cabinets. 1935.

Model 27 was the first Radiolette to use reflexed circuitry. Note absence of name on dial of cabinet. 1934.

Radiolette 27 in larger cabinet with 8-inch speaker. 1934.

Radiola 565B made by Radio Corporation of N.Z. Ltd. It was also sold under the Columbus name. 1955.

Fisk Radiola model 163 7-valve DW. Note use of pleated cloth covering the speaker opening. 1938.

The last valve-operated Radiola sold in N.Z. It was made by Allied Industries Ltd. Model MS100 1964.

By 1936 Radiolettes were available in cabinets having an imitation marble finish. This is a model 32.

By 1937 Radiolettes were available in two-tone cabinets as above or in coloured "Radalec" cabinets with a choice of four colours. This is a 5-valve, dual-wave model 38.

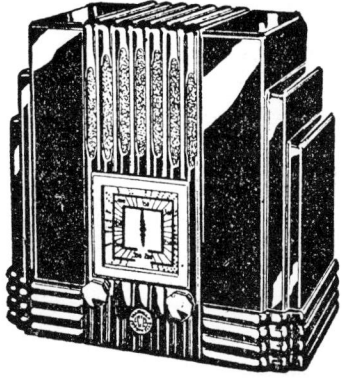

measuring only 8½ inches high, while the model 27 had a slightly larger upright cabinet. They were the first superhet Radiolettes.

For the 1935 season the model R28 was announced in December 1934. It was the first of the now classic models to use a step-sided 'Skyscraper' bakelite cabinet, nowadays much sought after for their art deco look.

The first dual-wave Radiolette, model R35, appeared in 1936 and in the same year coloured cabinets were introduced on both BC and DW models. Although from the name of the series it might be imagined that all Radiolettes were small mantel models this was not the case as some were available in small console cabinets.

The last AWA receivers were imported in 1938 and the name Radiola was not seen again in this country until 1952 when two models were made by Radio Corporation of New Zealand. Following this no further Radiolas were produced in New Zealand until after 1960, following the establishment of Allied Industries Ltd.

A feature of AWA's receivers has been their almost total Australian content, in fact AWA made nearly everything themselves. The only items obtained from outside suppliers seem to have been carbon resistors and electrolytic capacitors. Although imported valves were used up to about 1933 or later in some cases, the establishment of a separate valve factory in 1932, the Amalgamated Wireless Valve Co., in which valves were produced under the Radiotron brand, enabled AWA to eventually become self-sufficient in this respect, and in addition to supply a large part of the Australian market.

As far as New Zealand was concerned AWA's local office continued to import American rather than Australian Radiotron valves, probably because of the greater need for types not made by AWV. However, with the changed economic conditions prevailing after World War II Australian Radiotron miniature valves were used in large quantities by N.Z. manufacturers as well as being widely sold for replacment use.

With the advent of television in New Zealand in 1960 AWA apparently decided that it was time to become more deeply involved in the N.Z. industrial scene. In 1960 this led to the establishment of a new company known as Amalgamated Wireless (Australasia) New Zealand Ltd (what a mouthful!). Links were formed with a New Zealand company, Allied Industries Ltd, who undertook to extend their existing manufacturing activities to include the production of Radiola radios, Radiolagrams and AWA television receivers. As Allied was already involved in manufacturing Murphy radios under licence to the U.K. firm, arrangements were made to market AWA Radiola television under the Murphy name in addition.

Since then AWA in New Zealand have become involved in the production of such things as radio-telephones and hi-fi amplifiers and have been successful in marketing these items overseas. In 1967 the Amalgamated Wireless Valve Co. became a shareholder in Allied Industries and commenced the manufacture of picture tubes in 1970; production was continued until 1975.

CHAPTER TEN

Radio collecting

Amongst readers of this book there will undoubtedly be some whose interests extend to the collecting and restoring of old radios and associated equipment. Although one of the more recent additions to the vast area of 'collectibles', old radios are rapidly becoming more and more sought after. Particularly since the 1960s they have come to be recognised as legitimate collectors' items the same way as have old gramophones and phonographs of a slightly earlier period.

Where to start? What to collect? As with any other areas of collecting there is a generally accepted date or age which determines the desirability and value of a particular item. Although collectibles, unlike true antiques, do not have to be over 100 years old before they can become collectors' items, generally speaking the older they are the more sought after they become.

The term 'vintage' is often used to describe an old radio, but unlike the term 'antique' has no clearly defined meaning and has merely become a synonym for 'old'. Incidentally, in its original sense the word refers to the French grape harvest of a particular year and does not in itself mean old. In the case of household radios there were no true 'broadcast' receivers made before 1922, in fact, that year can well be taken as the starting point of their commercial production. At the time of writing (1985) any radio made in the 1920s is considered to be 'very old' while one made in the 1930s is just 'old'.

As time goes by it is obvious that what is now not yet considered to be old will eventually become so. To anyone, regardless of his age, the fact that any man-made object was produced before he was born must make it seem old, regardless of its relative age.

Instead of using a fixed date as a reference point another way of categorising an item is to adopt an arbitrary span of time, say 40 or 50 years, dating back from the present moment, after which time that item qualifies as being in the vintage category. This system is in line with the accepted practice whereby a true antique is classed as being over 100 years old.

Nowadays any radio made prior to World War II is generally considered as being in the vintage category, while one made before or during the First World War is regarded as antique.

However, age alone is not the sole criterion of interest or value; it is quite possible for a more recently made item to be rarer, and thus more valuable, than an earlier one. This may be because the later item was originally made in smaller quantities, leaving relatively fewer to survive to the present day. Then, too, there is the matter of an item having a personal, sentimental or nostalgic value on which a monetary value cannot be placed.

As regards where and how to start collecting, reasonably priced sets can still be obtained at garage sales or by watching classified advertisements in local or daily newspapers. Depending on how well combed-over a particular area is it may be worthwhile placing want ads in the same papers. Second-hand shops and auction sales are other sources, but nowadays prices tend to be a bit on the high side. Luck enters into the matter, too. Sometimes a casual conversation can provide a lead to the location of an old set which may have lain for years in an attic or shed. Unfortunately not all of such old radios turn out to be what is expected, but every lead has to be followed up, just in case!

While some fortunate few collectors may have had sets given to them, the majority have had to pay prices which have been escalating year by year. In the latter case the thought that resale values have likewise been climbing may perhaps help to ease the pain of paying a big price for a much wanted item!

So, having obtained one or more old radios the next thing is to decide what, if anything, needs to be done to it/them. If a set is in a presentable condition and appears to perform satisfactorily it may need no more attention than a cleaning of the chassis and polishing of the cabinet. Here it should be mentioned that there is a clearly defined distinction between 'polishing' and 'repolishing' of a cabinet. The latter term is used in the furniture restoration trade and means 'refinishing'; that is, the complete stripping of the old surface and refinishing in the original manner.

At this stage a word of caution is in order.

Don't be in too much of a hurry to start work on an old set, whether on chassis or cabinet. It is very easy, particularly for a beginning collector, to develop 'itchy fingers' and attempt some ill-advised 'restoration'. Here the author can speak from personal experience, having sometimes done things that he would later have liked to be able to undo! So, let your watchword be—proceed with caution. This way you will help to avoid making wrong decisions which may permanently affect the value of any item.

Although it is outside the scope of this book to provide detailed instructions on 'how to do it', a few generalities are offered in the hope that they may be of interest or use.

Because the cabinet is the first thing that meets the eye, most owners of old radios will desire to have their cabinets in reasonably presentable condition. Lucky is the person who acquires a set where the cabinet does not require refinishing. So often the cabinet has sustained damage in the form of deep scratches or dents or may even have pieces missing so that complete refinishing is the only course of action. In cases where minor damage such as the lifting of small parts of the veneer has occurred, careful patching of the affected area may obviate the need for complete refinishing.

Having made the decision to refinish the next step is to decide whether to attempt the job oneself or seek the assistance of a professional polisher. Practically all radio cabinets will have been originally finished in nitro-cellulose lacquer, which precludes a 'do it yourself' job unless the person doing the work is an experienced spray painter with the necessary equipment. French polishing was almost never used for radio cabinets, although this form of finish can look very attractive, providing bleached, and not orange, shellac is used.

Although there are the purists who may throw up their hands in horror at the idea of using a 'synthetic' varnish such as polyurathane, remember that lacquer is a synthetic too. Such people are probably thinking of examples they have seen of poorly applied polyurathane varnish resulting in a horrible 'treacly' appearance. Properly applied, polyurathane can be almost indistinguishable from a lacquered surface.

Having made the decision to refinish the next decision is 'high-gloss' or 'satin'. The person desiring a cabinet to look like new will choose the former, while one who likes his old sets to look old will opt for a satin finish which more nearly resembles the patina which comes with age.

Owners of early battery sets have slightly different problems as in nearly all cases the cabinets are made of solid timber, not plywood. Solid timber has its own weaknesses, it can shrink, warp or split, all faults which cannot easily be remedied.

Most early battery sets had front panels made from some insulating material. Many American sets used solid Formica panels and some used panels of hard rubber. The former was a most durable material with a high gloss that lasted for years and required only occasional removal of dust. Hard rubber, on the other hand, after a period of time, exuded a chemical which formed a disfiguring surface film which required periodic removal.

Radios in plastic cabinets require different treatment again. Bakelite cabinets can undergo a 'weathering' process, particularly on surfaces exposed to sunlight, which over a period of time results in the loss of the original finish. If the surface is not too badly affected it can usually be restored by a vigorous application of metal polish such as Brasso. In cases where the surface has become badly oxidised it will be necessary to first use a fine grade of rubbing-down paper used wet and then finish off with a cutting compound.

We come now to the innards. Early battery sets generally used a wooden baseboard on which the components were mounted. In such cases there was little or no iron or steel to become rusty as most of the metal used was nickel-plated brass or plain aluminium. Only through prolonged storage in damp conditions can corrosion of such metals become a problem. Where necessary brass can be replated but there is really no satisfactory method of restoring badly corroded aluminium.

Most mains-operated sets used a metal chassis, usually of sheet steel though sometimes of aluminium. The finish applied to steel chassis varied, the most common being cadmium plating. In the early days before cadmium plating came into general use dull nickel plating was sometimes used. Many New Zealand manufacturers simply spray-painted steel chassis using coloured lacquer applied directly without a primer.

In cases where a plated chassis has become badly rusted it will be necessary to remove all components before it can be cleaned and re-plated. This is rather a daunting prospect for even an experienced restorer and it is possible to avoid such extensive work by using a different procedure. Instead of re-plating a chassis the top and sides can be spray-painted using an aerosol can of silver coloured lacquer which gives a finish closely resembling slightly weathered cadmium plating. It is not necessary to remove all topside components before painting as they can be carefully covered or masked, as can valve sockets and other large holes. Obviously the same method of working can be used where a chassis has previously been painted; close colour matching can be obtained by using one of the small cans of automotive touch-up lacquer.

When it comes to the electronics of a mains-operated set not all hobbyists will have sufficient technical knowledge or experience to undertake other than the simplest work. Nevertheless, a determined person can learn a lot from some of the newer how-to-do-it books which have been published recently. In any case it is largely a matter of necessity that owners of old radios should learn how to do their own repair or restoration work, for professional work is liable to be quite expensive, even if someone can be found to undertake it.

Apart from any difficulties in actually doing the job there is another difficulty—the matter of obtaining any necessary parts. Two minor but much wanted items seem to be control knobs and speaker grille cloth. Satisfactory reproductions of many types of wooden knobs can be made by anyone with access to a wood-turning lathe; reproductions of bakelite knobs can be made using suitably coloured epoxy resin.

The demand for replacement parts, particularly valves, has led to the establishment of specialist suppliers in countries like England and the United States. Here in New Zealand there are also at least three suppliers of old type radio valves.

The growing number of people interested in old radios has also led to the formation of organisations catering for their needs. Vintage radio societies throughout the world offer their members the opportunity of obtaining needed parts or equipment by buying from or swapping with other members.

HOW OLD IS IT?

One of the questions most frequently asked by beginning collectors is—how can I find out how old this set is? Here are a few suggestions.

One of the surest ways is to look for an original advertisement as this will provide definite evidence that a particular set was sold during a certain year, or years. By referring to old newspapers or magazines it is possible to locate such advertisements, but many people will not have access to such publications.

In the case of American receivers there have been several books published in recent years which provide much good information on ascertaining their age. Recommended are McMahon's *Vintage Radio 1887-1930, A Flick of the Switch 1930-1950* and *Radio Collector's Guide 1921-1932*.

Although, by comparison, there were relatively few British radios seen on the N.Z. market there are similar books available giving

information on these sets—*Early Wireless, The Cat's Whisker 1896-1946* and *Vintage Crystal Sets*. Details of all these books are given at the end of this book.

Another source of dating information is radio service manuals, the best known of which are the annual volumes of Rider's *Perpetual Troubleshooters Manual*. By referring to the schematic diagram of the (American) receiver in question it will frequently be found to carry a date which can be assumed to be within a short time of the release of that particular model. In the case of British receivers it is possible to obtain photocopies of circuit diagrams by writing to one of the addresses given at the end of this book.

In the case of New Zealand-made radios many of the larger manufacturers issued service data which in some cases carried the dates of issue of each model. Nowadays, however, access to any remaining data is not easy as all of the firms except one, Philips, have gone out of business.

So far we have considered only printed material but there is another source of information which is always at hand, and that is the set itself. One way of obtaining the approximate date of manufacture is by noting the types of valves used in it. Once the release dates of individual valves, or series of valves, is known then a 'not earlier than' date for the radio can be established. Many of the earliest AC valves remained in current use for no more than a year or two, which makes the dating of receivers using them fairly easy. For example, the type 47 output pentode was released in 1931 and by 1933 had been largely superseded by later types. Valves having 2.5-volt heaters were introduced in 1927 and continued to be issued up to 1932. The first valves having 6.3-volt heaters were issued in 1932 and by 1935 this figure had become the industry standard in the United States and many other countries. American metal tubes appeared in 1935 and first became widely used in 1936. Octal-based glass versions of metal tubes followed later in 1935 and the shorter 'GT' versions were introduced in 1938. Loktal or lock-in type tubes arrived in mid-1939 and were first used only by Philco.

The first miniature tubes were 1.4-volt battery types which appeared in 1940. AC and AC/DC versions came into use in domestic receivers in 1946. British 8-pin miniatures and the Philips-Mullard 'Rimlock' series also appeared in 1946. The 9-pin 'Noval' series were first used in the U.S. in 1949 and in Britain in 1951.

To obtain more detailed information on the release dates of the various types of valves the reader is referred to the valve handbooks issued by valve manufacturers over the years. By noting the first appearance of a particular type of valve and the date of the relevant handbook it is possible to ascertain approximately when individual valves, or series of valves, were issued.

To be of much practical use this system requires the possession of a full set of valve manuals, something not many collectors are likely to have. A useful single source of valve dating information is this author's previous book *70 Years of Radio Tubes and Valves* which is still in print at the time of writing (1985).

Apart from technical considerations, the matter of cabinet and dial styling can provide a simple and easily understood way of ascertaining the period during which a given model was manufactured. Particularly this is true of early AC sets where cabinet styles changed rapidly during the first decade. It should be emphasised that the following is to be taken as a guide only; there were many individual variations to be found within a given period.

1921-27 (Battery sets) plain wooden boxes, composition front panels.

1926-29 (AC sets) metal boxes, separate speakers.

1929-30 (In the USA) large free-standing 'console' cabinets.

1930-34 Introduction of mantel and midget models, 'peep-hole' dials.

1931-33 Gothic or 'cathedral' style cabinets.

1933 First bakelite cabinets, 180 degree 'half-moon' dials.

1934-37 Upright 'flat-top' table models, circular 'aero' dials. Legless consoles, plain bars instead of ornamental grilles over speaker openings.

1938-42 Horizontal style cabinets, horizontal 'slide rule' dials, completely plain speaker openings.

1946 General use of plastic cabinets for small models.

Another useful guide to the dating of New Zealand-made sets are the patent licence notices affixed to the receiver chassis. These first came into use in July 1934 following an arrangement made with the newly formed Australian Radio Technical Services & Patents Ltd (ARTS & P). The first type of licence notice used was in the form of a white paper sticker which was serially numbered in the upper right hand corner. This type of notice remained in use until the end of 1935.

Commencing in 1935 a pale blue transfer (decal) came into use which had the letters ARTS & P as a background to the words on the licence. The serial numbers were prefixed by a letter, starting with 'A', which changed from year to year and had extended to 'H' by 1942.

Shortly after the end of World War II,

commencing in about 1946, a new type of decal having a dark greeny-blue base colour with the letters ARTS & P in red was issued. These were followed in 1950 by decals having a dark orange background with the ARTS & P letters in green. The serial numbers of both styles were prefixed by the letter 'I' throughout the period in which they were issued.

In 1952 a completely new and much smaller type of decal, measuring 45 mm by 25 mm, was introduced. The colour was pale blue with the ARTS & P letters in a darker blue and there was now no prefix to the serial numbers. This type of decal remained in use until the last valve radios were produced in the 1960s.

SUMMARY OF PATENT LICENCE NOTICES

Plain white paper label used from July 1934 to end of 1935.
Pale blue transfer (decal) used from 1935 to 1946 with serial numbers prefixed by a letter, thus:

B = 1935-36	F = 1939-40
C = 1936	G = 1940-41
D = 1937	H = 1942-46
E = 1938-39	

Dark green decal with ARTS & P letters in red. Use commenced in 1947 and continued to 1952. Serial numbers prefixed by letter 'I'.
Orange decals with letters ARTS & P in dark green. Use commenced in 1952 and continued to 1955. Same prefix as above.
Small pale blue decals with letters ARTS & P in darker blue. Use commenced in 1955 and continued to 1960s. No prefix to serial numbers.

MANUFACTURERS' CHASSIS DATE CODING

In cases where manufacturers used a date coding, incorporated in either the model or serial number, a knowledge of this code will provide a sure means of determining the year of issue. A simple system used by various smaller manufacturers consisted of a three-figure model number containing the number of valves in the set combined with the two last numerals of the year of issue, thus: 495 or 549 indicated a 5-valve set made in 1949.

Four manufacturers known to have used a system of date coding are Akrad, Collier & Beale, HMV and Radio Corp. Details will be found at the end of each manufacturer's section.

Rola speaker code dating

In those New Zealand radios produced after 1939 which used locally made Rola speakers, yet another useful pointer to the date of manufacture exists. From the inception of their production in this country all Rola speakers carried a manufacturer's date code ink-stamped on the rim of the cone housing.

The coding contained not only the year and month of manufacture but also the actual day as well! In the code the first numeral, or numerals, indicated directly the day of the month, the middle digit was a letter the sequence of which, running from A to L, corresponded to the month of the year, while the final numeral indicated the year within a particular decade. Examples are: 28J2 = 28 Oct. 1942, 9E7 = 9 May 1947, 23I5 = 23 Sept. 1955.

The only difficulty which might be encountered in deciphering the code is to decide in which decade the year of manufacture was. It is worth remembering that the first speakers were all EM types and none were made in the wartime years 1942-45, which meant that any having the numerals 3 or 4 as a final digit could not have been made in 1943 or 1944. From 1945 on only permanent-magnet types were made. Care should be taken not to confuse the date coding with any other figures stamped on the cone housing.

Station callsigns

After about 1936 most radios produced in this country had at least some station callsigns marked on their dial scales, but the markings were usually restricted to just the main YA and ZB stations. However, in cases where other callsigns were marked their presence can serve to indicate when a particular set was made, provided it is known when these stations first came on the air. One very definite landmark date is September 1948 when a big wavelength reshuffle occurred. For example, at that time 1YA moved from 650 Kc to 750 Kc, so any set having a dial scale showing 1YA at 750 must have been made after that date.

A question asked

"Why did the early Australian and New Zealand AC sets not have on-off power switches fitted?"

The reason had to do with electrical safety; the N.Z. Electrical Wiring Regulations prohibited the use of a single-pole switch unless the 'apparatus' was supplied by means of a non-reversible plug. Because many, or even most, radios were connected via a BC adaptor to a light socket in the early days there was consequently no means of ensuring that the switch remained in the live (phase) lead. Although the use of a double-pole switch was permissible on the set this type of switch was not available in the usual volume control attachment form before 1937.

With the steady increase in the use of 3-pin wall sockets to supply family radios, most N.Z. manufacturers started to fit on-off switches from 1937 on. It is assumed that similar conditions existed in Australia, although the fitting of power switches did not become commonplace until much later.

Bibliography

NEW ZEALAND BOOKS

Broadcasting, Grave and Gay
    Ken G. Collins (1967)
Scrim, Radio Rebel in Retrospect
    Les Edwards (1971)
Philips in New Zealand
    H. Leighton Lord (1961)
Broadcasting in New Zealand
    Ian H. MacKay (1953)
Voices in the Air
    Peter Downes, Peter Harcourt (1976)
History of Broadcasting in New Zealand 1920-1954
    J. H. Hall (1980)

NEW ZEALAND PERIODICALS

N.Z. Wireless & Broadcasting News 1923-1926
New Zealand Radio 1926-1931
The New Zealand Radio Record 1927-1939
The New Zealand Radio Times 1932-1938
Scott's Radio Handbook 1923-1931
N.Z. Radio Listeners' Guide 1928-1932

AUSTRALIAN BOOKS AND PERIODICALS

Radio Trade Annual of Australia 1936-1939
Wireless Weekly 1929-1934
Radio & Electrical Retailer 1939-1940

BRITISH BOOKS

The Broadcaster Trade Annual 1934-1936

The Economic Development of Radio
    S. G. Sturmey (1958)
Early Wireless
    Anthony Constable (1980)

AMERICAN BOOKS

A Pictorial History of Radio
    Irving Settel (1960)
A Pictorial Album of Wireless and Radio 1887-1929
    Harold Greenwood (1961) This book was later revised and enlarged by Morgan E. McMahon being re-issued under the title:
Vintage Radio 1887-1929
    Morgan E. McMahon (1972)
A History of Radio to 1926
    Gleason L. Archer (1938) (reprint 1971)
Big Business and Radio
    Gleason L. Archer (1939) reprinted 1971
Inventions and Innovations in the Radio Industry
    Rupert D. McLurin
A Flick of the Switch 1930-1950
    Morgan E. McMahon (1975)

In addition to the above listed publications, much information has been obtained from the many, many American, British and Australian periodicals of the day, all now defunct. Other excellent sources of information have been the many catalogues, sales leaflets and technical bulletins issued by various manufacturers of the period.

Index

Text: Phototypeset 10/12 Century Schoolbook
Paper: Klippcote matt art 100 gm
Book jacket: Topkote matt art 125 gm
Book jacket photograph: Ron Fitz-William
Book jacket design: Ellen-Marie van Empel
Bound by F. Cartwright & Son Ltd, Christchurch
Printed by Craig Printing Co. Ltd, Invercargill, New Zealand, 1986